capitalist humanitarianism

Duke University Press
Durham & London 2023

lucia hulsether

capitalist humanitarianism

© 2023 DUKE UNIVERSITY PRESS. All rights reserved

Project Editor: Lisa Lawley
Designed by Aimee C. Harrison
Typeset in Garamond Premier Pro and Antique Olive by
Westchester Publishing Services

Library of Congress Cataloging-in-Publication Data
Names: Hulsether, Lucia, [date] author.
Title: Capitalist humanitarianism / Lucia Hulsether.
Description: Durham : Duke University Press, 2023. | Includes bibliographical references and index.
Identifiers: LCCN 2022033007 (print)
LCCN 2022033008 (ebook)
ISBN 9781478019206 (paperback)
ISBN 9781478016564 (hardcover)
ISBN 9781478023838 (ebook)
Subjects: LCSH: Capitalism—Religious aspects—Christianity. | Humanitarianism—Religious aspects—Christianity. | Neoliberalism—Religious aspects—Christianity. | Economic assistance—Moral and ethical aspects—Developing countries. | BISAC: RELIGION / Religion, Politics & State
Classification: LCC BR115.C3 H85 2023 (print) | LCC BR115.C3 (ebook) | DDC 261.8/5—dc23/eng/20221025
LC record available at https://lccn.loc.gov/2022033007
LC ebook record available at https://lccn.loc.gov/2022033008

Cover art: Adam Pendleton's painting studio. Photo by Charlie Rubin. Courtesy of the artist.

for my brother Mark

contents

preface ix

introduction: Capitalist Humanitarianism 1

interlude one 19

one 25
May Analyze like a Capitalist: Fair Trade and Other Histories

interlude two 49

two 53
Ethical Vampires: Conscious Capitalism and Its Commodity Enchantments

interlude three 75

three 80
Marxists in the Microbank: From Solidarity Movement to Solidarity Lending

interlude four 102

four 106
Representing Inclusion: Humans of Capitalist Humanitarianism

interlude five 128

five 134
The Hunt for Yes: Archival Management and Manufactured Consent

interlude six 156

six 162
Hope for the Future: Reproductive Labor in the Neoliberal Multicultural Family

epilogue 183

acknowledgments 191

notes 195

bibliography 221

index 239

May 2017.

I lodged my cell phone in the straps of my bicycle helmet, freeing my right hand to walk a bike while my left dragged a duffel down the sidewalk. The jerry-rigged suspension system—which somehow broke down only twice during a two-mile trek—made possible the telephone call. My brother is the person I have always sought when I am on the verge of doing a new thing: crouching behind the starting line at a first cross-country meet, collecting myself in some dead-end hallway before a big presentation, settling in on the about-to-take-off airplane that will deliver me to research overseas, enduring a long drive home after a first heartbreak. That afternoon, another moment of transience, needed his voice. I was about to join the hunger strike that the graduate teacher union had called in a last-ditch bid to pressure the university into contract negotiations. We hoped that this action would be the culmination of our three-decade fight to win livable wages, decent health care, and a neutral grievance procedure for the people who do the lion's share of teaching and research at the university, as well as for the people in the city who live under its shadow.

The union's senior leadership had sprung this tactic on the mid-level organizers in what everyone knew, but nobody would admit, was a workaround to the fact that we were nowhere near prepared to pull off an actual strike. We needed a way to shame Yale into concession, fast, before new presidential appointees struck down the legal precedent that had allowed graduate workers to unionize at all. When I stopped lying to myself, I knew the win had already slipped our grasp. But this was why the hunger strike compelled me. The tactic was masochistic, yes, but it was also consistent with the experience of organizing. Rarely did our compulsory performances of movement optimism allow room to admit the costs of what we were doing: the sacrificed time with loved ones, the neglect of our own health, the dissonance between our internal practices and the world we said we were building, the friendships that couldn't endure the pressure. I'd lost count of the times I'd joined our standard chant—"I believe that we will win!"—only because opting out would indicate a flagging devotion to the cause. I never felt like explaining why my doubts had nothing to do with my resolve, so I played along. For me, the hunger strike was an overdue acknowledgment of how our fight was forged in loss. Still, the coordinating committee had elected this tactic not through democratic deliberation so much as brute arm-twisting on the part of the charismatic staff. I'd abstained from the last-minute vote on process grounds. But once the majority raised their hands in favor, I knew I'd get in line.

This was how I found myself stumbling, a human luggage trolley, toward the headquarters of UNITE HERE—Local 33. International staff flown in from across the country had transformed the space into a temporary home for eight hunger strikers at a time. Each student participated until the in-house doctor benched them for medical risk. It was mid-May, and some of my colleagues were going on fourteen days. Earlier that day a third-year geophysicist on day eight had fainted in the shower, and I'd been tapped to replace her. We just needed to last two more weeks to Yale's commencement. On that morning locals from across the Northeast would converge on New Haven to mark the conclusion of the hunger strike and its accompanying month of lobbying, protest art, and civil disobedience. The spectacle of self-denial at the center—a battle against biochemical balance, literally impossible to win—gave metaphor to the slow death that precarious workers in the late capitalist service economy faced, in different ways, every day of their (our) lives.

The fasting was not the hardest part. The real showdown with the possible happened in strained one-on-one meetings with skeptical colleagues adamant that they didn't talk politics at work, in the media frenzy that drew celebrity "delegations" to pay homage to starving graduate teachers, in the escalating ultimatums to ex-radical deans, in the street-theater preambles to another round of arrests caught on cell-phone camera, and in the see-it-to-believe-it sequence in which, in broad daylight, we borrowed the local Teamsters' flat-bed truck, loaded it with lumber and Ikea furniture, backed the whole thing onto the granite quadrangle abutting major administrative offices, raised a yurt-meets-boathouse encampment, decked it with twinkle lights and picnic tables and Astroturf, and somehow held this utopian ground for fifteen days and counting. We hadn't even expected the structure to last the night. My brother, Mark, had never been to New Haven, and I had not yet visited him in Milwaukee, but still each of us knew how the other inhabited space, how to focus the other's senses, how to make the other laugh at the end of the world.

I thought that Mark was the only person who could register the poignancy of a hunger strike for these days of Left melancholy.[1] It was the kind of spectacle we'd learned to revere, and to skewer without mercy, in Sunday school. Churches pastored by our mom, services populated by members who spent weekends trespassing at the nuclear weapons plant before the police booked them (again) in the county jail. The sermons were imprinted on our hearts. Adults told us constantly about systemic sin. Systemic sin—kind of like structural oppression but amplified by the fact that it was an affront to God herself— had poisoned everything. It didn't matter how good or pure an action or motive seemed; anything borne of human agency was bound to be rotten at its root. We heard about our own birthright crimes early. We were the children of two white people with high-level degrees and steady jobs as a professor and a pastor. We lived in a house whose mortgage would soon be paid off, enjoyed the golden-ticket mobility of our US passports, and were raised by adults who could afford to compel our year-round enrollment in team sports. They impressed on us that these were unfair advantages, inheritances of hegemonic power. Our father, who often rehearsed his undergraduate lectures to us at dinner, lobbed this term at us when we could still use our fingers to count our age in years. We learned early on that, for us, hegemony was just another word for sin.

. . . . . .

Both Mark and I had drifted away from the explicitly theological vocabularies of childhood, and we'd replaced them with a more sustained engagement with traditions of philosophical negativity and dialectical materialism that we'd imbibed as young adults. Both still prescribed a certain asceticism about one's footprint on the world; both had room for the resolute social antagonisms and hopes for an impossible utopia that we never didn't know. What I am saying is that, like many siblings, Mark and I had the natural solidarity of a weird upbringing. We reveled in it. We shared gallows humor about it. Mark was first to observe how the Local 33's hunger strike strategy incarnated in its constitution the slow death that capitalist economies inflict on their workers. The strike, in its grandiosity, admitted defeat. "Self-immolation is not a strategy of the powerful, my sister," he had quipped a couple of weeks prior. I could hear his smile. That the graduate union lacked any chance of getting our demands met—that we were going to lose spectacularly, and look arrogant and unhinged in the process—had little to do with the obligation to try.

We talked about the protests for about two blocks of that walk. Mostly I listened. You said you were probably going to lose your job. You had blown off work that day, and yesterday, and you would do the same tomorrow, to wander the city on foot. Leaving that Riverwest apartment where you scraped by without furniture, passing the hippie food cooperative in the gentrifying zone a few blocks south, cutting through the urban nature preserve and the middle school cliques gossiping outside, you eventually came to the lakefront. Spring arrived with you, all its creation overwhelming the fluorescent call center where you spent your daytime hours. The contrast reminded you again that, yes, there was an outside. You told me one more time how you hated work, the threats lodged at you from other cubicles, the surveillance and verbal abuse that you endured. You expected to be fired for excessive absence.

Neither of us acknowledged the other part of the story. It had to do with the news that for the past several months you'd proclaimed to anyone patient enough to bear with you in the sharing. Within the amorphous buzz of a thousand-person contact-center warehouse, you had discovered a subterranean language, its existence mostly unintelligible to bosses and other outsiders but revelatory for those who could decipher the tonal codes. For example, in order to greet a coworker stationed on the other side of building, you only had to answer incoming client calls in the normal way—"Hello!"—while projecting your voice in the direction of the colleague's assigned cubicle. You were sure the messages had gotten through. People were now angling greetings back toward you. A couple weeks later you decided to up the ante and try your hand at labor organizing. "I'm recruiting for the union!" you effused one day on the way from the call center to a jazz club gig. "Every time the word *union* comes up on the script I read for a call, I say UNION! really loud to spread the word." You confirmed that you had made yourself understood when the employee-of-the-month scabs in your area began to convey cease-and-desist warnings in this same code. Sentences that untrained ears heard as apologies to dissatisfied customers—"I understand you have *problems*. We *regret* to see you *go*"—masked doublespeak threats to workplace troublemakers. You cut out early. You'd take attendance demerits over the parking lot beatdown that the goons had reserved for you. You knew that they were waiting for their chance. It was clear in how the guy with the tattoos whispered *regret*.

This hyperreality still flickered on the fringes of our catch-up, but for the first time in a while, it kept a steady enough distance. You restated what we both took for granted—that you had to get out of the call center, that the place wasn't good for you. Then you'd interrupt yourself to describe, again, the Lake

Michigan horizon, indigo waves against the rocky shore, a rainbow-spiral disk that glided through the turquoise sky until it touched down at your bare feet.

I have tried to understand that walk as your last *fuck you* to the service economy that sold you the barest physical subsistence at the cost of your incandescent perception. But any sense of a victory here is my fantasy alone, a palliative for moments when I want to forget how you twisted in the grip of supercharged meaning. That day in the park, you swung between the ecstasy of your immediate senses and—you finally allowed—your shame. "One second," you interjected. You set the phone on the ground, tossed the Frisbee toward the pickup game that had thrown it askance, and nodded to people who, if you had a second try, might have become your friends. It took all of three seconds, enough time for me to buckle under what you had shared. You came back, and I tried to overwhelm your feelings so quickly that I didn't even ask what you were ashamed of, and I still am unsure. Was it about you asking me to float you some money again? Was it that you'd finally found language for what was making your job so cruel and scary, but your friends failed to follow the terms you used to explain it? Was it that, when you plotted a rebellion against the company's racist labor practices, your confidants inquired into your *mental well-being*? Was it that your friends thought you were slipping away from your musical gifts? If they had intended to be subtle, they had failed. You had majored in psychology and had memorized the diagnostic euphemisms. Did you see the writing on the wall? Did you worry that they were right?

I did not ask you those questions. Instead, I told you what is true, which is that I get mixed up about the lines between regular sibling loyalty and wishing that I could fade into you. I want to trade my compulsive rigidity and risk-aversion for the mind of a person who at three years old composed an original song to celebrate our relocation from Minnesota to Tennessee: "Knocking on Knoxville! Knock Knock! Knocking on Knoxville!" You hummed it, then sang it in full voice as the movers unloaded boxes-made-drums in the sunroom, as you and everyone else tried to ignore the melting-down sibling across the hall, outraged that her brother had a capacity that she lacked. I wish that I were so porous to the atmosphere, to pick up the world's soundtracks and weave them into rhythms, lyrics, and music. I wish that those gifts came at less of a cost. I told you that when I in my life think of you in yours, the word *shame* does not occur to me.[2]

Then I continued the mental health first aid protocol. Step 1: Affirm the person's life and its value (check). Step 2: Confirm their immediate safety (no plans to self-harm). Step 3: Brainstorm actionable, positive steps they are capable of taking right now (send Obamacare enrollment form, look up local

preface   xiii

therapists). Step 4: Schedule a time to talk again so that they have a concrete commitment (this Wednesday after work). The final step involves allowing the person their space and saying good-bye with the confidence that their fragile life is not your burden: we are autonomous agents, responsible for ourselves only. This step is a scam.

. . . . . .

What is it to lose the person who lost their mind? You would write a song about the violence of these abstractions; I would exhaust every possible avenue to try to find a precise answer, to pull you, to pull both of us, back from that brink.

I began writing this book thirteen days, four hours, and thirty-eight minutes after that phone call from New Haven's main drag. Thirteen days, three hours, eight minutes after I began the Local 33 hunger strike. Fifteen days after Mother's Day, 2017. Ten days after my brother left his apartment, drove onto Interstate 94 westbound, pulled over to the shoulder just across the Waukesha County line, and stepped in front of a cargo truck. Nine days, fourteen hours, and three minutes after two university security guards approached the graduate student protest site searching for Lucia Hulsether, hunger striker, and triggered our defend-the-structure elbow-linked circle. *This is not a drill. No. It is a false alarm. Nobody is under arrest.* The police left our utopian boathouse and headed to the church where the fasters slept, having ceded the main encampment to our peers' snack-fueled outdoor slumber parties. The police told the union staff lookout that I should call my mother. She picked up. She said: Your brother is dead. I said: Hold on, you sent the *police* to our base camp because of that? *Do you know what police do?* Also, me: *Did you just say that to your mom? Her kid died. She isn't thinking. Don't make it worse. Don't make it worse.* I grabbed the next flight south from Hartford. Hammered out an obituary somewhere in the water vapor above North Carolina. Time passed as events: cousins at the terminal, visitation, funeral, commencement, cremation, bulldozed encampment, nothing.

I will never stop replaying how the cardboard box glided, like a suitcase at an airport, down the conveyor belt and into the incinerator, one sibling trapped inside, the other's body made useless by a tangle of orphan arms that restrain her on the wrong side of the Plexiglass barrier. There is an almost feral clarity: how I do not want to exist, want to have never existed, in the world that made possible this ending, even though I realize, too, that my desire is self-indulgent and that my mourning has revealed my ugliest propensities, like how I react to my brother's death as if it is special when, in point of fact, death by capitalism is a multigenerational norm, and if this particular loss registers as outlier, it's probably because the corpse on the highway belonged to a white boy with a safety net, which is just evidence that this event feels apocalyptic for one reason, and it's because I became assimilated to an anomalous reality where twenty-six-year-olds don't die, and I let my body learn everything was fine even when her primary, and to others abrasive, character trait was the obsessive fumigation of hypocrisy in others and myself, but in the case of the latter it was apparently no use, since I was frozen squarely in the storm path of a Category Five nostalgia trip for some lovely reconstituted suburban white family that not only has never existed but that I have never actually wanted to want, so before this goes any further I need an emergency exit *now*, like the rope ladder I imagine unfurling from a window in the sky, swinging me into the air, catapulting me into a canopy of words where I know I can stay, suspended, freed from sense, over the life that is no longer mine. I tell my parents I am going back north. I have a writing project, and it has a deadline.

. . . . . .

The writing project was the first draft of the manuscript that later evolved into this book. I had conceived the project as a cultural history of the idea that capitalism could be made "socially responsible." I was interested in the conditions under which it became possible to even imagine that a political-social-economic system built on plantations, sweatshops, and foreclosures, as well as ongoing histories of slavery and settler-dispossession, could be bent toward a humanitarian good. Three years into my doctoral study, I'd front-loaded my fieldwork. I had road-tripped to fair trade archives, shadowed microfinance bankers overseas, and collected dozens of case studies about socially conscious companies. Mark's day job was in one such firm, a call center with an ethics pitch about delivering accessible sound communication technologies to people with hearing loss. The steady poverty wages supplemented his even sparser income from the jazz and hip-hop circuit that he hoped could eventually become his full-time pursuit. Always my first interlocutor, he brought both his artistic vision and his experiences at the call center into our conversations about research and writing life. When he drifted into a realm of perception that not even his most synesthetic friends could access, then toward the only exit door that he could see, I did not know how to continue with the project.

. . . . . .

My fieldwork took place at a time when I could hear my brother's voice on the other end of the line. I composed the manuscript without that possibility, in a partitioned time-space continuum. Loss can explode all systems of measurement and, from the grief and debris, make the most intricate map of existence, memories the sole coordinates on a desolate landscape. The most sheltered among survivors—here I speak to and about most white survivors, and in general anyone accustomed to being protected by present orders—can afford to forget that these apocalypses happen all the time, are the architecture of everyday life, to the point that grief itself gets meted out as luxury. This means that, insofar as I am inclined toward the vocabulary of the apocalyptic to describe intimate loss, then there must be another kind of ending not to dread but to welcome: the overthrow of a system founded on the theft of life from the racialized and feminized poor. Before my brother died, I had not wavered from my negativity, at least in the abstract, but my experience of personal loss threw it into incoherence. Now I simply wanted to get back the life I had before or, failing that, to bargain a halfway covenant with the universe.

......

Back in the Smoky Mountains where we had grown up, pounding twilight laps around the high school track, I couldn't outpace these thoughts. I imagined Mark grimacing at my bad faith. I had spent three years interfacing with the embarrassed beneficiaries of neoliberal surplus. I had seen how their episodic bids to manage their own conflicted attachments had evolved into a vast life-support infrastructure for a white supremacist patriarchal capitalist empire that was torpedoing into even deeper crisis. Profits *and* people. Capitalism *and* care. And other bullshit conceits whose seductive power lay in how they defer any reckoning with the magnitude of capitalist abandonment and in how, through their deferral, they both ransack the loss of its politics and held up sentiment as the universal remedy. How mortifying to catch myself propelled by a twin affective current. Not unlike the people I wrote about, I was running after private palliative that, if it was available at all, would enfold me right back into the original violence.

I collapsed on the cleat-pecked grass and allowed myself one more memory of a someone who would have known the course of action. I could almost hear his voice. Ban exception. Ban repair. Ban the sentiment that triggers both. Meditate on the endlessness, all of the losses, the pleas that echo after: stay in this existence; don't die. This book begins from that ground.

introduction

CAPITALIST HUMANITARIANISM

This book is about what is happening when power reproduces itself through performances of self-critique, historical awareness, and progressive repair. It takes as a launching point an idiom of historical consciousness that is now part of the background to late capitalist institutional life. Notice it in the ribbon cuttings for corporate social-responsibility offices in Fortune 500 firms or in the smiles of farmers from the global South who pose on the product labels of B-corporations and multinational conglomerates. See it in the eclipse of state welfare programs by "public-private partnerships" focused on entrepreneurship training and "social-impact bonds." Read it in the bookseller niche for executives who tell the rest of us how a neoliberal economy can solve structural racism, stop climate change, empower women, and, in the words of one economist, "save capitalism from its own excesses."[1] All betray a hope not only that corporations and firms can remedy the forms of privation that they have entrenched but also that free markets generally might promote feminist, decolonial, and antiracist solidarity. I call this hope, as well as the pedagogical projects and institutional arrangements it inspires, *capitalist humanitarianism*.

. . . . . .

Public reflection on history is central to capitalist humanitarian projects. A venture capitalist learns about land-acknowledgment statements at an annual professional gathering and adds one to their website. A microcredit bank envisions a new line of credit products for indigenous women survivors of ethnic cleansing and civil war. An entrepreneur of luxury clothing understands her start-up as a bid to preserve artisanal traditions whose survival is threatened by the influx of sweatshops and cheap plastic from overseas. A philanthropic foundation studies its ties to transatlantic slavery and affirms its commitment to black lives. Such understandings of a past that is not past—settler occupation, war, neocolonialism, transatlantic slavery—draw the coordinates of a present-day capitalist moral geography, political theology, and redemption arc. The goal of the capitalist reformer is not to cover up history so much as to use it as a springboard to remediate its consequences.

A litany of confession follows on the heels of this historical recognition. The enlightened beneficiary of neoliberal order recognizes the calamitous consequences of modern so-called progress, with its planetary murder sprees and casual abandonment of entire populations to abject misery. Then they acknowledge their personal complicity in this economy, how their relatively good life or at least somewhat-more-bearable-existence is predicated on the dispossession of countless others who, by design, they probably cannot name but to whom they absolutely owe a debt. Finally, they will commit to doing what they can to repair these relationships and eke out any sliver of hope from the matrix that enabled them. This is where the recourse of capitalist humanitarians to historical narratives—with history signifying either a repository of bad relations to overcome or subterranean possibilities to retrieve—becomes a preamble to the question of what to do now. What if my commodity attachments could express solidarity with exploited and oppressed people? What if the workplace could promote networks of care and friendship? What if a corporation caught poisoning reservoirs or murdering labor activists could rededicate its resources to repairing those harms?

Such questions are a method for managing the dissonance that arises between, on one hand, claiming a commitment to collective liberation and, on the other, benefiting from racist and heteropatriarchal economic violence on a massive scale. Meanwhile, on every platform where converted elites tell the rest of us about their plan to devise a socially just version of capitalism, a platoon of skeptics will pillory their hypocrisy. Each morning I power up my device and let the social media algorithms browbeat me out of my self-deception. "No ethical consumption under capitalism!" scolds the same meme that I have used to scold my boomer parents. I scroll and click and scroll and click, letting my angst generate profit for the billionaire who wrote the code for the feed. I see that yet another hate read on the "elite charade of changing the world" has made it to the top of the *New York Times* best-seller list.[2] An ad from an outdoor gear company tells me not to buy a new jacket, since habits of fast fashion fuel climate collapse. A bank markets its services by condemning the scam artistry of other lenders. A cable news broadcast livestreams protesters as they storm the network's headquarters. At some point I remember that many if not most plutocrats are in on this game of self-critique and self-reform. I am never sure how to point this out without joining their self-aggrandizing chorus.

. . . . . .

This book attempts to critique the cultural politics of capitalist reform in a way that avoids repeating, or at least forestalls, the conventions of exposé that are already fully factored into neoliberal institution building. Toward this end, I put analytical pressure on not only the organizational networks that pervade capitalist humanitarian historical archives and ethnographic fields but also the overlapping and contested institutional contexts that have conditioned the actual composition of this book: the state, the family, the corporation, the university, the union, the church.

Capitalist humanitarianism is a pervasive and understudied expression of neoliberal institutionality. The major thread of this book tracks how cacophonous critiques of capitalism on the Left have settled into streamlined efforts to reform, and rebuild, capitalist institutions. The key players in this story are multiply situated. They are missionaries whose opposition to the US global Cold War inspired them to create entrepreneurship programs in military occupations from Puerto Rico to Palestine. They are Central American solidarity activists who transferred their liberation theology into microfinance ventures and food cooperative chains. They are middle-manager bankers dedicated to facilitating financial literacy trainings for rural Guatemalan women. They are global North consumers who feel happy about purchasing eyeglass lenses from a company that provides vision testing for the poor, or who are eager to buy organic fair trade coffee if the profits are reinvested in farmer cooperatives. They are social entrepreneurs who doubt the efficacy of nonprofit aid. They are venture capitalists who attribute their investment philosophies to the radicalism of Harriet Tubman and César Chávez. All share an abiding discomfort with an imperial economic calculus that would section enormous swaths of the planet, and the life that endures there, into glorified sacrifice zones. All remain socially and psychologically tethered to capitalism as an existential plausibility structure. All strive to overcome their dissonance with best-of-all-world ventures, where one can luxuriate in private surplus while also divesting from, even dismantling, late-capitalist systems of expropriation. Their plural efforts, rooted in self-critique, have helped to reify neoliberal markets as a portal into some semblance of freedom.

For example, as chapter 1 describes, some of the earliest champions of conscious consumer practice were the Anabaptist missionaries who founded global fair trade chain Ten Thousand Villages. They did so by brokering two discourses: a tradition of disciplined asceticism with respect to secular modern temptations *and* the siren song of US benevolent supremacy. The founders found practical synthesis in a new model of consumer citizenship that, borrowing from their theological vernacular, would be *in but not of* the world into which it was born. The proposition was a win-win. If I am charmed by a vanity item that, say, was handstitched by a war refugee who received fair compensation from the Christian aid group that hired her, how can that be bad? What if my transaction is a way of turning away from the hollow excesses of mass production and toward solidarity and mutual aid with refugees? From the retrospective outlook in which "conscious capitalism" has gone mainstream, an experiment such as Ten Thousand Villages may look destined for success. But don't be fooled by the impression of smooth consensus. The dominative structures that even now are managing and concealing the conflicts immanent to them were themselves born out of antagonisms that finally could not be contained.

This book is full of stories like the above, in which radical social critiques come into dialectical tension with hegemonic forms, and something new emerges. Many of these accounts run against the grain of recent scholarship that has portrayed neoliberal capitalism as an ends-oriented rationality that captures institutions that could or should stand independent of its logics. For example, political theorist Wendy Brown argues in *Undoing the Demos* that neoliberalism is a "peculiar form of reason" that "transmogrifies every human domain and endeavor, along with humans themselves, according to a specific image of the economic."[3] The new subject of neoliberalism, *Homo economicus*, has turned her entire life into a hustle. She curates her online image until it reflects her "personal brand." She runs her household "like a CEO." She approaches her friendships as "investments" in a professional network. She relates to her government as a consumer of its services. She is, in every respect, an incarnate Kantian disaster. But she may also be on her way to obsolescence. Where does this subject fit within the turn toward socially conscious capitalism?

To the conscious capitalist, the recent efforts to infuse free market systems with humanitarian passions would be an optimistic reversal of the trends that scholars like Brown decry. Instead of a horror house where returns calculation infiltrates a social or political realm that once upon a time offered relative shelter from economic predation, the pundits for a more humane capitalism are confident that the sentimental postures of our closest relationships can be rehabilitative blueprints for free-market transactions that have lost their pastoral touch. Thus the savviest companies hawk their luxury goods as tokens of solidarity with global South laborers on the far ends of the supply chain.[4] A maverick of social investing excoriates Wall Street greed and calls for a "Church of New Capital" that approaches finance as "directed energy" to "manifest [the] impact its stewards intend."[5] Microfinance officers assign credit scores based on the credulity with which loan applicants perform "hope for the future."[6]

At an earlier phase of this project, I planned to argue that the direction of neoliberal cooptation had been inverted. I would have said that the distinguishing quality of capitalist reform movements lies in how it they resignify zones of formal production, such as factory fulfillment centers and corporate megacomplexes, as select centers of social reproduction. That is, champions of privatization and austerity have fought for hegemony as much through discourses of intimate care as through injunctions to rational self-management. But this initial direction turned out to be a false start. As with the claim that neoliberalism has "undone" a prior social world or subjective ideal, my thesis would have reified and reinvested in the conceptual separation between "social" and "economic" processes. Worse, it risked reiterating the capitalist humanitarian axiom of the "double bottom line," except instead of lauding the merger between profit margins and philanthropic mission, I would have condemned its self-deception.

The liberal distinction between the social and the economic—whether deployed by political theorists defending the democratic public sphere or by finance bankers promoting the possibility of humanitarian markets—is unprepared to reckon with its own immanent contradictions.[7] Several generations of feminist theory have established the contingency of capital accumulation with socially reproductive labor.[8] Moreover, the same liberal-settler regimes that are parasitic on this labor achieve structural coherence through the expulsion of dissonant life from their commons.[9] If late modern institutions are unraveling because of their capitulation to logics of economic utility, this development will be nothing new to those for whom capitalism's "racial calculus and political arithmetic" have been the rule, not the exception.[10]

The problem with neoliberalism is not one of overreach or collapse of spheres. And it is cruel optimism to imagine that projects of accumulation by dispossession could or should be made more humane, less predictably racist in their modes of expropriation, less overtly corrosive of democratic processes, or more beneficent in how they "give back to" and "reinvest in" the life they brutalized.¹¹ Rather, the problem with neoliberalism is and continues to be racial capitalism and the settler dispossessions, racist propitiations, and murderous abstractions that are its animating structural premise—and whose expressions adapt in relation to the conflicts and pressure points that are never not emerging. Capitalist humanitarianism is one of these adaptations. All the more crucial, then, to refuse its seductions and organize toward its crisis, so that other solidarities can come to light.¹²

. . . . . .

Like all secular modern institutional forms, capitalist humanitarianism arises in dynamic relationship with its wider contexts. The career of capitalist humanitarian intervention is in some respects a story about Christian political theology and Protestant secularism. Proponents of early fair trade and microfinance ventures were often affiliated with white Protestant churches. These actors were adamantly *not* the pro-business evangelical organizations so often featured in the historiography of capitalism. Rather, they would be quick to insist that their faith called them to resist war, support feminist politics and queer liberation, destroy white supremacy, and never cross a picket line. Their stories complicate studies of twentieth-century capitalism that have laid blame for neoliberal privatization and debt discipline almost exclusively at the feet of the political Right. Within this literature, religion rarely appears, and when it does appear, it usually references strategic alliances between free-market hawks and conservative evangelicals who wish to roll back feminist gains and legislate sexual morality.¹³ The association between Protestantism and capitalism has been especially apparent in scholarship on religion in Latin America, which often tells a story about how Left revolutionary energies sagged when the poor masses turned away from Catholic liberation theology and toward Pentecostal doctrines of personal salvation. The best of this literature demonstrates the elective affinity between the latter theological anthropology and market technologies of credit, debt, and labor asceticism.¹⁴ This argument is not wrong and, in general, has offered important insights into the production of neoliberal ideology. Taken on its own, however, the singular construal of evangelicalism as imperial shock troop and dasher of redistributive aspirations has a secondary effect of making "liberation theology" and "social Christianity" into relative moral safe zones.¹⁵ But there is no such thing.

The apparent demographic anomaly of Christians who are also leftists who also built an infrastructure for neoliberal capitalism is of secondary importance. More primary is the question of how capitalist humanitarianism comes to resemble a political theological discourse. Recurrent motifs in capitalist humanitarian formations—such as history and agency, contract and accountability, debt and redemption, responsibility and hope—are long-standing tropes in debates over the boundaries of Christianity as a popular movement, as a collective identity, and as a set of disciplines that format everyday life. I do not much care whether readers remember how scrappy bricklayers for (at least one major expression of) neoliberalism operated out of sanctuary churches. I am more invested in demonstrating, with these examples, how a more developed vocabulary around religion can be a jetpack for the task of ideology critique.

This point belongs to the Raymond Williams and Stuart Hall tradition of cultural studies. In a 1983 lecture on "Ideology and Ideological Struggle," Hall theorizes religion as a discourse that needs to be considered in the work of cultural interpretation—alongside and overlapping with popular culture, law, literature, and grassroots coalition building—and cautions against ascribing independent or transhistorical meaning to religious forms.[16] Reading the lecture can feel like trailing Hall through a series of equivocations. Hall insists that religion "has no necessary political connotation" and that you can't do cultural studies without recognizing "the continuing force in modern life of cultural forms which have a prehistory long predating that of our rational systems, and which sometimes constitute the only cultural resources which human beings have to make sense of their world." Obviously, Hall continues, "In one historical-social formation after another, religion has been bound up in particular ways, wired up very directly, as the cultural and ideological underpinning of a particular structure of power." But such "lines of tendential force" between religious formations and dominative ideological ones are neither given nor predetermined. They can be transformed through creative disarticulation and rearrangement of their constituent elements: "It is not the individual elements of a discourse that have political or ideological connotations; it is the ways those elements are organized together in a new discursive formation."[17]

I take Hall to be warning cultural critics against twin patterns in many treatments of what we take to be religious forms. One approach treats religion generally, and often Christianity specifically, as a shorthand for a stultifying secular modern order that has failed to cast off its irrational and exclusionary past.[18] Here religion is paradigmatic shorthand for what Williams would call "residual," but without any allowance for how these forms may carry dangerous memory or "flash up in a moment of danger."[19] A second approach to religion recovers this lost allowance and turns it into implicit valorization. Religion again becomes paradigmatic, this time as the wellspring of fugitive spirituality and otherworldly imagination that secular modernity has failed to contain.[20]

Between these two analytic styles, we end up with a bifocal framework in which religion looks in one instance like governing normativity and in another instance like a revolutionary, very often racialized, transgression or evasion of those norms. Both approaches run a high risk of abstracting religion from historical-material processes—which is the opposite of what Hall aims for when he writes that the "meaning [of religion]—political and ideological—comes precisely from its position within a formation."[21]

Hall does not travel alone. Core thinkers in Left cultural studies have engaged religion in tandem with, or as an explicit vocabulary for, the critique of ideology. For Cedric Robinson, who maps the collision of Marxian and Black radical traditions, a critique of religion helps to identify racial antagonisms at the heart of a capitalism forged in the transatlantic slave trade *and* as a way of identifying the metaphysical, mythic resources that fuel rebellion.[22] Silvia Federici's Marxian-feminist analytical frame recasts timelines of capitalist origins and Christian interventions in her excavation of the gendered class relations embedded in, and necessary for, modern divisions of labor.[23] Antonio Gramsci develops a theory of religion as the convergence between philosophy and action. In his *Prison Notebooks,* the Sardinian antifascist explains his concept of hegemony using an extended analysis of the cultural power of the Catholic Church. Against contemporaries inclined to reduce religion to hegemonic dominance, he shows the revolutionary potential unlocked when subalterns rearticulate religious forms in service of counter-hegemonic struggle.[24] Karl Marx, who is not as reductionist on the point as some of his readers have claimed, offers religion as a vehicle for interpreting dynamics of alienation, possession, and liberation in contexts structured by labor exploitation and the pursuit of surplus value.[25] All of these theorists engage religion in order to better diagnose, and to bring to crisis, structural antagonisms whose dissolution, for them, would be a basic reordering of existence.[26]

It can be bewildering to behold the extent to which Left cultural studies has been underused, and sometimes altogether absent, in scholarship on religion and capitalism. For example, numerous scholars situated in the academic study of religion have been more consumed with building a constructive case that modern capitalism is itself a religious form and thus worthy of scrutiny from religious studies scholars. This argument has gained traction in a larger effort to disarticulate the academic study of religion from the study of the narrow set of phenomena that settler states, university departments, and ordained clergy have historically defined as "religious."[27] One of the most clarifying voices in this renegotiation of the field's internal boundaries has been Kathryn Lofton, whose scholarship reanimates the writings of nineteenth-century social theorist Emile Durkheim in the name of a more capacious disciplinary mandate: "Whenever we see dreams of the world articulated, whenever we see those dreams organized into legible rituals, schematics, and habits, we glimpse the domain that the word religion contributes to describe." Lofton nominates consumer culture as the paradigmatic example of a modern religion: "Where our social and ritual interests are placed now is not in denominational tradition but workplace culture, not in inherited objects but recently purchased goods; not archaic icons but an endlessly rotating cast of minor and major celebrities."[28]

Lofton has done as much as anyone to crack open an academic field for those of us who no longer wish to collude with the colonial claustrophobia of a "world religions" model. Perhaps it is the potency of Lofton's intervention—the momentum of which carries into this book—that explains the surprising thinness of discussion on how her methods relate to the Left cultural studies critiques of people such as Hall and Williams. Which is partly to ask: Why Durkheim? What baggage does one take on board, and what tools do not fit on board, if we make functionalist sociology the preferred framework for interrogating religion and capitalism? A theory of religion, like a theory of capitalism, is never simply descriptive. It is also instantiating a world.[29] For example, as chapter 3 discusses in detail, Durkheim's theory crowns a lifelong quest to discover the possibility of "social solidarity" to counteract the antisocial effects of industrial capitalism. Disavowing the paeans to class revolution that had gained momentum during his lifetime, both on the page and in a transnational labor movement, Durkheim planted a flag for liberal reform. He wagered that modern workplaces could be transformed from anomic death traps to totemic hubs for social belonging and collectivity; he insisted that they could be, and should be, the new predominant religious (which is also to say social) organization.[30] A century later, Lofton's *Consuming Religion* refurbishes a version of this position in a statement about what higher-education workers can learn from investment bankers at Goldman Sachs:

> Universities are places where it is rare to hear people speak with easy fondness about their institutions. Very often you hear resignation about and disdain for their employers. This is a critique inlaid with examples indicating how far their institutions have fallen from the ideal of higher education. Goldman employees like where they work. We could call this a dislikable greed, a moral bankruptcy, or a convenient delusion. If you want to find hatred toward Goldman, there is plenty of it, filling Tumblr pages and Twitter feeds, sitting in comic punchlines and newspaper editorials. Rather

than sit in that aversion, I ask what other institutions besides Goldman could we imagine to be worth creating, and worth sustaining? And what do we think our work, our culture, our commitment is supposed to make, to do, out there?... Goldman persists because it has made—for better and for worse, for richer and for poorer—a religion. If its religion isn't ours, what is?[31]

Thinking in terms of contested articulations, there may be a way to read this statement as a call for politically engaged scholarship and pedagogy, presumably as a better alternative to Goldman's religion. But whatever potential is blunted by the rest of the paragraph, which recycles tropes that have been used to malign radical and deconstructive critique in and beyond the academy. Lofton suggests that those who excoriate the power of a major investment bank have been railroaded by negativity. They "sit in that aversion" just as "hatred toward Goldman" is "sitting in comic punchlines and newspaper editorials." These critics forfeit the battle to create the world otherwise—unlike Goldman analysts and scholars who, learning from the workplace that is the investment bank, happily make their own reality.[32] A straw impasse between uncompromising critique and commitment to transformative worldmaking is how a bid to sharpen our tools for understanding corporate consensus backs itself into a treatise about reinvesting in the workplace.

This case rhymes with larger debates, which are resonant in feminist and queer studies, on critique, post-critique, and reparative reading. Riffing on the classic essay by Eve Sedgwick, scholars have penned polemics against what they view as an academic tendency to reduce the work of interpretation to the relentless unmasking of repressed violence in texts, rather than as open-ended reading staked in generosity, care, and potentiality.[33] Too often the banner of post-critique has been used to defame critical negativity, as if in refusing to make a last-ditch punt toward pragmatism or hope, they are sabotaging Left solidarity. For all of their emphasis on generosity to readers, post-critical interventions hinge on a presumptive collapse of feelings with politics.[34] What is experienced as pleasurable or life-sustaining is imagined to correlate to political solidarity and radical futures; that which is experienced as negative or hostile is imagined to signal political cynicism and social resignation. "From this perspective," Patricia Stuelke writes, "racial capitalism, settler colonialism, and empire often emerge as structures only in need of repair and remediation, rather than as ever-shifting violent structures whose nuances must be perpetually, collectively apprehended if they are ever to be destroyed."[35] There is nothing necessarily revolutionary about the satiation of desire; a chance at radical transformation may well require many people to become much more unhappy with life as they have experienced it so far.[36] The same critique that triggers a depressive spiral for a C-suite executive or an economically stable tenure-line professor may be to the precariat an incandescent promise of another possible world or, at the very least, a pure affirmation that their suffering is real, that what they see is not paranoia, that life really can be this bad.

. . . . . .

Writing this book was an experience of constant preoccupation with how the prose would interface with the arrangements of power that I am seeking to understand and interrupt. If the seduction of neoliberal capitalism lies in how it metabolizes and absorbs dissent, on what grounds can radical critique proceed? What performance could throw a wrench into these machines of reification, or interrupt their processes of abstraction, even if just temporarily? If a writer celebrates alternative ways of being and knowing, under what circumstances can this gesture spark dreams of a world otherwise, and when is it one more way of casting a carceral searchlight on what had tried to remain undetected?

Questions like these cannot be answered with any closure but must be worked through continually across contexts. Moving with their pressure, my thinking has found its shape as much through decisions about written form as about what parts of my research to highlight. I have divided the book into six chapters, each of which theorizes a dynamic of capitalist humanitarian reform, and each of which is preceded by an interlude that situates the following chapter in the conditions of its creation. Readers will notice a permeability between the traditional chapters and the first-person accounts that divide them; their blur of first person and third person is one way that the book asks its audience (and author) to reckon with the immanence of all critical gestures and the unreliability of all narrators. Porous as their boundaries are, however, the interludes and the chapters do different kinds of analytic and affective work. The interludes can be read as formal pauses, devoted to the narrator's realization and unraveling around questions of loss, repair, and critique. The chapters connect those themes to currents in academic research and discourse. Combined, these pieces are an effort to bend lines between public analysis and private seeing, between acknowledgment of a context and critique of that context, between argument and form.

Now a word on how the research for this book developed. My initial fieldwork involved two three-month trips to Guatemala in the summers of 2015 and 2016, a more condensed follow-up visit during summer 2017, and extended engagement with US-based organizations and their archives during the concurrent academic years. My research methods included participant observation and interviews with microfinance, fair trade, and responsible-investment organizations that operated between these two countries. I initially chose to focus on Guatemala because of its history as a ground for United States– and World Bank–led adventures in neoliberal economic reform and austerity.[37] Despite or because of this history of exploitation, Guatemala has become a destination for eco-tourists, missionaries, and self-described "social capitalists" who seek to contribute to the region's economic development while immersing themselves in neocolonial fantasies about the indigenous people there. Capitalist humanitarian groups often invoke Guatemala's long history of civil war, entrenched anti-indigenous racism, and CIA-backed dictatorships—and then pitch their own ventures as the incipient pivot from grisly past to glorious future. After three-plus summers shadowing financiers and fair traders, however, it became clear I had limited the project by tying it to the nation-state borders of the United States and Guatemala. I drew this conclusion not because states and localities become moot under neoliberal reform; we know that state power is almost always central to neoliberal policies and that the effects are variable depending on scale and context.[38] I stretched my lens because I was struck by how programs of humane capitalism—these quests for a free market defined by multicultural reconciliation, interpersonal care, and political freedom—had gathered momentum. I wanted to comprehend how this happened.

Over time, this study became less like a typical history or ethnography and more like an interdisciplinary hermeneutics focused on attachments that capitalist humanitarian projects rely on and reproduce. My time with people and organizations in Guatemala—all of whom are assigned pseudonyms, sometimes with inconsequential identifying details changed—remains core to the analysis. But of equal importance are conferences of Silicon Valley investors, visits to microfinance institutions' headquarters in sleepy US suburbs, adventures in the archives of corporations and nonprofit aid groups, trips to churches that boast about their Christmas fair trade bazaars, attendance at conferences for scholars who study capitalism, and everyday encounters in a university that trains future elites in the vocabularies of neoliberal multicultural humanism. Each scene in this book is a clue to how an imperious capitalist humanitarian consciousness is contested and reproduced in a local context. Together they tell a story about how grounded critiques of neocolonial dispossession and racist dispossession found symbiosis with a sweeping ideological project to make anticapitalist dissent into a neoliberal raison d'être.

There are multiple routes through these pages. One approach would divide it into two parts. Chapters 1–3 detail historical practices out of which capitalist humanitarianism emerged and evolved. Chapters 4–6 are concerned with how those histories manifest in recent missions to bring finance discipline to the global South. That said, there's no clean break between the two halves. The chapters that draw primarily from capitalist humanitarian archives also attend to how more contemporary capitalist reformers have both domesticated and derived knowledge from those archives; the parts that highlight live encounters with financiers, investors, and reformers also reckon with the historical and material conditions through which they came to be in those places, in those ways. The same principle holds for the relation between the interludes and the chapters. A reader could hypothetically sever them from each other, approaching the interludes as creative essays and the chapters as sequential installations that add up to a more traditional monograph. But I recommend that they be read together: they are designed for mutual enrichment, with each conceived as a kind of photographic negative for the other. Moved by authors who discovered that their losses could be a starry portal to some different or more demanding kind of existence, I am writing against the fallacy that the creation of knowledge could or should be sequestered from the life that bears it.[39]

. . . . . .

The opening chapters introduce the liberal and Left reformers who laid the groundwork for an idea that participation in market exchange could under certain conditions ameliorate the worst of capitalist ravages. Chapter 1, "May Analyze like a Capitalist: Fair Trade and Other Histories," revisits the post–World War II missionary roots of the modern fair trade movement. It illuminates a genre of historical consciousness that manifests in "conscious-capitalist" projects. Qualifying a historiography of capitalism that has tended to privilege the role of religious conservatives in the dismantling of New Deal policy, it excavates the role of Left Christians in the rise of the neoliberal order.[40] I focus primarily on the pioneering fair trade chain Ten Thousand Villages, which was founded by Mennonite missionaries stationed in Puerto Rico and Palestine. They sought to design systems of exchange that would both empower poor women as income earners and provide a way to monetize, and thus preserve for posterity, artisanal crafts that the missionaries saw as threatened by globalization. Their practice of historically conscious self-critique not only rationalized their foreign interventions but also modeled a kind of reflection that would become a hallmark of capitalist humanitarian projects: an impulse to recognize and confess how the present bears a debt to a past violence, and then to offset this debt through monetized transaction. As historical exposé emerges as a discourse of neoliberal institution building, this case is instructive for critics who want to clarify how the production of historical knowledge on capitalism relates to movements for popular democracy.

The next two chapters address legacies of the early alternative-trade movements: the cultural mainstreaming of fair trade models and the ascent of microfinance. Chapter 2, "Ethical Vampires: Conscious Capitalism and Its Commodity Enchantments," illustrates how the pioneering coffee cooperative Equal Exchange retheorized the commodity fetish. Rather than assume commodities always index alienated relation, Equal Exchange discovered a *conscious* and *fair* kind of commodity, which glimmered with its powers to reverse exploitation and broker solidarity among oppressed people. The fair trade commodity spoke on its own behalf, transmitted messages back to its producers, and initiated the purchaser into a gift economy, where ethical transactions in the global North saved peasant farmers from industrial plantations and backbreaking maquiladoras to which they would have otherwise been condemned. Fair trade products even resisted Ronald Reagan's imperialism in Latin America. And still, the career of the responsibly reenchanted commodity had barely commenced. Enter the "conscious-consumer" ideologies of the new millennium, when entrepreneurs began not only to define conspicuous consumption as an act of charitable giving but also to insist that the acts of earning and spending money comprised an "energetic exchange" infused with spiritual potential. By working through an evolving mash-up of the commodity fetish and the bonded gift, chapter 2 tells the story of a transition from fair trade dissent to conscious-consumer saturation.

The arc wherein proudly leftist fair trade ventures give way to the spiritual entrepreneurship of millennials resonates with another story of strange bedfellows and counterintuitive outcomes: the rise of microfinance as an antipoverty instrument. Chapter 3, "Marxists in the Microbank: From Solidarity Movement to Solidarity Lending," explores this convergence. It follows the dual trajectories of two pioneering but politically opposed microfinance institutions (MFIs): ACCION International and FINCA International. ACCION, established as a Kennedy-era international volunteer program with anticommunist objectives, had by the late 1970s endorsed commercial "microenterprise" as a route to hemispheric soft security and economic returns. FINCA, in contrast, had opposite allegiances. Its early backers were liberation-theology-reading and anticapitalist Christians politicized by the Central America solidarity movement. These supporters believed microcredit could help small-scale indigenous farmers stand up against the financial austerity and free-trade policies ripping through Latin America. Alongside Muhammad Yunus's Grameen Bank, by the late 1990s these organizations had put microfinance at the top of the US international development agenda. Moreover, they had seeded a model of aid with enough ideological ambiguity to unite social democrats and Sandinista sympathizers with exponents of free enterprise and trickle-down economics. Blending historical and ethnographic analyses of microfinance, I argue that this convergence should be seen as a watershed moment not only in a manufactured neoliberal consensus around antipoverty strategy, but also in the embrace of free markets as a domain of political solidarity.

The second set of chapters turns to contemporary landscapes of capitalist humanitarian interventions in the global South, with emphasis on their pedagogies of financial selfhood and multicultural reconciliation. Chapter 4, "Representing Inclusion: Humans of Capitalist Humanitarianism," takes stock of the representational conventions of social capitalists and the racialized sexual-reform projects that they support. Two tropes of gendered financial subjectivity took hold in the aftermath of the 2008 stock market crash, recession, foreclosure spree, and Wall Street bailout. The first was the fiscally bootstrapping global woman-of-color microentrepreneur. The second was the racialized subprime borrower, disgraced after she squandered her chance at the American dream of home ownership. More than the mere colorwashing of racist economic violence, this discourse of qualified citizenship and liberal freedom ties both ideals to the reproduction of financial infrastructure. In making this claim, chapter 4 extends recent studies of post-1970s "predatory inclusion" in the subprime and microfinance industries while situating these financial schemes within a longer history of "philanthropic banking."[41] It finds a precursor for financial inclusion in an early twentieth-century progressive campaign to legalize small personal loans for specified segments of the working poor—namely the white ethnic immigrants that social-workers-qua-credit-officers deemed assimilable into normative racial and sexual citizenship. To revisit this moment is to cast a harsh light on calls among financial reformers for "universal financial inclusion" for "unbanked" people, exposing the ways that these discourses undergird the expulsion of entire populations from a circle of neoliberal multicultural citizenship.

The final pair of chapters draws most heavily from fieldwork with financiers who work between the United States and Guatemala. Chapter 5, "The Hunt for Yes: Archival Management and Manufactured Consent," concerns cultures of data collection and knowledge production in MFIs. It moves between the bare corporate suites in midwestern US suburbs to Guatemalan highland towns where credit officers amass data that they then transmit back to headquarters. I show that the challenge of information management in these settings is also a problem of how to procure something like a moral warrant for continued interventionist presence. The capitalist humanitarian fixation on record keeping—the surveys shoved into clients' hands at the end of each loan cycle, the quarterly due-diligence reports jerry-rigged by unpaid interns, the account-book photocopies that credit officers file and never look at again, the wall-to-wall charts on every conceivable variable—is less about game-planning the future than affirming the immediate urgency of MFIs' institutional endurance. Immersed in such paperwork, one is already and always falling behind, already and always having to rush to master whatever data point has so far escaped its domestication into the total system. The principle of capitalist humanitarian accounting is the following: whatever difference or dissonance one encounters in the field, there is a larger system of knowledge that contains it. Here there is no such thing as an archival silence or a rebel interruption.[42] The capitalist humanitarian archive asks its subjects to consent to their own inclusion in it. Then it translates every yes, every no, and every nonresponse into a license for further expansion.

Chapter 6, "Hope for the Future: Reproductive Labor in the Neoliberal Multicultural Family," reflects on capitalist humanitarian visions of the future, especially ones that vest hope in a "next generation" that will inherit its predecessors' labors and strivings, wealth and debts. I meet MFIs that provide in-house reproductive health-care services as a perk of membership, entrepreneurs who mobilize rhetoric of "youth empowerment" to rationalize child labor, and loan officers who determine creditworthiness by how well mothers convey optimism in their children's upward mobility. To observe these practices as they are enforced in various locales—the bank, the family home, the factory, the hotel, the vans shuttling between them—is to reconsider frameworks that understand neoliberalism as the subjection of all domains of being to an economic calculus.[43] These scenes also dramatize the colonial politics of what Melinda Cooper has identified as a neoliberal and neoconservative alliance around a Protestant secular regime of "family values."[44] Attentive to how finance discipline refigures theological tropes of inheritance and salvation, I show how capitalist humanitarian reproductive surveillance aims to capture any kinship formations that would escape the bank's reach. In the process, these technologies legitimate the factory and the firm as privileged zones of social reproduction, standing ready to adopt the lost and vulnerable into the care of a global corporate family.

The epilogue reflects on a latent tension within this book. I have repeatedly tripped over the expectation—from readers, from interlocutors, from myself—that such a heavy account of consuming violence and compounding loss should also make an explicit nod toward that which is not subsumed. Another version of this book could draw attention to the everyday flights to freedom, pleasure, and creation that people make daily. I could lift up grassroots organizers and popular uprisings that in their shared governance processes and their models of mutual aid manifest the social democratic vision that they seek. I could sketch out a vision of life lived in solidarity and care, and I could make a list of things that one could do or create or look at right now to see a glimpse of that life. It's not as if I don't have ideas. I could recite a reason to believe that a win is either immanent to our present or at least coming down the pike.

This book is more reserved on such gestures. It is conceivable, then, that it will be encountered as a disavowal of possibility in struggle or a treatise on how all difference is subsumed into the death-dealing itineraries of racial capitalism. How a book is read, of course, is not for an author to decide. Still, I invite readers to stay alert to the utopian refusals and radical experiments that not only shatter delusions of neoliberal consensus, but which in their defiant incarnation are nourishing other possible worlds even now. We might begin to see capitalist humanitarian reform not as the capture of movements, but as the counterinsurgent response to the everyday people who have held ground against full tidal wave of neoliberal austerity. Is there any better explanation for why investment bankers would rebrand themselves as heroes in a battle with economic predation, if not out of a sense of their own vulnerability now that grassroots democratic movements have persuaded a critical mass of people that free markets will fail to deliver the prosperity they promise, and that there are more compelling ways to distribute resources, labor, and care?

Insofar as I did not focus on popular freedom struggles and their emergent strategies, this was an expository decision. As I comprehended the scale of capitalist humanitarian surveillance and incorporation of local knowledges, I could not justify another way through this material. I have circled back to the question: How does context inform our choices about when and how to perform a commitment to hope, when and how to perform a commitment to negativity, and when and how our expositions are received as such by our readers? This book's core research is based on thousands of hours immersed in an industry that literally specializes in capturing instances of insurgent worldmaking, precisely toward the commodification of their signs and the theft of their tactics. The days of translating field notes into readable prose became a long confrontation with how the sentences and paragraphs I wrote would interact with those processes—processes that I was convinced had colluded in the murder of my brother, times a million others whose names I do not know. For all of these reasons, I have staked this text in a more negative, sometimes apophatic, pitch. This does not mean that the narrator ends up in the same place that she begins or that she is confused about the substance and stakes of her demands. Even less does it mean that the stories shared in the coming pages deny the immanence of freedom for those who tune themselves toward its rhythms and signs. When I say there is no way out, this is another way of saying: begin.

Late May 2017.
Woke up this morning.

A *New Yorker* profile opens with an image of an academic superstar who is a paragon of ascetic excellence or of a frigid, callous bitch. You decide. The night before she is set to give a lecture in Dublin, this scholar of law and philosophy learns that her mother is dying in Philadelphia. She goes back to her hotel room, proofreads her speech, delivers the talk the next morning, and then spends the transatlantic flight composing the keynote she'll give two weeks later. Should you happen to flinch at this scholar's coldness, the article slaps you to attention. You think that's cold? Listen to *this*. She wakes up every morning and runs a half marathon. She accompanies those runs with Beethoven symphonies that she plays to herself in silence, in her own head, *from memory*. When she gets back to her twelfth-floor Hyde Park condo, she practices for her weekly opera lesson. Then she heads to campus to hold court over the legions of graduate students competing for her attention. So committed is she to this regimen that, last year, when she had to get a colonoscopy, she refused anesthesia, lest it compromise her ability to work. More shocking: she felt it was appropriate to share this with a journalist. Soon it will be 10 a.m.

The article casts its subject—this acclaimed author of twenty-five books and nearly five hundred articles, this recipient of sixty-one honorary degrees and counting—as an effigy of a certain kind of female intellectual. But on the moral of the story, the narrator equivocates. Is the reader supposed to admire the ferocity of her work ethic? Is the point to share an inside joke about the pathologies of second-sex celebrity academics? Entrusting the audience to do its own guesswork, the article steers away from the arguably more pertinent question of how this particular style of sublimating maternal loss became more available than, say, canceling the talks and taking a day off. All we know is that there are two choices: yield to pain, or work.

She works. The profile makes the professor's laboring body its hook and its nod/wink at a highbrow audience that, if asked, would swear that what matters about this scholar is not her body but her corpus of ideas. The article gets there, eventually. Between intimidating her graduate students and polishing off the single-serving yogurt cup that is her standard lunch, this ice queen writes treatises in defense of liberal arts education. She is hopeful that the Greek and Roman classics, with some other Great Books thrown in, can help the under-cultured masses overcome their natural instincts to barbarity and, instead, cultivate their capacities for humanity, empathy, and citizenship.[1] Critics condemn her program as a civilizing project: it is a narrow, Eurocentric account of what constitutes the human and what it would mean to live a good life, which seeks to bring aberrant forms of being into alignment with its norms.[2] To witness this discipline and its potential effects, look no further than the routinized accomplishments of the neo-Stoic philosopher herself.

That I share these critics' concerns about this scholar's brand of liberal humanism and its pedagogies of virtue formation makes it all the stranger that, within hours of my brother's death, I remembered the *New Yorker* profile. A few weeks earlier, I might have cited it as an example of the kind of universal discourses that I was trying to understand and dismantle—capitalist humanitarians also speak in terms of a global civic ethic framed in their case by a market that transcends nation-state boundaries—its use value had changed. I received the piece as a step-by-step emergency incantation against a chorus of advisers who urged time away from work and, with that withdrawal, a practice of worldly detachment that loss makes necessary and, for people who can afford it, possible.

Sitting in a café across from another dissertation reader, scrutinizing a strawberry salad that I forgot I had ordered, I registered a voice urging me to take a leave of absence, no doubt to forestall me going the way of my brother. It took me a beat to realize that this check-in might be the endgame of the lunch. She waited for my answer. I thought, baffled, *Does she realize I am writing a book about that?* The corollaries had not stopped screaming since Mark died: sometimes you feel complicit in the global warming burning down the rainforests, so you go buy some shade-grown, cooperatively farmed coffee and feel like you're at least not making things worse. Sometimes you feel gutted by your loved one's suicide in a global service economy that kills people all the time, so you can pause and consume and rest toward a shallow approximation of a psychic repair. Both scenarios confounded the apocalypse into the most trivial thing: how the bystander feels.

I heard concerns about my well-being as political sabotage. If my reaction didn't play fair with someone just trying to name what she saw—a person in denial that she was spiraling—it was honest in its perception of cliché. How many representations do we have of white women and girls, bereft of parental care, drilling themselves toward crisis, needing intervention from Mature Adults before they harm themselves? *I am not your fucking black swan*, I snarled back, in my head.

People say that grieving a loved one's loss is a process and that there is no wrong way to do it—the unspoken part of the reassurance being *so long as you are feeling your feelings and moving toward closure*. What is closure when the death is part of a bigger story, a wound that keeps bleeding? What does it mean to grieve a loss when how one performs that grief will tell a public story about what caused it? To retreat from my work, as if Mark's death justified pausing a critique of capitalist reform projects, as if it should not have the opposite effect on my motivation, seemed unconscionable. I ventured into the summer with that *New Yorker* profile in my back pocket.

. . . . . .

At that point I'd finished most of my fieldwork, minus a few loose ends. One was an event hosted by Equal Exchange, which is one of the most established and recognized fair trade brands in the United States. Company executives, thrown by the rise of Wall Street wolves posturing as fair trade lambs and by the elevation of a real estate tycoon to the White House, had invited their customers to a "Citizen Consumer Summit." Held near the company's headquarters in conjunction with a nationwide staff retreat, the summit would strategize toward a movement to "take back control of the food system" from the megacorporations now calling the shots.

I had signed up for the event months ago. The rhetoric of consumption as civic involvement caught my attention. Eyebrows raised at the mass email invitation, I wondered if the organizers knew that historians of US capitalism coined "consumer-citizen" to describe a self-interested, benefit-maximizing national subject of Cold War suburban sprawl.[3] The conference's low bar to entry sealed my attendance. Most industry conferences were bankrolled by four-figure registration fees fronted, in most cases, by angel investors and executive-retreat budgets. This conference was free. They even provided room and board. I just had to fill out an interest form and claim an annual expenditure of $100 on the brand's chocolate, tea, and coffee. Honesty came easy. Their whole beans had monopolized my local co-op's caffeine section. Every week, the smiling Buddha pictured on the "Mind, Body, and Soul" roast's bulk bin thanked me for my solidarity with small farmers.

A harsher bodhisattva might have called out my class allegiance. That I spent 25 percent of my weekly food budget on this cheapest of the bourgeois options had less to do with my justice consciousness than my reticence to purchase coffee from supermarkets that stocked Folgers. Did my niche commodity dependence qualify me for "citizenship" in a humanist anticorporate collective? And did it matter that my coffee consumption was an instrument for eking out the last of my productive capacities, to put one more writing session in, to give a few hours to side gigs that would pay next month's rent? Both issues seemed debatable.

When I drove onto the campus of the Catholic liberal arts college hosting the event and pulled up among a clique of Subaru hatchbacks and proud-to-be-fourth-hand Toyota Camrys, their bumper stickers an impious chorus of BLACK LIVES MATTER! WE ARE ALL IMMIGRANTS! BUSH LIES! SORRY I MISSED CHURCH I WAS OUT PRACTICING WITCHCRAFT AND BECOMING A LESBIAN, I did so, adamantly, as an observer. I was there for research. That's all.

Two millennial women, both dressed like me in khaki shorts and sporty button-ups, opened the doors. One pressed a tin coffee mug into my hand. "Its handle is a carabiner, like for camping! Sustainability!" she beamed, while I side-eyed a crucified Jesus retrofit into one of the conference-center walls. The sculptor hadn't skimped on the blood. The women pointed me toward the ballroom, where about one hundred citizen-consumers milled around making small talk. I headed past gory Jesus—*Is he side-eyeing me?*—toward them.

I checked the room's demographic. Boomer-generation white people draped in linen made up half the crowd. Twenty-something white women, like the greeters and like me, added another third. The leftover minority included everyone else. Almost everyone in the latter two categories worked for Equal Exchange. The rest were regional co-op members, buddies of western Massachusetts farmers, and semiretired chairs of their local Working Families Party committees—people who could have been my own parents or their friends. The parking lot was a dead ringer for the one outside my childhood church, and many of the socially conscious drinks on the summit's breakfast bar mirrored the refreshments served each week at after-worship fellowship hour.

I grabbed a cold brew and steered around the parental demographic, finding an empty seat at a table with people who I would learn were three guest speakers from Peru, Colombia, and Guatemala. I jumped into a one-upping conversation about the best hiking trails in Central America, happy to be transported elsewhere by stories of high peaks, rainy season gusts, and backpacking trips gone wrong.

I had almost forgotten where we were when off-pitch singing jolted us to attention. Strumming his guitar at a microphone, a white man, later identified as a co-president of the company, bellowed the lyrics to an old civil rights ballad. "Woke up this morning with my mind stayed on freedom!" The more enthusiastic participants answered back: *Woke up this morning with my mind stayed on freedom!* More people joined the chorus, some swaying and clapping, others gritting out halfhearted mumbles. The direct object changed. *Woke up this morning with my mind stayed on JUSTICE! Woke up this morning with my mind stayed on PEACE!* The verb changed. *Singing and clapping with my mind stayed on freedom!*

I had heard this song a million times. It was standard at liberal Protestant churches and leftist protests of my childhood, where it rotated with other black freedom anthems like "Eyes on the Prize" and "We Shall Overcome." These late twentieth-century performances evoked an institutional memory of black and white collaboration during the civil rights movement. Not long after these songs stopped being sung on freedom rides, they found their way into the hymnals of white Protestant churches and seminaries, where they came into heavy rotation at protest marches and during Black History Month. During the 1970s, white folk musicians such as Pete Seeger and Guy Carawan performed these songs at protests, expanding audiences while drawing the focus away from the black cultural workers who developed this music in oral tradition.[4] The performances began to signify the white singers as inheritors of the black freedom movement. Now, at the 2017 Citizen Consumer Summit, the song was extending the black freedom legacy to a new cause.

Conscious consumption was being transposed into a kind of civil and human rights globalism that values consumer practice as solidarity and global South production as a foretaste of utopian freedom. Public narratives of capitalist humanitarianism have a fairly consistent cast of characters. The consumer citizen is the global North actor who abjures racist, colonial, and patriarchal capitalism in order to bend economic exchange toward a more universal justice. The scrappy farmer-producer embodies this justice, her testimony a glimpse of the simple, honest labor that remains uncorrupted by profit motive—and that can stay that way so long as the demand for fair trade goods stays strong. Ultimately, this story is about the redemption of the consumer herself: it is by rescuing the Christlike worker from the jaws of the plantation and the sweatshop that the convicted beneficiary of neoliberal capitalism finds her own salvation. The longer story is much more complicated: it took its form over time, melted and glazed in the kiln of the US Cold War empire and disappointed Left movement politics.

. . . . . .

Woke up this morning with my mind stayed on freedom! Sort of. Today I woke up. I poured a cup of fair trade coffee. I went to work. I tried again to make sense of these capitalist reformers and the world they (we) have created. The guitar player stopped. He introduced himself as a copresident of the company, thanked us for being here, and dismissed the room to our morning session. Mine was a workshop organized under the description "What happened to fair trade?"[5]

may analyze like a capitalist   1

FAIR TRADE AND OTHER HISTORIES

A person can observe "what happened" to fair trade by strolling through almost any gentrified urban shopping district. One will inevitably stumble across some window display of colorful textiles and niche gift baskets arranged alongside images of their makers. Walk in, and you will be bathed in the warm glow of hanging paper lanterns, immersed in the woodwind melodies that you can't quite place but that you know falls into the vague catchall genre "world music." Inhale, and you breathe an unplaceable smell—sandalwood? lavender?—that might also waft through the nearby yoga studio.

    I last entered one of these stores with a friend, Sophie, who swooped in for consolation coffee and mental-health checks in the weeks after my brother died. On one of these outings, she asked if we could stop by the Ten Thousand Villages in downtown New Haven. She needed to buy a wedding present for her friend and had determined to avoid the online megastore where the couple had registered. I agreed. I was eager to prove my wellness, and to me this meant proving that I'd lost none of my snark about the issue of "ethical consumption," which—along plenty of memes circulating on social media—I doubted was possible under capitalism. The two of us wandered through the sections: jewelry (chunky, colorful), textiles (lots of scarves), pottery (handmade, heavy), children's knickknacks (again, with photos of the child playing somewhere across an ocean), and single-origin coffee (in packages that depict black and brown farmers above food-centric captions such as "zesty, spicy, a little sweet" and "dark, bold, smoky"). I had anticipated exoticism, but these hit a new level of extreme. I gaped at the packages, even snapped covert photos

1.1 Equal Exchange released the comic book *The History of Authentic Fair Trade* as an educational tool. The goal was to inspire the reader to "make a conscious decision about where she stands in relation to small farmers, co-operatives, and democratic movements, as well as corporations, certifying agencies, and alternative trade organizations."

of them, while Sophie chose a handcrafted-by-Ecuadorian-farmers birdhouse. As the graying checkout clerk wrapped the package in maroon tissue paper, she asked Sophie if she was familiar with the history of Ten Thousand Villages. Was she aware that it was the first fair trade chain in North America? Had she heard that it was founded by a missionary in the 1940s to help refugees in the aftermath of World War II and that, despite the cynical appropriation of the "fair trade" label by conventional enterprises, Ten Thousand Villages has remained faithful to its "authentic" relationships with small-scale producers?

Just one week earlier, at Equal Exchange's Citizen Consumer Summit, I had spent a full day entertaining similar proclamations about authenticity. I'd even nabbed a complimentary copy of the company-published comic book *The History of Authentic Fair Trade*. The plot followed two consumers who, while drinking coffee in a café, suddenly find themselves on a Magic School Bus–style whirlwind tour of the historical struggles out of which fair trade was born. *Don't you know the history?* one of the café patrons asks her date, before the two of them are slingshot to a coffee plantation somewhere in nineteenth-century Latin America. From this encounter with backbreaking labor, the time travelers encounter the radical priests who helped the farmers unionize; the alternative trade organizations, including Ten Thousand Villages, that created networks for vulnerable people to sell their crafts at fair prices; and the appropriation of "fair trade" certifications by human-rights-trampling megacorporations. The structuring antagonism of this cartoon history is between "people" (whose fair trade projects are genuine) and "profits" (who appropriated the fair trade label for their own gain). The reader, like the café patron, must decide whose side she is on. The pages read like an evangelical tract, where the point is to convince the reader of a past consumer sin and inspire her conversion to a countervailing ethic: no to drinking "the blood and misery" of farmers, yes to "authentic fairness." In both the book and in the mouth of the Ten Thousand Villages salesclerk, the historical narrative sets a foundation for future moral action. This moral action involves commodity purchase.

Back on Chapel Street, sulking near the earring display, I indulged my internal monologue. *I know this history better than this clerk does*, I seethed, defensive at the world, ready to mobilize the same archives toward a bleaker lesson about false salvation. The moment we stepped out of the wind-chime-accessorized doors, I launched into a fact-checking diatribe, forcing my friend to tolerate the spiel for a second time. *And did you know*, I demanded, *that that person in the store probably is not even getting paid for her labor?* I had arrived at the true offense. Ten Thousand Villages, I told her, is a nonprofit venture of

1.2 The second chapter of *The History of Authentic Fair Trade* depicts fair trade shopping as a means of supporting the livelihoods of refugees in the aftermath of World War II.

1.3 The third chapter of Equal Exchange's fair trade comic book reviews the history of farmworkers organizing in Latin America, with an emphasis on the role of nonprofit organizations and the clergy in the labor movement.

the Mennonite Central Committee and most of its staff are church volunteers. To sell those products, to repeat the myth of their founding, is understood as Christian mission work. I ranted at her, relishing the irony in disconnected fragments—*like, the layers of exploitation, fetishizing global South labor while not even paying your own workers in the US*—as if the crime were obvious. I was confident, correct. They had their myths; I knew the history.

. . . . . .

To say that a product, an emotion, a belief, or a history is "authentic" is often to contrast it with something less true, something fake, lurking in an implied background. The claim to authenticity is common within capitalist humanitarian projects, but it isn't unique to them. The market reformers who handwring over illegitimate statements about producer relationships and ethical products have kindred spirits among public intellectuals who confront violence they believe to be fueled by historical confusion, and who brandish *better history* and *setting the record straight* as antidotes. Think classicists who correct white supremacists for their flawed depictions of ancient Greece or historians debating the founding principles of US democracy.[1] Fights over historical truth convey hegemonic contestations in the present.[2] In the case of fair trade and other capitalist humanitarian interventions, the twin instincts to expose historical oppressions and litigate the "ethical" provenance of commodities function as a settler move to innocence. It can suggest that having become aware of capitalism's colonizing violence, it is now possible to avoid and overcome the worst of it.[3]

Scholars of capitalism and architects of market reform share a love of historical data. Tracked to the sites of their narrative production, the threads of the clerk's origin story and the plotlines of the fair trade comic-book preview a main argument of this book: a core pattern of capitalist humanitarian thinking is one in which the relative beneficiaries of neoliberal spoils awaken to their complicity with racialized economic violence, pledge to leave behind their destructive habits, and seek to offset their moral debts through acts of reformed market participation. It repeats whenever free-market beneficiaries—entrepreneurs, investors, historians, corporate executives, everyday consumers—attempt a program of capitalist harm reduction. These aren't always empty actions; a fair trade latte probably inflicts less suffering than one whose ingredients were sourced from a plantation. Still, it's worth underlining the ways that comparatively less brutal infrastructures of monetized value and private property can become political arguments unto themselves, when pitched in comparison to a worse alternative. The crimes of capitalism are converted, piece by piece, into arguments not for, say, democratic socialism or a feminist anti-work politics, but for the installation of a *more humane capitalism*. With their wails of error and calls for repentance, capitalist humanitarian projects launch their subjects into a process of expiation of the moral debts they have accrued and the reparations they can make with more-enlightened transactions. As the cases of fair trade pioneers Ten Thousand Villages and Equal Exchange have already shown, the process often begins with a question: *Don't you know the history?*

......

Sophie and I navigated the streets around Yale while I held forth on all I had discovered about Ten Thousand Villages. Most accounts of the project's origins portray it as the shoestring passion project of Mennonite missionary Edna Ruth Byler. The idea came to her when, as part of a church service trip, she traveled to Puerto Rico about one year after the end of World War II. While there, she encountered levels of privation that were, at least within the limits of her own experience, unprecedented. Missionaries with longer-term placements on the island had tried to facilitate income-generating opportunities for local women by holding embroidery lessons and then selling the needlework crafts, but they needed a bigger market. Byler joined them in brainstorming: What if she sold the products to her network of churchwomen back in Pennsylvania? And, assuming her plan worked, could it be scaled to other places and people? The answer turned out to be yes, and the Overseas Needlework and Crafts Project was born.

......

Needlework rose under the star of United States benevolent supremacy, when key geopolitical watchwords—international peace, human rights, unity—operated as euphemisms for US soft power.[4] Responding to the perceived threats of communism and socialism, state agents and mass media outlets portrayed Western-dominated markets as a privileged domain where "free choice" and "democracy" were uniquely achievable.[5] This free-market boosterism informed the creation of the World Bank, founded in 1944 to finance Europe's postwar recovery, and the establishment of the United Nations, charged with keeping the international peace.[6] A legion of private aid organizations, such as Heifer and Oxfam, also cropped up alongside these formal alliances, and urged them to approach humanitarian intervention with an eye to seeding the long-term economic vitality of local communities.[7] Meanwhile, mass consumer infrastructure had ballooned in the United States. Big-box stores cropped up like dandelions, suburban enclaves sprawled out, credit became available to everyday shoppers, and direct-sales brands such as Avon and Tupperware transformed living rooms into theaters of entrepreneurship. Whether Mennonites would be changed by the dawn of this consumers' republic was an open question; they were, after all, the inheritors of a long Anabaptist ascetic tradition premised on a commitment to living in, but not of, the world.

Needlework brokered a treaty among US neocolonial power, mass consumer culture, and church teachings about simplicity and restraint. Whereas some commercial enterprises lured people into excess and vanity, Needlework sought only "to glorify God by serving people, to love the poor in obedience to the teachings of Jesus, and to be designs of God's continuing love and care."[8] Byler downplayed her economic savvy—"I'm just a woman trying to help other women"—even as she laid the groundwork for a new genre of consumer citizenship.[9] She taught a cohort of global North Christians to not only to cultivate beauty in their own homes, but also to enable poor women to "help themselves to do the same."[10] Through this conscious consumer ethic, Needlework's customer base could experience their evolving consumer desires less as materialistic indulgence than as a form of asceticism, which oriented them toward humanitarian need outside of themselves.[11]

Within ten years, Needlework had established outposts in places where strong humanitarian need correlated with a high demand for indigenous and locally produced textiles: Puerto Rico, Jordan, Jerusalem, Hong Kong, and Haiti.[12] In Puerto Rico, missionaries worked amid rapacious foreign speculation in the colony, as well as the US military crackdown on the national independence movement. Needlework's inaugural customers would have included the thousands of soldiers and tourists flooding the island.[13] In Jerusalem and the West Bank, missionaries employed Palestinians to sew textile designs that were then sold to the Israeli soldiers who had expelled them from their homes in 1948.[14] Stationed in Haiti during the Duvalier regime, the missionaries expanded their inventory to include woodwork by artisans thrown into disarray by major hurricanes and, presumably, the dictatorship.[15]

So rapidly did Needlework grow in the early Cold War years that by 1962 Byler had turned over its management the Mennonite Central Committee (MCC), the umbrella office of the Mennonite and Brethren churches in the United States and Canada. The MCC moved the project's headquarters to the church offices in central Pennsylvania, expanded retail operations to Canada, hired Byler as full-time director, and rebranded the project as SELFHELP Crafts (SHC).[16] By 1975, what had begun as a one-woman shoestring venture had proliferated to more than a dozen countries and raised $200,000 in revenue.¹⁷ The next two decades saw further growth—additional shops, dozens more countries, multiplied staff—before rural Pennsylvania and rural Ontario Mennonite country hit a saturation point. The executive leadership, to rise above the plateau and continue to create jobs for artisans overseas, needed to initiate a "dramatic culture shift," starting with a "new corporate and visual identity." Taking guidance from advertising consultants, they zeroed in on a new target demographic: "middle- to upper-income" women, ages twenty-five to fifty, who lived in "urban centers," boasted "an above average understanding of global cultures," and felt "concerned about their own status and the status of the products they buy."¹⁸ The SHC identity was centered on the philanthropic aspects of shopping; the new Ten Thousand Villages identity would celebrate products' fine quality, cosmopolitan cache, and ethical upside in equal doses.

Commercial success had a way of exposing conflicts, fantasies, and fears about the organization's future direction, several of which surfaced in debates over the new name. A "common visual identity" committee generated, and vetoed, hundreds of options before narrowing the list to ten finalists. "The Banyan Tree" emerged as frontrunner but was nixed by consultants when they discovered a technology advertising firm by the same name. "Touch the World International" attracted votes from members excited to convey how shoppers were "literally touching the world (smooth Pakistani onyx, rough Philippine fibre baskets, smooth Vietnamese lacquerware)" in the stores, but the name was jettisoned for "sound[ing] like a 'how-to' seminar for molesters." Others liked "Upside Down Trading" as a fun title for their "producer-driven not consumer-driven" business, until they thought twice about broadcasting that "merchandise will arrive upside down and broken." The naming team landed on an official winner in the pun-happy "Far Fetched"—but retracted after their colleagues revolted, objecting that possible connotations with "wild and crazy things, outlandish and not useful [items]" cut against the mission of a "religious/Christian" enterprise and could "burn bridges" with their most loyal patrons.¹⁹

Each new phase provoked internal debate about whether the project had broken faith with the original mission. To enter the fray, one needed to know something about the traditions of North American Mennonites and to defend a vision for how the enterprise formerly known as SELFHELP should interface with the church's evolving identity. To do justice to this debate, this book would have to dedicate many more pages to the matter. A fuller account of Ten Thousand Villages feasibly could begin with their roots in the sixteenth century's radical Reformation, the centuries of persecution that followed, and the migration and settlement of Anabaptist sects throughout the Americas.

To underline the commitment to mutual aid and humanitarian response to suffering, the story of their fair trade project could include a synopsis of how the Mennonite Central Committee formed in the 1920s—mostly as a way of organizing North American Anabaptists to give mutual aid to their persecuted comrades in Eastern Europe. The narrative could recall how in the 1930s and 1940s Mennonites multiplied their missionary infrastructure to accommodate conscientious objectors to military service and to provide a witness to international peace.[20] And, insofar as the goal of this historical rehearsal is to critique capitalist humanitarian projects, it should underline how in the name of mutual aid the MCC threw its resources behind the massive, violent colonial settlements of Mennonite refugees in Bolivia, Mexico, Paraguay, and Argentina.[21] All of these details would fill out the Mennonite relationship to the state and to empire, and to humanitarian and communitarian ideals, as they played out in their fair trade projects. An arsenal of historical facts could become the proofs and counter-proofs of accounts given by MCC members themselves, always with the implicit demand to know the history.

The archive of Ten Thousand Villages is replete with consternation over how to reconcile the values of ascetic restraint with the fact that church missionaries seemed to be encouraging consumerism. People wondered: Was the MCC's entrepreneurship-and-sales initiative a *service* or a *business*? Did it promote consumerism, and, if so, how did this track with Mennonite values? What crafts could Ten Thousand Villages appropriately sell? Could participation in capitalism ever promote social justice, or was this just a wishful delusion?[22]

The answers tended to circle back to issues of survival. Vulnerable populations around the world needed nourishment and shelter, both of which were more easily secured with the income streams that SELFHELP generated. On the issue of overindulgence, SELFHELP only stocked "products that are utilitarian and that do not violate the more-with-less lifestyle, hand-crafted items that are labor intensive and products that do not compromise MCC values (no ashtrays, wine bottle openers, erotic dancers, excessively expensive jewelry, carousels that play jingle bells)." Distributors also screened out "objects of worship used in non-Christian religions," even as they acknowledged that "the line between religion and culture is not always clear."[23] The ambiguity about the inventory anticipated even tougher conflicts over whether the MCC should be involved in a commercial enterprise at all.

Here, leaders of SELFHELP reasoned not only that their work provided income to artisans but that it also protected artisanal forms that capitalist modernity threatened to extinguish. Thus the missionaries in Puerto Rico "learned traditional embroidery designs from women in the mountains and taught them to city dwellers who had forgotten them."[24] Their counterparts in the West Bank took pride in marketing "Palestinian needlework patterns [that] had been passed down since the time of Abraham and Sarah" and worried that the vagaries of consumer demand would corrode their "truly Arab" character.[25] In both cases, commodities count as "authentic" to the extent that they can be associated, however dubiously, with the traditions of the people targeted for settler displacement and colonial occupation. Fair trade was like a bad consolation prize: if capitalist modernity and its military enforcers threatened indigenous life, here was a way to preserve it by working with, rather than against, free markets.

It is unlikely that the MCC missionaries would have understood their presence in terms of settler colonialism. Yet SELFHELP could not exist without an implied account of its relationship to occupation, given that occupation was the literal precondition and enabling condition for their work. The query *Are we a business or a service?* hinted at a sharper question: *Who and what are we serving?* Extraction? Genocide? A suffering and displaced population? Women? Can a business be a net good? Or at least be neutral? The answer can never crystallize beyond a "both" or a question mark. The undecidability of the issue guarantees its recurrence. Table the question, and you make certain that it boomerangs back, with its history, its futures, its postponement, again.

. . . . . .

Historians understand that to lack a record of what happened is a liability for the present. Corporate enterprises know this as well, and never as sharply as when they are divining their possible futures. If Ten Thousand Villages gives one front-row seat to how historical deliberation shapes the trajectory of capitalist humanitarianism, then Equal Exchange witnesses to the corporate investment in origin stories. Several months beyond my foray into the MCC file folders, at the Citizen Consumer Summit, I nabbed a seat in the final workshop: "From Audacious Idea to Impactful Social Enterprise: The Founding of Equal Exchange." Its description addressed the reader/consumer/citizen in the second person. "Maybe you know there is something kind of special, different about Equal Exchange," it began. "And so you wonder, how did this thing begin?" The contention is that in order to comprehend what makes Equal Exchange exceptional, you need first to behold its roots.[26]

The first speaker introduced himself as the current copresident of Equal Exchange and the only founder still involved with the organization. The purpose of the session, he explained, was to honor the "human investment" that made the "fair trade movement." Then he rewound the clock to the 1980s, when he and his two friends were scraping by in entry-level jobs stocking the warehouse of a cooperative grocery store. Wanting more for themselves and hoping to make a difference in the world, they determined to strike out on their own. Specifically, he reminisced, they would launch a coffee cooperative whose top-notch products would be matched only by the quality of the founders' solidarity with Central American producers. The friends set their sights on Nicaragua, where small-scale farmers were buckling under a trade embargo that Reagan had passed in retaliation against the leftist Sandinista government. Equal Exchange routed its first product, Café Nica, from Nicaragua, to third-party countries like Canada and the Netherlands, and finally to the United States. It was unbelievable, Founder 1 glowed, that these days of upstart activism had bloomed into the established institution we know today.

I recognized the basic outline, which permeates Equal Exchange literature—except for one rhetorical snag. Founder 1 could not stick to the ragtag-to-riches landing; he kept jumping between plots. The main story featured three idealistic young adults building a fair trade movement against the odds, but a barely repressed subplot kept interjecting with hints of strained friendship. "We left at different times," he reminded the room for the second time, right before he swerved back to their shared work and legacy. "People at Equal Exchange owe us so much. We built this model," he declared, or pled. He talked this way for five minutes: rehashing the split, affirming the role of the leavers, reminding the room of our debt to all of them.

The more cracks in the nostalgia, the more awkward the session felt. Privately, I spun scenarios to explain the tension. Did someone leave in protest? Was it weird that Founder 1 expressed such magnified gratitude to his cofounders for coming, even though both of them were local? Hadn't they wanted to come? I also wondered if in my fatigue I was projecting drama where none existed. Still, I saw less camaraderie than what I would have expected in a reunion of three friends turned business partners. I had anticipated exuberant storytelling crowded with interruptions, shared laughter, knowing eye contact, and "oh-my-goodness-can-you-believe-how-young-we-were-then" reverie. What they performed was a rote rehearsal of "three perspectives on the founding" with little cross-pollinated dialogue and almost no laughter.

. . . . . .

Later on, I'd understand this awkwardness as key information about how narrative operates within capitalist humanitarian projects. Somehow the genre of founding-story reminiscence had become familiar enough to me that, despite my predisposition to criticize it, I could be disappointed when a version of it fumbled the delivery. How did I come to expect an affective payoff?

One explanation: I came to the Citizen Consumer Summit fresh from four months as a student ethnographer in a Yale School of Management class titled "How Companies Can Align Profit and Purpose." Two-thirds of the curriculum was based on hearing founding stories of publicly avowed socially responsible companies, as told by their executives. The assignments required us to identify and write essays about our personal "mission." The speakers—who included an executive of a private weapons contractor committed to offering its employees excellent health insurance, the "vice president of philosophy" for a high-end apparel company, and financiers who "stand with the poor"—had modeled this narration. I learned in this class that being a good narrator—and "good" always involves a mash-up of hardship and humor—is central to the success of a company. Whether it was the weapons manufacturer or the philosophy VP, their project cohered in how they narrated them into unity. The stories they told had a common arc, which went like this: *Once we were young and naive activists, and then we realized that our social-justice energies could be scaled up if we worked with, rather than against, capitalist systems. We could never have imagined this then, but look at us now.*

We heard from one multimillionaire business executive who left his corner office job at a private equity firm to become an independent angel investor for social enterprise start-ups. Addressing our windowless seminar room, our five-deep rows of oblong tables and rolling chairs obstructing anyone inclined to stage a walkout, he testified to how the United Farm Workers influenced his approach to personnel management and investment banking: "The important part of social change is movement building. There is a guy at the Kennedy School named Marshall Ganz who has worked with César Chávez and others on narrative [and] how do you get people on the ground to buy in through narrative." In other words, this venture capitalist (VC) situated a militant labor union primarily made up of migrant workers as the moral precursor to impact investing. Bowled over by this counterintuitive claim to affinity, I asked him to elaborate on the relationship between grassroots labor movements and impact investing. He did not miss a beat:

> Yes. It's exactly the same. We are setting up new systems now because the old ones—religious orders, Rotary Clubs, and so on—have broken apart, and we need to find ways to reconnect. We are working in silos, need to find another way. Building a movement is not just about saying no to business. You know, Marshall Ganz in the early days was working with Chávez. He

hated business. But when you do that you exclude the people who can be very helpful. Now people are figuring this out. They are learning that the system can be helpful. We can't be religious about structure. Movement building is a tool. Impact investing is a tool.

The investor was telling a story. It was a story of secularization, of conversion, of enlightenment, of persuasion. I asked our visitor to explain something about his experience, and he jumped to what Ganz might call the *story of now*: the collective action required to mend a present injustice.[27] The problem of the present, in the mind of this VC, is a "siloed" community suffering in the absence of plausibility structures and mutual trust. When I presupposed an antagonism between venture finance and anticapitalist labor organizing, I had exacerbated the issue—and then was called to the carpet for it. For the VC, the incommensurability between these entities was a dialectic that had already worked itself out. *We are setting up new systems now.* Or, as he concluded, "Capitalism figured out at some point that I need to do something to change, because otherwise communism is going to own us. They are in a system; that's what happens when you are working in a system. They begin to bring in women, minorities, be more responsible to workers." The course instructor chimed in to say that "capitalism is very adaptive"—*yeah, the workers have noticed*, I thought—and to move our conversation along.

It all felt smooth. That is the magic of that kind of story. There is conflict, but we already know that it is headed toward some resolution. The firm would, as the title of the School of Management course suggested, "align profit and purpose."

. . . . . .

It was this posture of resolution that, back at the Citizen Consumer Summit, Founder 1 could not seem to pull off and that the second founder would reject. Revolutionary peasant farmer movements bequeathing a legacy of socially responsible capitalism? Bullshit, said Founder 2, in so many words. But first he wanted to open, he said, by "recognizing where we are." "From my perspective, we are on occupied land," he announced. Then: "I raise this to say this is how the world works." He did not elaborate.

This statement is another historical act, which reminds the audience that our presence on that campus is an outcome of dispossession. Once again it is a litany familiar to me from political gatherings. Whatever the event, the call to order often includes an acknowledgment of the indigenous land on which we stand, led by someone from the local university's Native American Cultural

Center. If these speech acts are attempts to surface a colonial situation that is most often whitewashed and denied—and thus involves a risk to the speaker, who may find herself censured or worse—their valence changes when spoken from a position of elite power. It is now common for liberal settler states to publicly atone for genocide by confessing wrongdoing and then celebrating generic indigenous difference as essential to the nation's cultural fabric.[28] Capitalist humanitarians share this tendency.

Three months after the Citizen Consumer Summit, I again found myself party to a land acknowledgment that was transposed into an apologetics for colonization. That time it took place in a San Francisco auditorium with about three thousand other specialists in impact investment and social entrepreneurship, gathered there for the 2017 conference of Social Capital Markets (SOCAP), an association "dedicated to the acceleration of new global markets at the intersection of money and meaning."[29] That year, the opening plenary session featured a dance by a teenage member of the Ohlone Nation. "We want to recognize that this *once was the land* of the Ohlone people," a SOCAP point person announced by way of introducing the guest. The articulation grated: if Founder 2's phrasing made settler colonialism sound like a matter of subjective viewpoint, these words sounded to me like an unfortunate (if unintended) gloat, as in *We realize it was your land, and we are kind of sorry, but it's our land now*. Both statements hat-tip toward restitution, but neither manages the follow-through on the Implication: If this is an occupation of indigenous land and the speaker regrets the situation, then why are they here? Or, as Elizabeth Povinelli asks, "What is the nation-state recognizing, capital commodifying, and the court trying to save from the breach when difference is recognized?"[30] I am contending that one of the things being recognized and commodified is the capacity to enact self-reform through transaction. It starts with confession.

. . . . . .

Founder 2 transitioned from his acknowledgment to the familiar warehouse origin story, plus one added detail about the source of their start-up funds. Equal Exchange's angel investor was his grandfather, who bankrolled the project with money that he inherited from *his* grandfather, who was "an itinerant Jewish peddler who went to the south to be a slaveholder and got rich doing it." The great-great-grandfather's descendants still benefited from the wealth accumulated through slavery, he admitted, and so do Equal Exchange's employees, farmer partners, and citizen-consumers.

Founders 1 and 2 put Equal Exchange in a position of indebtedness to its past, but they parted ways on the question of where the debt lies, who owes what to whom, and who can rightly claim the position of creditor. Founder 1 charged a moral debt to current Equal Exchange employees, who *owe so much* to him and his friends. For Founder 2, the creditor was the great-great-grandfather, whose traffic in black life not only defames his legacy but also casts harsh light on the social justice mission that Equal Exchange continues to claim, not to mention the summit's opening black freedom hymn. Founder 2 further suggested that the debt of Equal Exchange's beneficiaries—including everyone in that room—was to the Wampanoag people who stewarded the land we were on and to the black people whose slave labor created the wealth that built the company. Founder 1 hoped to respond to these moral debts with "fair" transactions; Founder 2 insisted that this was impossible.

Listening to their dueling presentations, it was still unclear to me what the stakes of Founder 2's historical announcement were supposed to be, even if I shared his proclivity to myth-busting. It lands less like a prompt for reflection than the retread of a stale quarrel, a personal-political history served as a pent-up rebuttal to an old trigger. The trigger, in this case, was the fair trade evangelism that had resounded throughout the day. Founder 2 had had enough. I tried to disaggregate his concern about Equal Exchange's ties to slavery from his consternation at a relationship gone sour, but they were too tangled up. He would allow that he left Equal Exchange because of a "stalemate" over "whether marketing leads sales or sales lead marketing." Then he would announce that the "more success you have, the more integrated [into the market] you become." *This is how the world works.* Then his story would disintegrate, and he would be all over the map. He would describe a personal foray into transcendental meditation that stoked his passion for systemic change. He would hope for a united Left that could stand up to corporate interests. He would interrupt his colleagues with barrages of questions about their motives.

I struggled to follow. I resented what registered to me as a display of masculinist bravado, stark against the performances of feminized humility among the quilting Mennonite women. Does capitalist reform always swing between these gendered poles of righteous awareness and sheepish self-deprecation? I rolled my eyes as I considered the question, at the same time as I told myself that Founder 2's critique of incorporation should be heard. I remembered that when people name things that others do not see, they often sound overwrought and incoherent to everyone else. Still, these righteous announcements have come to feel as obvious as the mission drift that their speakers put on trial. So I wish that what we were asking is this: What is this place where the business founders can recite the critiques of capitalism lodged at them by the rioters at their gates? What becomes of the critique of capitalism when the idiom of capitalism, and of the empires it raises, is an idiom of self-critique?

These are not the questions that Founder 2 asked. He spewed rhetorical accusations at Founder 1: What is success for you? Is it scaling up? Is it building incremental power with the procurement of the powers that be? Does success mean that producers don't need you anymore because you have become irrelevant? He already knew the answers—that Founder 1 would define success as growing his relatively more ethical business in a world where there is no realistic alternative to capitalism—and didn't like what he'd heard. So he used questions about future success to state a grievance with the history that his former partner had told; he introduced historical facts that were, at least in the eyes of Founder 1, at odds with the official origins of the company. But insofar as the two founders clashed on the level of interpretation, they did not clash on the assumption that a story had to be told. Polarized as they were, Founders 1 and 2 shared their drive not just for a coherent narrative but for a narrative of success as well. "What is success for Equal Exchange?" Founder 2 asked again. "Is it that they don't need you anymore?" I heard him asking: How can you valorize your own institutional survival when that survival is premised on a moral debt that you cannot settle?

. . . . . .

The leadership of Ten Thousand Villages likewise wondered to whom they owed their upward thrust and to what values they should hold themselves accountable. The Six-Day War in 1967 forced an institutional reckoning with the questions. In an offensive secondary only to the Nakbah of 1948, the Israeli Defense Forces (IDF) expelled hundreds of thousands of Palestinians from their homes and seized control of the West Bank, the Golan Heights, Sinai, and the Gaza Strip. The war also spiked nationalisms on all sides, redrew borders, undermined diplomatic negotiations, and subsequently opened the gates to Israeli settlers and international tourists.[31] Needlework benefited from this latter development. "The political situation itself," admitted missionary Helen King, "seemed to be the thing that helped us break into the 'big time.'"[32]

As King reported from the field, the years between 1967 and 1970 had been difficult for everyone. For the missionaries themselves, the problems mainly concerned the hassles of military bureaucracy and new regimes of customs enforcement. Their daily rhythms had been all but hijacked by the tariffs and customs regime that, even prior to the latest war, had regarded Needlework with suspicion.[33] King also feared for the well-being of the project workers.

"A number had husbands in prison since the war, prices of staple foods and ready-made clothing climbed steadily, and they lived in constant fear of the Israeli army," she reported, "Whenever a grenade was thrown at a passing army vehicle in the night, the nearby villages were placed under curfew and many arrests were made."[34]

Still, they tried their best to stay out of the politics. Although King rebutted official representations of the Israeli state as a non-aggressive party seeking only to coexist, her passive voice evaded any assignation of responsibility for the occupation itself. The topic at hand was not Palestinian grievance but the "fear" felt by women. Arrests *were made* and curfews *were placed,* no agents involved. Into this rhetorical lacuna the MCC entered as a mediator. Circumstances are bad, King's letter said, but we are making the best of it. They planned to do so by generating income opportunities for Palestinian refugees. She was telling a story. *Once upon a time, there was this situation, and we found ourselves in it, so we had to figure out how to navigate it. This is what we did.*

King's acknowledgment of Palestinian fear was bound up with her orientation toward Palestine as site of ancient biblical history. From her description of Israeli tanks rolling through town, King conjured a vision of the pastoral Palestinian everyday:

> The majority of village women were uneducated and lived simple lives, rarely leaving the village where they lived because they saw no reason to do so. Life was straight out of a Bible story picture book. A familiar scene was one of a long-robed woman walking to the well with a five-gallon can on her head. They stood ramrod straight from carrying heavy loads on their heads. Those from families with property worked long hours in the fields during the spring and summer months tending to their olive trees and plots of grape vines, tomatoes, cucumbers, and other delicious fruits and vegetables.... The fortunate ones owned a donkey; the others used their backs to carry their harvest from the fields.[35]

The verbal illustration recapitulated a cultural discourse of "the Middle East" that had circulated in the United States during the mid-nineteenth century and that amplified in conjunction with mounting US economic interests in the region following World War II.[36] Gazing out at occupied Jerusalem, King narrated a clash between, on one hand, the ambivalent advance of military technology, capitalist globalization, and Western liberal education and, on the other, the implied historical anachronism of Palestinians performing manual agricultural labor, taking trips to the well, and walking alongside donkeys. The allegedly simple lives of Palestinian women—echoing the simple lives of Anabaptist women who also embroider and tend the land—are figured as vessels for modernity's biblical "before."

These missionaries, as well as their eventual successors in the mainstream fair trade industry, began to transpose the categories of occupier and occupied into categories of consumer and producer. As Israel anticipated its twentieth anniversary as a state, government officials sketched plans for a parade through a newly captured area of East Jerusalem. The route passed by the Needlework storefront.[37] King remembered how "regular Israeli customers" put the shop on "the sightseeing list they had prepared for their visiting family and friends." Their demand overwhelmed supply. We stared openmouthed at these tourists who bought large size tablecloths without asking about prices," King wrote, awestruck even in retrospect, "Many of these were businessmen from New York, and I could hardly contain the questions I wanted to ask them about outlets for our needlework in their areas. I hesitated though because I knew we could never fill more orders with our present number of village women."[38]

Needlework staff recruited labor from the exact population of "village women" displaced by the occupation. Then they grew their humanitarian enterprise by selling their crafts to settlers. The approach yielded high, if also self-reinforcing, returns. With news about the textile products "spreading like wildfire" among Israelis, the high-end fashion house Maskit approached Needlework's front office with a collaboration opportunity. Maskit, established by the Israeli government in 1954 to provide jobs for settlers in the absence of other labor opportunities, was in the process of reinventing itself around an cosmopolitan desert chic aesthetic.[39] Maskit CEO Ruth Dayan intended to accessorize her next collection with "wares made in the newly-occupied areas of West Bank and Gaza." For a line of winter wool jackets, Needlework's embroidery fit the bill.[40] The association with Maskit further augmented the project's reputation for stewarding Palestinian history and culture. Curators at the Israel Museum consulted Needlework staff when they were "researching the clothing and embroidery patterns of Palestinians" and, once the exhibit was live, promoted their storefront when tourists "inquire[d] where they could buy authentic Arab embroidery."[41] When MCC staff took exception to the "Made in Israel" tags that state-backed venues had affixed to Palestinian textiles, they wrestled over the potential price of public dissent. The Needlework Project had, at its apex, generated more than nine hundred jobs in Jerusalem and the West Bank alone.[42] What would happen to the workers if the revenue dried up?

Without an obvious path forward, these fair trade pioneers wove a tapestry of myth, history, and fantasy, until the threads lost their beginnings and ends. One story summoned the Holy Land to endorse Israeli settlers' world historical claim to the territory. Another dwelled on the desperation of refugees who could not have survived without outside help. A final story cast the missionaries as keepers of a fragile peace, wherein commodified relics of Palestinian tradition would find affirmation in the modern state of Israel—even and maybe especially when the makers of those crafts were exiled.

Less present in the MCC record is reflection among missionaries about why settlers wanted needlework produced by Palestinian refugees in the first place. Was it a desire for some myth of a biblical past, preserved on the mantles of the new occupants? How did Palestinian workers feel about being asked to sew the Rose of Sharon into pillowcases for citizens of an occupying state? How soon after the conquest can you start selling representations of the people who used to live there? How long until the commodities on display have rewritten the prior histories with new authentic truths? How long until the objects testify? When they do, here is what they will say: once I was ripped away from my home; now I celebrate historical difference. Once there was an invasion; now the land is rich with citizen consumers. Once your people lived here; now they live on this wall. Don't you know the history?

. . . . . .

My own knowledge of historical facts and my amendments to the historical record are how I make my living. I am trained to locate Helen King and her fair-trade contemporaries in the larger history of empire, capitalism, and missions; I have learned to make hard sense of her life and its milieu in ways that she might not have seen herself.

So, when I seek clues about her milieu in the growing body of literature on Protestants abroad, I am struck by a trend in which scholars underline the personal good intentions and moral ambivalences of the missionaries they are studying. Even more, I am alarmed when these chronicles of feeling have been used not to interrogate the affective regimes of colonial rule, but to dispel one-dimensional caricatures of Christians as imperial zealots.[43] Even if they were involved in dubious operations, one influential argument has maintained, at least they learned lessons about multicultural tolerance that they could put into action once they returned home.[44] This lens occludes many possible arguments about the complicity of King or her MCC colleagues with colonialism. Instead, insofar as their presence sometimes lubricated Israeli occupation, the major takeaway point would be that they went for humanitarian purposes, and that scholars should center on their goodwill. Clearly, I could proclaim, they built authentic bonds with the people they met there, who would have had diverse positions and stakes in the future of Israel and Palestine. Clearly, they were moved to connections that might not have existed otherwise. But care and solidarity are not mutually exclusive with colonialism. They are just as likely to be conveyors of it.[45] Feelings of sincere attachment can be an affective production of coloniality, such as when occupiers experience themselves to be personally invested in the lives and future of the people they dominate. In repeating a story where the emotional attachments of Protestant missionaries double as one litmus test for the virtue of their projects, this historiography can morph into quasi-apologetics for *respectful occupation, sensitive colonialism,* and *humanitarian capitalism.*[46]

When I try to locate these early fair traders in the historiography of religion and capitalism, I runs into an almost inverse problem. When this literature has attended to religion, it has primarily been to call out a specific sort of actor: the evangelical Christian, usually a man, who hatches strategic alliances with laissez-faire economists to build the post-Depression New Right. This actor is calculating in his desires for power and zealous in his conviction that Christian witness requires faith in US-dominated free markets; he is unaware or dismissive of groups such as Ten Thousand Villages and Equal Exchange.

Even less is he aware that these latter organizations, if given a moment in the limelight, might qualify the outsized role that evangelical corporate executives and trickle-down economists have played in mainstream economic histories. Looking at the religious roots of fair trade, a student of capital, labor, and culture can reencounter contemporary "conscious-capitalism" movements as a partial outcome of a liberal Christian combat with the injurious historical effects of colonial land seizure, forced labor, crackdowns on socialist regimes, and structural adjustment. Their stories, mixed as they are, reveal a cohort that saw the military-flanked ascent of US soft power and sought to make that power more humane. Part of how they did so was through recovering images of the pasts they sought to restore and by fighting over how to best live out their traditions in technological, networked modernity. Appealing to past tradition as a guide for their interventions—*Don't you know the history?*—they began to reproduce the systems of exchange much like the ones that sparked their initial intervention.

History is never just a method that scholars bring to bear on capitalism. History is one of many transactions that take place within a matrix of monetized value. That is, history becomes a transaction in capitalism because that is what capitalism needs it to mean. *We are working within a system,* says the VC, before he credits the United Farm Workers for his managerial style. *These patterns have been passed down for centuries,* says the salesperson, in an effort to secure your purchase. Both statements do interpretive work in that they try to salvage a sense of ethical urgency from an imagined past, whose changes over time should be marked and interpreted. Historians also do this work. Case in point: the advent of a disciplinary subfield organized under the banner "the history of capitalism." So prominent was this humanistic turn that the *New York Times* spotlighted its consolidation at major universities.[47]

Observers have debated whether the history of capitalism subfield signals a step forward for struggling Humanities departments or a simple rebrand of economic, business, and labor history (but maybe with downplayed class conflict and even less critical race analysis than before).[48] If nothing else, this new history seems to have earned its keep. Universities have created new faculty lines in its name. Presses have launched book series.[49] One prominent East Coast university even identified an unmet professional demand generated in its wake. A team of professors realized that their colleagues were trying to understand corporate archives but that they lacked skills to interpret the accounting spreadsheets, investment portfolios, and earnings forecasts they discovered there. The History of Capitalism Summer Camp at Cornell University commenced 2015. Many summers since then, it has accepted applications from approximately forty people who, at the end of the two weeks, have experienced something like a mini-MBA. They will have covered basic principles of microeconomics, macroeconomics, accounting, corporate finance, and statistics. They will have gained membership in a network of humanities scholars, both senior and junior, committed to bringing quantitative skills to bear on the stories they tell.

. . . . . .

I learned about this camp from a colleague who attended in the inaugural year. After so much time with capitalists charmed by the notion that historical reflection would grow their margins—but who were almost nonchalant about math—I was transfixed by the notion of historians who sought to understand capitalism using regression analysis. The reversal was too rich: fund managers imagine that the humanities knowledge will instill charismatic meaning and moral value into their quarterly reports while humanists unlock parallel significance in the cold quantities of investment bankers, summoned just in time to rescue humanities departments from their own subjective excess. If one is looking for an example of why knowledge is both a discursive production and a product of contingent value, there may be no better proof than this inverted mutual regard between economists and historians.

I had to attend. I wrote an essay about my desire to be a token ethnographer among this cohort of historians, and, a few weeks later, cashed in my efforts for a slot at Capitalism Camp 2018. I watched Khan Academy mini-lectures on statistical principles and puzzled over word problems in accounting textbooks. Then hit the road to Ithaca.

On the first day of camp, a staff leader advised the room of humanists to approach the upcoming lectures from economists as if we were "anthropologists inhabiting the worldviews" of people in a foreign culture. "The idea is to get you literate, engaged, and empowered in how you think about [capitalist archives]," they explained. "It is about setting aside the kinds of questions that historians ask and are rewarded to ask. As Joe is talking about a balance sheet you might say, 'Joe, what would Foucault's notion of biopower be in this rendering of an accounting sheet?' There are places for that, and that place is a bar." Historians, caricatured as nonsense theorists, were to be reformed in order to understand better the capitalist scene. Questions about a proverbial *history* and *theory* were the prohibited substrate against which the real analysis of capitalism took place. The implicit suggestion here was that "capitalism" could be sequestered from the humanities and approached as objective math. "History" involved translating that math into narrative. At the opening of our weeklong frog march through statistical regression, I gaped from the stadium-seat auditorium as a management consultant turned academic historian dangled out the carrot we would earn for paying attention. At the end of the week, he promised, we would collectively get to "calculate the dollar value of being white in America in 1864."

Bug-eyed in the top row, scribbling enraged notes to the friend who had already lost patience with my negative attitude, I considered giving the historian the benefit of the doubt. He was an awkward dude trying to rally our room of math-phobic bookworms to enjoy our algebra lessons. He would capture our attention by connecting the content to something we might actually care about: the history of slavery. Technically, the exercise involved isolating whiteness as a dependent mathematical variable in historical time. But—the question hung in the air—why would someone find this activity compelling? And what about the implications? Dependent variables can change; they can have *negative* numerical value; they can be manipulated by other variables beyond their control. The effort to hammer racial capitalism into a set of equations was telling us a story. Its premise was that we could pinpoint the racist violence of Civil War–era slave capitalism and perhaps even *make it solvable*—using the quantitative tools of business school students.

Dazed from fluorescent lighting and my diet of granola bars, listening to lecturers spin hypothetical scenarios about IRA investments and the effects of outsourcing on a company's bottom line and how all these numbers can supercharge archival research, torturing my roommate with my repeated failure to compartmentalize the angst or at the very least shut up about it, I could not decide what disturbed me more: capitalist humanitarians consumed with their own world-historical significance or academic historians hoping to temporarily bracket a humanistic impulse in the name of better understanding. The cognitive dissonance toppled me in the end. I cut out early, betting that the camp wouldn't notice one fewer body in a lecture hall. We'd already paid.

A flat cardboard envelope arrived at my apartment several weeks later. Mindless, I ripped it open on the walk back up my fire escape. Only back in my 95-degree attic hatch, alone with my luggage-strewn floor and scattered accounting worksheets that I hadn't bothered to file, did I investigate the contents. Sweat dripped from my forehead onto the certificate as I read its blocky Word Art: "Lucia Hulsether has survived two amazing weeks of boot camp. Lucia may analyze like a capitalist, but critiques like a historian. Lucia may calculate like an accountant, but tells stories that matter. Lucia may graph like an economist, but draws the right conclusions. Lucia Hulsether is ready to historicize capitalism!" But capitalists are already historicizing capitalism, and numbers are not really the name of that game.

June 2017.
It's great to be a Tennessee Vol.

Twenty-four hours after I returned from the Citizen Consumer Summit, eighteen days after the death of my brother, it hit me that I had left my most important personal possession behind. My orange Nalgene water bottle—translucent, sixteen ounces, scrawled with my name in Sharpie, $9.99 to replace—sat forlorn in a classroom at Stonehill College.

When I misplaced things as a teenager—and I did, all the time, especially keys—my mom would tell me that my losses were a sacrament. If I asked her what this meant, she would give me a theology lesson: a sacrament is "an outward and visible sign of an inward and spiritual grace." Sacraments distill a bigger story into a symbolic act. For example, my mom would tell me again, when a person celebrates communion, the bread and wine they consume are like "little shots of a whole story of Jesus and of the power of his death to overcome death itself." "It just makes sense to me that negative power goes the same way," she would say. "Every time I lose my keys, it's an outward and visible sign of inward chaos. I know my life is messed up because I can see I'm not keeping up with basic things." This is how my mother modeled a certain peace in the face of lost material possessions: they were the most meaningful, had the most to teach, in their absence.

Not so with the water bottle; its loss was a miniature apocalypse. I'd received it as part of UNITE-HERE's standard-issue supply kit for graduate student hunger strikers. As we nestled under blankets in our encampment or surfed around campus in wheelchairs, this mass-produced receptacle marked us as tributes to the cause and bonded us to the group. Our assigned handlers, present at all times to enforce rules against solo bathroom trips and to discourage the consumption of seltzer, which apparently some of our buzz-kill colleagues had deemed too much of a luxury, seemed capable of just one positive speech act: telling us to hydrate. Still, the Local 33 staff forbade us from carrying our own water bottles; they told us that the public optics relied on a certain display of uniformity.

I didn't mind. All annoyance faded against my extreme pleasure that our union color, and thus the color of our swag, was the same shade of orange as the uniforms of the University of Tennessee women's basketball team that I'd worshipped since first grade. Just as I once counted every Lady Vol victory as a premonition against evil—a sure indication that I'd ace the weekly spelling test, or that my soccer club would prevail at our upcoming tournament, or that my parents would make it home from work safely—the magical-thinking girl still inside of me had registered the orange as proof of our union's preferential option in the cosmic order. Once upon a time, Tennessee basketball losses meant that I would retreat under my covers, refuse to go to school, and boycott cruel reality until further notice. (Luckily for my truancy record, those years coincided with the Pat Summitt dynasty, when Tennessee dominated the NCAA and almost never lost.)

Now, caught in the ruins of a fallen basketball empire and a far-right takeover of the United States government (and that whisper from the past: *Are the two related?*), I took the orange as company and comfort for an impossible but necessary labor mobilization: an outward and visible sign of an inward and spiritual grace. "It's great! To be! A Tennessee Vol!" I'd chirp through ravenous exhaustion when a handler refilled my bottle. Chanted into a tent of over-serious leftists, it was an absurdist attempt to cut the tension. Nobody even knew what I was talking about. Probably they thought sports were false consciousness. This made the joke more hilarious to me. I assumed that the water bottle agreed and that we were best friends through the long days.

. . . . . .

What I am saying is that I understand attachments to inanimate commodity objects. And if this is the point of the book where a different scholar would insert a tangent on transitional objects and childhood regression—whether induced by nutrient deprivation or shattering grief—all I can say is that the hunger strike was a weird time of hypervisibility and body surveillance. We were hungry. Our rows of cots afforded us no privacy. Showers were available only every couple of days, and they required shuttling to the off-campus hotel rooms of staff organizers here from out of town. There were public weigh-ins. The infrastructure built around the fast replicated that of an eating disorder treatment center, except that the regulations enforced food abstinence rather than appropriate sustenance. Few of us acknowledged this similarity out loud, but I suspected that I was not the only person sliding into the universe of body-image distortion and calorie obsession that had once held me hostage.

On the morning of the last day of Mark's life, I sat cross-legged on the shocking-green Astroturf and confided my doubts to a friend. Was I playing with fire? Should I quit the hunger strike early? She didn't think it was worth the trade-off: considering the climate of antiunion backlash and the verbal abuse that organizers were enduring from antiunion peers, almost any activity was preferable to another day pounding the pavement in a futile effort to get more people on board with the action. My body did not belong to me at the moment, but at least I got a reprieve from canvassing. The hunger strikers were all but canonized for our sacrifice; the better-fed organizers might as well have been human boxing bags. We coped how we could. It could have been a water bottle, or a blanket, or a book, or anything else: people had their comfort objects. These attachments are a documented effect of starvation, but beyond that, it does not take a psychotherapist to predict that my relationship with the Nalgene escalated when, just as it had become an extension of my own body, my brother left this world.

Released from my union obligation, I refused to drink out of any other container. I cradled the water bottle on the airplane ride south. I carried it into meetings with police detectives and funeral home directors. I touched it on the brink of panic attacks. I made it my bond to colleagues still sleeping under the stars and hoped it would spirit me back to them. I hydrated.

I also recognized that my attachment might raise alarm in family and friends. Psychologists consider strong adult bonds with "transitional objects" to be a red flag for a personality disorder. The informal and derogatory name for these attachments is the "teddy bear sign." As in, adults are walking around with teddy bears.

In preemptive defense of my own mind, I began to chronicle instances of humans who have social relations with inanimate objects. I thought of the queer theorist who got mercury poisoning and experienced an altered intimacy with their couch. This was not a fetish relation or a pathology, they had argued, but a relation of interdependence anchored beyond the normative human subject.[1] Maybe readers should try it, the author seemed to say. Then there was the industry for fighting commodity attachment by further enshrining those same commodities. Lifestyle consultant Marie Kondo swore that material possessions could feel pain and "spark joy."[2] Therefore, we should treat them with empathy and probably declutter our homes while we are at it. I thought of how smart devices had become glorified appendages of the human body. That spring I had made frequent use of a phone app that rewarded screen-free time by planting trees in a cartoon orchard. Touch your device while the app is activated, and trees die. I am using this app now.

As I type and avoid distraction, the so-called teddy bear sign does not sound so exceptional to me. It feels like the baseline condition of life under neoliberal capitalism. If our limited brains are unable to process the scale of losses necessary to support everyday life—when climate disaster death statistics feel unreal, when I compartmentalize the planetary suffering that must have taken place to get me the off-season blueberries I had for breakfast—these simple objects absorb a nomad empathy. I could say that this is a destructive rerouting, condemn myself for how I cared more about the water bottle than I did about the dead. I could also say that in the abandonment of feeling, this attachment kept my senses warm.

. . . . . .

As for the water bottle itself, I did stop caring so much in the end. I moved on to different objects. Before that happened, the bottle got lost three more times. It left me for good when I forgot it on an airplane. By then, I felt almost relieved to be rid of the thing. But the first loss was like losing a tether to Earth's gravitational pull. That time, I emailed the two conference door greeters and asked (really, pleaded with) them to find the bottle and mail it to me. They were happy to help; it arrived at my house three days later.

I think now that they must have known something about the affective bonds that one can make with material objects, how those objects can be portals to other kinds of relationships.[3] I remember their kind smiles when they handed me a souvenir coffee mug at the door of the conference, the certainty with which the leaders talked about the social solidarity incarnate in a fairly traded commodity. They must have known how a vessel for nourishing the physical body can approximate a connection with another person in a faraway existence—even if that existence is beyond reach, even if the recognition is fantasy. *Fantasy* doesn't have to be a bad word.

ethical vampires   2

CONSCIOUS CAPITALISM AND

ITS COMMODITY ENCHANTMENTS

"Excuse me, waiter!" shrieks a cartoon café patron, "There's the blood and misery of a thousand small farmers in my coffee."[1] The iconic scene first appeared in a late 1990s campaign by pioneering fair trade brand Equal Exchange. The company had placed full-page ads in national magazines to warn readers that when they consumed items derived from situations of labor abuse, they became vampires, parasites of mortals who had no other option but to spill their blood for people who could afford to pay. "If you drink an ordinary brand of coffee," the caption to the caption explained, "you're inadvertently maintaining a system which keeps small farmers poor while lining the pockets of rich corporations." Luckily, the ad continued, readers could opt out of that system. "By choosing Equal Exchange Coffee, you can make a change," the text reassured them, noting that the brand's producers earned a living wage for their work. Best of all, the decision to patronize the brand "need not be completely altruistic" because Equal Exchange takes "as much pride in refining the taste of our gourmet coffee as we do in helping the farmers who produce them." Solidarity, it turned out, could taste even more delicious than blood.

The Equal Exchange messaging campaign waffles between two theories of consumer power. Speaking in the voice of the woman who rejects her drink and alerts the waitstaff to its contamination, Equal Exchange seems inches away from leading a boycott of plantation-grown coffee. But the omniscient voice of the explanatory text can only circle the perimeter of such an escalation, and it dares not mention the b-word. To the extent that militant action

2.1 Equal Exchange placed this advertisement in several major periodicals in 1999 as part of a nationwide advertising campaign for its fair trade products. The metaphor of conventionally produced commodities drenched in the "blood" of workers—as opposed to ethically produced commodities that are pure and even life-giving—has offered a potent and long-running rhetorical device within many capitalist humanitarian projects. Equal Exchange ad in *Mother Jones*, Sept.–Oct. 1999, p. 8; https://mronline.org/2018/09/19/labor-and-human-social-metabolism-part-1.

is a logical outcome of the scene, the text redefines its terms. The ad campaign suggests that politicized consumption is defined as much by a negative choice to abstain from "ordinary" coffee as it is by the constructive impulse to buy what Equal Exchange is selling. In implying that brand loyalty exists proximate to anticapitalist dissent and international solidarity, the cartoon anticipates a more sweeping strategy of neoliberal capture that, in the coming years, would pose serious challenges to the organizing Left.

Years before it became common for companies to make humanitarian promises to their consumers—*for every pair of shoes you buy, we will give one to a child in need, this granola bar saves lives, your purchase helps indigenous women preserve their culture*—there were other conscious-consumer movements. These skipped bromides about "ethical" purchase and cut straight to the heart of the matter: *stop cooperating with the enemy*. A ticker tape of social movements railed against the rippling terror of capitalist complicity, from nineteenth-century abolitionists who wailed that each time a northerner donned cotton clothes or added sugar to their tea they ate the flesh of an enslaved person to the Progressive-era unions that demanded price controls and wages that reflected the cost of living to the international boycott of apartheid South Africa to the contemporary boycott, divestment, and sanction (BDS) movement against companies operating out of Israeli settlements.[2] These movements shared in common a use of public refusal—refusal to buy, refusal to invest, refusal to work—as a political tactic.

Early fair traders developed this prior discourse toward one that grounded solidarity politics in rarified acts of brand loyalty and conspicuous consumption. Their strategies built on a fairly standard Marxian understanding of the commodity: that the assignation of an exchange value to anything, whether the product of labor or to labor itself, maligns a whole web of human and planetary relations. To mark something as a commodity, to assign it an exchange value, is to disfigure and obscure a "definite social relation between men" by transforming it into a "fantastic form of relation between things." Marx reserves derision for the capitalist who fetishizes and consumes the labor of wage workers by deriving surplus value from what for Marx is the most basic activity of existence: creative productivity, pursued in conjunction with others. "Capital is dead labor," Marx writes, "which, vampire-like, lives only by sucking living labor, and lives the more, the more labour it sucks."[3] Insofar as Equal Exchange marketing materials nodded to the Gothic insult, it was with a twist. They left room for a more virtuous sort of commodity relation and then scripted what that relation should look like.

Fair traders would allow that most commodities are laced with the body fluids of exploited workers—*there's the blood and misery of a thousand small farmers in my coffee!*—but they would also add an enticing qualification: What if you could support your caffeine addiction, and your commodity dependence in general, without leeching the "blood and misery" of workers? Better, what if some commodities could transmit renewed life to people down the supply chain? The alternative-trade organizations nurtured by these questions—having drawn the conclusion that, yes, commodity exchange could be like gift giving—would soon find their signs appropriated by conventional corporate players. Within three decades, the legacy of early fair trade was barreling, full-throttle, into the realm of the absurd as group after group of millennial entrepreneurs began to redefine the most flexible and immaterial commodity of all: money. Not only could commodities reverse alienation, not only did supply chains facilitate gift exchange, but capital itself pulsed with spiritual energy that could heal broken relationships and elevate the consciousness of a generation.

"We Come from Plantations": Commodities

Launched in 1984, the fledgling Equal Exchange company left no ambiguity about its intended customer base. "Introducing (at last) a coffee that keeps Ronald Reagan awake," declared an early flier. Tacked on the cluttered bulletin boards of food cooperatives next to ads for meditation retreats, community-supported agriculture (CSA) subscriptions, and open slots at the local Waldorf school, it bet on an audience gripped by two political feelings: rage at the political Right and solidarity with the Central American Left. The first Equal Exchange product, released in 1986 and known as "Cafe Nica," circumvented a US presidential embargo on imports from the Sandinista-ruled nation—hence Reagan's insomnia. As the ad explained,

> He knows Nicaraguan coffee is delicious and has mass appeal.
> He knows the campesino farmers live better today than before 1979, the year the dictator Somoza was thrown out of power.
> And he knows that Equal Exchange's work—keeping the spirit of the Nicaraguan people alive in the hearts of the North American public (*despite the U.S. embargo against Nicaragua*)—makes it harder to mobilize for war.[4]

The advertisement doubled, clumsily, as political education. It assumed that the reader remembered how six years back, the revolutionary Sandinista Party had ousted a US-backed dictatorship and created a program of land reform for the country's poor, and that this regime change had ignited a civil war. The ad assumed, too, that readers knew how the Reagan administration had shored up an ex-dictator's paramilitary death squads, had locked everyday Nicaraguan farmers out of international commerce, and had justified all of these measures with red-baiting screeds about how Managua was just a day's drive from Houston, meaning that communists had camped out on America's doorstep.[5] Equal Exchange set its sights on the retaliatory trade policies. Unfazed by the rule that all Nicaraguan imports undergo "substantial transformation" in a third country before entering US Customs, Equal Exchange allied with partners in Holland and Canada to triangulate the process. Now the three founders just needed buy-in from US consumers.

Equal Exchange set about promoting a consumer-centered notion of solidarity. The public relations blitz endorsed Reagan's certainty that commodity practices and trade policies made for effective political weapons. It then advocated a counter-deployment of these weapons on behalf of underdogs like the "campesino farmers." With economic solidarity from US consumers, the coffee could unlock powers to haunt the president and revivify a Nicaraguan "spirit." The interpretive long jumps—from commodity as blockage to commodity as solidarity to commodity as partial container for an immaterial force that exceeds it—invited consumers of Café Nica to compose a new chapter for the history of US-Nicaragua relations and for the agency of the commodity itself. That is, consumer buy-in was the activating ingredient of commodity solidarity; Café Nica possessed only *potential* agency until the moment of transaction. So long as Nicaraguan coffee lay marooned outside of a buyer-seller bond—whether because of the US embargo on Nicaragua or because shoppers chose another product—the coffee could neither resist war nor "keep the spirit of the Nicaraguan people alive in the hearts of the North American people."

Focused on the consumers already attuned to the social consequences of their consumer practices, these early marketing campaigns began to articulate a revised theory of the commodity fetish. The Equal Exchange vision of its commodities both riffed on and departed from standard critiques of commodity capitalism. Marx and most of his inheritors identify commodities by the two kinds of value they hold: use value, related to the commodity's physical qualities, and exchange value, which exists when the commodity enters into commercial circulation. These forms of value lack natural connection; they relate to each other only in the context of a whole network of labor-capital relations, which are obfuscated in the pretense of objective exchange values. For example, if I pick tomatoes from my drooping porch garden and put them in my lunch, they are not commodities. This is because they exist in direct relationship with my labor power at all stages, from the moment when I planted them in my flimsy plastic pots to their transformation into energy units for my afternoon run. Still, I am consuming these tomatoes within a capitalist economy, so they will always be *potential* commodities.[6] Perhaps this year my tomatoes won't die, and I'll decide that it would be better to sell them to my friends. In that case, the tomatoes would assume an additional value in the context of an exchange. Exchange value can fluctuate; it does not have any necessary relationship to the specific quality of the labor that produced it or the potential specific uses of the tomato. It is, in Marxian terms, an abstraction. It is a story I tell about the potential value of my labor and my property. Each time I repeat it, at least if I agree with Marx, I become more alienated from its physical truth. To tell the history of commodities—to demystify their conditions of production and denaturalize exchange value as a natural quantity—is a primary goal of Marx's critique.

Right now, though, Marx's warnings are not my concern. I'm just trying to turn a profit from the tomatoes that I managed not to kill. Now that I've subjected them to monetized exchange, it's possible to make direct comparisons between them (and the labor that produced them) and any number of fundamentally different objects, activities, and qualities. I can sell my haul of porch tomatoes to a friend for $25 and then use the money to buy some new yoga accessories. It turns out, though, that my friend with a back injury needs the props more than I do. She offers me $30 in laundry quarters for them, having noticed that I'm always scrounging for change when my clothes pile up. I take her up on the deal. But then, that same day, I am at the bookstore and realize I've forgotten my credit card, so I use one of her $10 coin rolls to purchase the newest issue of *n+1*, which I'm supposed to discuss at the Left Literary Reading Group tonight. I end up using the leftover coins to pay an undergraduate to fix some footnotes for me. He invests the money in a music-streaming subscription. The monopolistic tech corporation that owns the platform distributes a negligent amount of that $20 to its contracted artists. It invests the rest to develop a next-generation smartwatch. Considering the bad trade, it occurs to me that my original yield of porch tomatoes is worth about one-fifteenth of the gadget's sticker price, but maybe if I quit graduate school and find work on an organic farm, I will be able to afford it one day. I do the calculations in my head, considering how I might trade the commodity of my labor for other commodities that I want and need.

This kind of comparison is what exchange value, manifest in the form of a price, makes possible. It allows me to create equivalencies between what are otherwise incommensurable qualities: my mediocre gardening skills are like yoga props are like the chance to do laundry are like the newest copy of a leftist magazine are like a streamed song that neither the musician nor the listener owns. Exchange value is a story that arises in the context of a transaction. For Marx, this story is a horror script. The fear factor lies in how exchange value carves up the most basic of social activities—interdependent labor and productivity—into a fun-house distortion of themselves. When *Capital* (vol. 1) refers to the commodity as a fetish, Marx is referring less to a specific kind of consumer product and more to a misdirection of agency and power: social life is displaced through relationships with inanimate objects. This commodification and its alienation extend to labor, which no longer belongs to the laborer but rather has been seized by the capitalist to whom it is sold.[7] Enter the hellscape, where the elemental violence that is capitalism forces me to mediate through inert, opaque *things* my relations with living beings, with the Earth, and with my own labor. To grasp the extent of the abstraction, Marx says, "we must have recourse to the mist-enveloped regions of the religious world" where "the productions of the human brain appear as autonomous figures endowed with a life of their own, which enter into relation both with one another and with the human race."[8] So assimilated are subjects of capitalism to this warped state of affairs that we have begun to insist that commodity-mediated social life is a natural way of being. Moreover, because for Marx freedom rests on my relationship to my productive activity in concert with other beings and the natural world, the consequence is a collective degradation. Collective liberation would require divestment from the commodity form.

I rehearse this story of the commodity fetish in order to observe a disjuncture between Marx's concept of *commodity* as the elemental violence of bourgeois capitalism and the way that Equal Exchange—as well as other capitalist humanitarian projects—reformulate the commodity as an instrument of emancipation. On one hand, fair trade participates in and extends a Marxian project to demystify relations of production and labor. Usually this means that fair trade organizations are telling a story about labor that produced the good you are buying. The coffee bag is a collage of farmer photos; the corporate annual report begins with a vignette about the family who benefited when you bought those curtains. It also means that on the plane of company structure and business practice, fair trade organizations try to align the exchange value with the human and material costs of production, which stop skulking behind abstract prices and show themselves in the light of day.

"Fairness," of course, is subjective. Companies might define fairness by the commitment to pay a price minimum to suppliers, regardless of how capital conglomerates price the commodity at a given time. They may define their fairness as a posture of "cutting out middlemen" who typically triangulate interactions between farmer/producers and the consumers who buy what they grow.[9] Likewise important is how fair trade highlights the qualities of these relationships in public. The announcement completes the point: bourgeois capital tells stories that deceive, but fair trade tells stories that reveal the truth. It is not the commodity's quality of third-party mediation that is the problem. It is that the commodity has been mediating bad relationships.

Whereas for Marx the enchanted commodity provides an analogical way of naming an abusive relationship that is vanquished only through working class revolution—when, in effect, the workers secularize their own labor—capitalist humanitarian consciousness revalues the commodity as a reparative force. The rightly enchanted commodity can be the opposite of alienating; it is a spiritual agent with the potential to break, or to rehabilitate, the strained producer-consumer bond. Not all commodities index alienated labor and the obfuscation of capitalist violence. Some commodities can resurrect humanity from its ruins. The question is about what agency that I, consumer-citizen, choose to activate and affirm once I know what Reagan knows. Reagan knows the commodity has world-historical power and that this power can be channeled toward a number of ends.[10]

. . . . . .

If you don't want to ask Reagan, consider asking the commodities themselves. Another Equal Exchange ad, this one from 2004, depicts anthropomorphized produce items in a grocery store. A cartoon cashew, a coffee bean, a banana, a pineapple ring, and a tea bag smile at a group of their scowling counterparts. These latter unhappy figures wear clothes. The banana sports a suit coat and tie, and the frowning tea bag wears an eye patch as if injured. A speech-bubbled conversation between the two cohorts unfolds from left to right:

> SMILING CASHEW: We come from small farmer coops.
>
> SMILING BANANA: Yeah, where do you come from?
>
> SMILING PINEAPPLE RING: We're authentic fair trade. Can you say that?
>
> SCOWLING CASHEW: We come from... Where was it again?
>
> SCOWLING BANANA: We come from plantations, but *shhhh*, don't tell anyone![11]

These commodities testify to their value through appeals to their respective provenance. The items routed to the supermarket through "small farmer coops" speak with pride at the process of their commodification. The ones who "come from plantations" try in vain to hide a history that bruised them. *Don't tell anyone.* If one line of interpretation would decry the fantastical ventriloquism of inanimate objects, this fair trade frame turns the tables: the problem is not when ostensibly inert commodities speak; it is when commodities are smothered into silence about their origins in abuse, exploitation, and slavery.[12] You know which commodity is liberated and liberating based on whether it can testify.

The effort by fair traders to reanimate the commodity for a global labor justice project evokes racial capitalism's long history of traffic in black flesh. Fred Moten has observed, against Marx's insistence that commodities cannot speak, that in a world structured by slavery and its afterlives there is a literal "historical reality of commodities who spoke—of laborers who were commodities before, as it were, the abstraction of labor power from their bodies and who continue to pass on this material heritage across the divide that separates slavery and 'freedom.'" This means, for Moten, that the history of blackness is "a testament that objects can and do resist."[13] In other words, the idea of the animated commodity is not new and, in fact, the idea that the nonhuman object is saturated with the workers' blood evokes the transatlantic slave trade, even as it displaces slavery as a governing context for articulating the commodity form. If the speaking commodity is, for Moten, found first in the screams of the slave, those screams are now sublimated into the announcements of a cartoon banana and the protests of the white café patron. The patron is singing: *Woke up this morning with my eyes stayed on freedom.*[14]

The recuperation of commodity agency positions fair trade as the outgrowth of black freedom struggles and also as their fulfillment: they are universalized and made fungible in global exchange.[15] The rightly enchanted commodity does not scream. Instead, it announces, happily, the conditions of labor that produced it. The testimony creates drama for capitalist humanitarians. When and how does the commodity give you away as not as conscious and not as careful as you promised? How can the positive mediating powers of the conscious commodity be scaled for maximum impact? How might they exert their powers in places inundated with plantations and lies? The questions swirl among the entrepreneurs who took the fair trade mantle and scaled it into multinational start-up phenomenon.

"It Feels Amazing": Gifts

I cannot stop running into these conscious entrepreneurs. They are in the bar, in the hostel, at the juice stand, on the shuttle bus, in the markets, and at the one grocery store in town that sells cashew milk: entrepreneurial millennials who have relocated to Guatemala and are betting on the conscious-capitalist profitability of their cosmopolitan aesthetic. It was late spring 2016, and from my home base on the shores of Lake Atitlán I had lost count of the ethical fashion houses launched by people in my exact social demographic. That morning I sat with one of them, Madison, on the doorstep of an expat-run coffee bar on the main tourist drag. Her boyfriend founded the place with a fellow South Korean expat who, upon handing me an iced hazelnut latte on the house, told me to call him "Buddha." I sipped it while a mutant-sized dream catcher, six feet in diameter and operating as a makeshift screen to divide storefront from street, wafted into the back of my neck. I tried to ignore the bumping and focus on my companion. My companion had already described her work of sewing—rather, hiring local women to sew—secondhand Guatemalan textiles into garments that she could sell at markup to expensive US clothing companies and exhibit at Paris Fashion Week. Now she had moved on to what I gathered was the thick of the matter: her competition and, specifically, their commodity crimes.

I've been around this block before. I had heard about Madison at a bar down the street, the hangout for expatriates who had flocked to Guatemala to either improve the overall conditions of human life in the region or carry out a transnational gentrification of it, depending on whose perspective one heeds. I had a stock introduction. *Hi. I'm Lucia. I'm a graduate student doing a project about socially responsible capitalism—things like microfinance, impact investing, and ethical consumption.* Somehow these were magic words. I became an instant confidant. One by one, these white women of airy dresses and tailored jeans leaned toward me. *Great. Tell me what you want to know.* I learned that when they said this, they meant *tell me what you want to know about my competition.* Competition meant the other regulars at these same happy hours, where "networking" implied dishing dirt on whoever happened to miss the party that day. I heard a litany of accusations, always lodged with the same structure: she says she is one thing but actually she is something else. *She claims to be empowering local women artisans, but how is that possible when you can see on the textiles she sells that she doesn't let them sew their own traditional patterns?* Or: *She says she's honoring weavers by bringing their patterns to a global market, but she's just appropriating indigenous designs.* Or: *She claims to be working with women artisans, but, you heard it here first, those are huipiles she bought at pawn markets, cut up into new shapes, and rebranded as "vintage" so she could sell them to Urban Outfitters* (see figure 2.2).

The focus would turn to other expat-run development groups. I heard about an education nonprofit that erected a school on an earthquake fault line and, despite this choice, still scored dozens of celebrity sponsors, who plugged its cause at Hollywood awards ceremonies and in lifestyle magazines. I raised my eyebrows at a lampoon of the understaffed, jack-of-all-trades relief organization that allegedly made indiscriminate applications for in-kind grants that they couldn't actually use, including one for several tons of dry rice that moths and mold were devouring in a warehouse somewhere. I never found the bottom of the gossip well. It seems that being a socially conscious entrepreneur requires that you debunk the self-deceiving stories of other capitalist humanitarians.

Madison's competitors charged her with appropriation and pawn-shop slumming; she accused them of a tacitly genocidal suppression of indigenous

2.2 Pawned textiles are piled up at outdoor market stand in Sololá, Guatemala, where they are sold at a fraction of their original value.

women's traditional art. Listening to her on the stoop as I slurped the dregs of my latte, I made noncommittal noises and a mental note on where these women located their ethical proofs: in the commodities themselves. The products that a business sells are imagined to reveal the extent to which an enterprise delivers on its ethical claims and the odds that its wares are drenched in blood. Humanitarian capitalists treat commodities as testifying witnesses and sometimes as moral agents. Animated, except this time in a way that spoke rather than hid the truth, the conscious commodity was made to reveal the conditions of its production.

. . . . . .

The reenchanted commodity is imperious with respect to its interrogators. The operative question is no longer "How can we reveal what is really going on with the conditions of production?" or "What is the real provenance of this commodity?" Capitalist humanitarians and their ventriloquized products make these announcements daily. To the extent they confess a crime, the subsequent apology clears territory for the next reparative expansion. The better question is "Through what processes is the critique of expropriation, alienation, and theft disappeared into the positive idea of ethical consumption?" We know that the first step involves the reenchantment of the commodity, now infused with the capacity to announce its historical truth and broker new futures. The second step is to rewrite the story of the supply chain so that it's no longer a circuit of alienated production and vampire capitalists but is instead a circuit of reciprocal gift exchange between parties.

"What if the delicious box of chocolate you give to your wife could help teach children in South America to read?" asks Fairtrade International.[16] "What if the sugar you use to bake cookies with your kids could help ensure farmers in the Philippines have the supplies they need?" Scholars have shown how commodity capitalism teaches people to project their fantasies onto external objects, so consumer practice is as much about the pleasure of imagining potential fulfillment as it is about actually satisfying the desire (which is likely to be disappointed, thus giving rise to new fantasies, and the cycle repeats).[17] The capitalist humanitarian commodity adds a second beneficiary to this psychic drama. Fair trade advertisements and their derivatives invite their audiences to project onto the commodity both their own ideal pampered life—one spent charming their spouse and rolling cookie dough with the kids—and the rescued future of a deserving poor person across the ocean. The latter outcome, the questions seem to hint, might even be contingent on the prior indulgence. Through this lens each potential transaction carries the burden of the lives, worlds, and agents that now pulse through it. Lines between subject and object begin to blur; each purchase is a reckoning as the agency of conspicuous consumption collapses into the reciprocal expectancy of the gift.

Anthropologists of religion have long looked to cultures of gift exchange and reciprocity as proxies for their debates over the possibility of life outside of free-market capitalism.[18] The idea of a social system based on gifts, rather than commodity exchange, can channel wishes for an other-than-capitalist economy. It can sometimes moonlight as a nostalgic hope for return to life "before" a money system. The capitalist humanitarian revaluation of commodity *as* a gift economy helps underline that the gift and the historical associations attached to it are not always an alternative to neoliberal reform. They just as easily become rationales for its continuation.

The earliest fair traders might have intuited the multiplicity of gift discourse when they marketed their products in terms of a humanitarian sacrifice—the gift of a better wage, the gift of a relationship, the gift of keeping a spirit alive—to hardworking producers. By the early 2000s, however, companies had started to take this idiom further. They stretched the plot points of the commodity chain to include the in-kind materials that will be donated, like a carbon offset, to someone in need. The shoe company TOMS popularized the now-widespread "buy one to give one" model. Its branding campaign would teach a generation of well-off millennials to align their modern capitalist desires with the world's great unmet needs. Company founder and "Chief Shoe Giver" Blake Mycoskie describes traveling through Argentina, meeting local children who could not afford shoes, and feeling flooded with a desire to help.[19] He considered and then ruled out the idea of a charity, for this "traditional model of philanthropy" would "last only as long as I could find donors." The situation of barefoot kids was too daunting:

> I wanted something more sustainable. These kids needed more than occasional shoe donations from strangers—they needed a constant, reliable flow.
>
> Then I began to look for solutions in the world I already knew—business and entrepreneurship. An idea hit me: Why not create a *for-profit* business to help provide shoes for these children? It was a simple concept that I call One for One: Sell a pair of shoes today; give a pair of shoes tomorrow.[20]

In Mycoskie's account, giving is possible because of consumer agency and, even more, because of the profits gleaned from that commodity practice. TOMS trains its audiences to associate their economic activities with the potentiality of specific young lives, which can transform only if they get—you buy—that pair of shoes. Directed toward my shoes, my imagination comes to life, senses life, and sees me imparting life. I am not just wearing this pair of TOMS shoes; I am wearing it with a destitute brown child on the other side of the world, with whom I have something in common, about whom I care, who is now empowered for production at work or at school. Global North elites are now encouraged to occupy this vexed solidarity with racialized children when we pull out our wallets. Mycoskie advises his listeners that if they want to change the world, they should raise a cash surplus to do it, lest the whims of philanthropic foundations compromise their mission in the long term. It is in effect an acknowledgment that the children in that place will always be too poor to afford the shoes the capitalist humanitarian donates. Just on the edges of Mycoskie's caution against dependence lurk the smiling, playing children made to sit down long enough for the media crew to record the envoy of voluntourists sliding standard-issue moccasins onto their tiny feet. "It feels amazing," the underling shoe givers repeat in videos of their potlatch.[21]

It's worth asking: What, exactly, feels amazing about an up-front encounter with racialized poverty? What makes the attendant exchange so alluring that companies now urge potential consumers to buy not just shoes but also glasses, underwear, granola bars, backpacks, and condoms in solidarity with people of color in the global South?[22] If you are wondering these things, start with theories of gift exchange. Most of these theories are built on a classic premise that the act of giving is what creates the obligation to give.[23] If I give you something, you now owe me something. You give me something back; now we are even, or maybe I owe something to you. Gift giving "can be, simultaneously or successively, an act of generosity or of violence," writes one anthropologist. "The violence is disguised as a disinterested gesture, since it is committed by means of and in the form of sharing."[24] Gift giving can cement networks of interdependence or be a way of fighting with what you have, or both at once. A scene of interdependence can also be a scene of mastery and debt.

. . . . . .

Here is a revolutionary theory of obligation and debt: they are not material facts so much as historically contingent feelings that organize social life. The sense of outstanding debts develops in conjunction with the human capacity to remember the past and to make promises about the future. When I can recall what happened in the past, I know the wrongs I have done to others and the suffering others have inflicted on me. When I am capable of imagining a future beyond my present, I can also anticipate how I will have to settle accounts with people I have harmed or who have harmed me. Historical thinking thus presupposes a concept of debts owed and credits gained. This, at least, was the argument Friedrich Nietzsche made—that the emergence of historical consciousness had locked human life into a pattern of intolerable constraint, which is manifest anytime a person suppresses their basic desires in order to act on their felt social responsibilities. Nietzsche warns that to direct one's actions based on attachments to what happened in the past is not only alienated from the desires that make her alive but also acting from a position of weakness. The powerful do not perseverate on what they owe or are owed. They take what they want and watch the rest grovel.[25]

Of course, sometimes taking what you want involves manipulating other people's ressentiment. Case in point: Blake Mycoskie. This is a person who knows how to manipulate people's debt feelings in service of his own power. "We weren't selling shoes," Mycoskie admits. "We were selling the promise that each purchase would directly and tangibly benefit a child who needed shoes." A promise is a debt relation. Mycoskie's conditional-perfect pledge is that the potential buyer *will have done* something to gain credit relative to the shoeless child or to offset some vague obligation that she feels toward her humanitarian need. It goes like this: I buy the enchanted commodity. I activate its power to broker a relationship with a poor person in the global South. I can see myself as a giver or—if I don't go that far—at least someone who attempts some measure of harm reduction into her commodity practices. I tell myself that I am helping, or at least not making things worse. I get a little boost from occupying the position of someone who can give. Even if I feel powerless in the rest of my life—because my loans are adding up, because job prospects are bad, because my friendships have atrophied, because we are destroying the planet, because sometimes I am too tired to care—at least I can do this one thing. I can, for a moment, step out of my dependent posture and have the benefactor's upper hand. It feels amazing.

......

A past incarnation of me refused on principle to buy TOMS products. The paternalism was tacky. None of this gooey imagine-the-child-in-your-shoes projection for me! Secretly, I was pining for the day someone would give me a pair. The shoes would have paired perfectly with my Creation Museum Tyrannosaurus rex hoodie or my State-Farm-Insurance-Celebrates-Pride T-shirt, even if nobody got the joke but me. Then, on a summer night in 2017, I was out with some friends in Antigua, talking about run-ins with missionary groups, and somebody mentioned that an evangelical church had held a "shoe drop" in his town a couple of years back. "Those shoes were shit," he shrugged. We were in a haze, made goofy by the long week, and my wish slipped out: I had always wanted some TOMS. Maybe we could find some secondhand ones, or knockoffs, in the local market?

It was an instant mission. We cackled all the way down the block. The contest commenced: Who could find the glorified canvas slippers, size 6 with the big patched-on logo, first? The people working the stands joined in the search until, twenty minutes in, the cousin of a friend emerged triumphant. He presented a pair of faded gray fake-alpargatas that are Mycoskie's trademark product. I accepted the trophy. By the next day, the soles had disintegrated in the summer rain, and the concrete streets had bloodied my exposed toes. I never saw the cousin again. I still think about him. I scold myself for not finding him to pay back the two US dollars or at least to reciprocate with a joke gift of commensurate value. I can't get over how, when I mocked the capitalist gift economy, I pulled myself deeper into its network of disappointed fantasies and unreciprocated dependencies.

"We Made It Up": Exchange Value

My moments of failed irony can trigger a crisis of responsibility. Where and how are my attachments undermining my principled arguments? Then I remember: the thing about the reenchanted commodity relation and the figuration of the supply chain as a gift-exchange circuit is that there is no opting out. My actions either originate in "the blood and misery of a thousand small farmers" or they don't. Am I a malicious vampire or an altruistic vampire? Am I sucking out the life source of the worker or replenishing her store for the next time that someone visits? Choose.

Sometimes I pose these questions and then drop the mic. I want to leave the audience in a fugue of bad decisions about which self-deceived posture of commodity enchantment they planned to pursue. I used to hope—if I am honest, still hope—that they will pick the latter option. I did not want them to feel good about this choice; I wanted it to torture them. I sought bubbling nausea, self-recrimination, and the claustrophobia of needing an escape hatch and finding oneself walled in, stuck in the sense that the political horizon is less about doing good than about mitigating harm. But then I start to wonder if I am just making the ethical gestures that conscious capitalists make all the time, except my tone is bitter and theirs is jubilant. Commodities are enchanted! A social relation between people becomes a social relation between things! The supply chain is a circuit of gift giving! Consider the relationships that you are establishing through your purchases! My suspicion that my graduate education has made me a more bitter mimic of my more entrepreneurial peers crested in March 2019, when a fellow alumna of Harvard Divinity School tipped me off about an event that our alma mater had been boosting on social media. "The Business of Spirituality: On Money, Branding, and Other Taboos" would feature "spiritual and wellness entrepreneurs" advising theological studies students on how to market their ministerial gifts.

The event happened in the amber lecture hall where for generations the most-storied voices in the field of religious and theological studies have held court over their student acolytes, who look down at the speaker platform from stadium seats. Although I had tuned in remotely from my New Haven studio apartment, I could almost teleport back to my old top-left-corner hideout, where friends passed overconfident notes about our instructors' intellectual shortcomings. Instead, I settled at the polished pinewood board that, balanced between two file cabinets salvaged from the dumpster zone of a University of Tennessee parking complex, constituted my writing desk. An external monitor flooded my apartment with the livestream's machine-generated light, which showed five women perched on Harvard-branded chairs and five side tables where a production assistant had propped their glossy business self-help books. My eyes landed on the white woman who wore saffron robes and a headwrap for her dreadlock updo. She chatted with an iron-jawed blonde in a black power suit. A third speaker wore a black top hat. I was mid-wonder whether there had been a costume party memo—my disintegrated TOMS would have been perfect—when a person dressed in leather leggings and solid glitter-gold shirt called the virtual room to order. Tonight, she announced, our four guests would help us feel "more comfortable or at least less tortured about making good money for [our] spiritual work."

The introductions cued, I wandered the eight paces to my galley kitchen for a LaCroix, listening to the prebaked bios as I went. First was Kate Northrup, a mother and a social entrepreneur of undefined industry, who wrote the best-selling financial-advice book *Money, a Love Story*. Second was Rha Goddess, former US cultural envoy to Rwanda turned "entrepreneurial soul coach behind hundreds of breakthrough change makers." I was unsure what this meant, but we had already moved on to the third speaker, the one in robes. She was introduced as Guru Jagat, a kundalini yoga master "defining the new feminine matriarchal archetype" now that "Piscean and patriarchal energies [are fading] into history."[26] The fourth panelist, Miki Agrawal, followed. She had just published an advice book based on her experience as a cofounding CEO of the menstrual-blood-absorbing panties company Thinx and now at a bidet company called TUSHY. I recognized her as the executive from a *New York Times* exposé on labor conditions at the underwear company. Workers had alleged that their self-identified "She-EO" boss had, among other behaviors passed off as feminist leadership, went nude in the open-plan office and held mandatory remote meetings from her toilet.[27] The board fired her. She moved to TUSHY after that.

Tonight's organizers had other taboo topics in mind. The student facilitator didn't pull punches: "How do you know how much to charge [for your services] and how much it is appropriate to charge?" she asked. Northrup responded by discussing how she discerned fees for her feng shui consultant business:

> I would go do a session charging a certain amount, and then I would walk away with the check in my hand and feel: Did that feel equal to the energy

I just expended? And if I didn't, then I charged more to the next person. Which may seem a little bizarre, but that is what I did. I just really checked in with the feeling of walking away, or I would imagine the feeling of walking away from a consult and feel like, okay—whatever I was charging, I don't remember—but how did that feel in my purse walking away essentially? Because, I mean, really money, it's just like we made it up. It doesn't exist. It's just, what is it? It's nothing. We just all agreed that it exists.

Recap: money is a socially constructed way of balancing the energetic expenditure that was Northrup's labor. I was coughing on her use of the first-person plural—*who* agreed?—when Agrawal lurched in Northrup's direction. "I actually literally talk about that exact thing in [my book] *Disrupt-Her*!" she exclaimed, her gesticulations blurred by the spat-out-seltzer dripping down my external monitor. "Money is a made-up energy exchange that we all agreed to!"²⁸ "But," she paused for a micro-beat and pondered, "when you take that further, *everything is a made-up construct!*" It spilled out: "Literally, like the fact that there are these weird borders on this planet where these weird people in these costumes are like wearing uniforms that we made up, and you have to get past them with little pieces of paper called passports that we made up, and we're like yeah, we're going to do that on this made-up thing, but with like imaginary lines. And then the same thing with time, the same thing with, I mean, literally careers, professional failure."

Somewhere I'd stood up and begun to pace the three-meter distance between my unmade bed and the desk. To Agrawal's ramble I could log extra steps on my smartwatch. She was explaining that because geopolitical arrangements are "made up," we can "literally invent any new possibility we want if we give ourselves permission" (8,622 ... 8,640 steps). Case in point, her recent venture. When she gave herself permission to innovate (8,702–8,737), an idea seized her: "Why am I wiping my ass with dry paper? This is fucking weird!" Enter TUSHY (... 8,800). For each bidet sold, TUSHY will donate to a start-up that builds pay-to-use toilets in India's slums and thereby solves the "defecation problem."²⁹

I stared open-jawed, frozen a few steps back from my keyboard. It wasn't like I couldn't have predicted the social-responsibility turn, but there was something about *how* she ended up there, how she reasoned her way to *this* innovation. Now I figure that what stopped me in my tracks, even evoked my awe, was how these women had mastered a language of deconstruction-lite. They used terms and methods of social theory to situate the substance of their success—including the capital made available to them, the high returns they've gleaned, the employees they supervise—in terms of a reciprocal energy exchange with the universe. At times it sounded like they had read "The Power of Money in Bourgeois Society" and came away galvanized to spread this gospel: *Yes! Precisely! Isn't capital GRAND?*

. . . . . .

"The extent of the power of money is the extent of my power," Marx writes in his early manuscript. "Money's properties are my properties and essential power." (*Did that feel equal to the energy I just expended?*) Money transforms "image into reality and reality into a mere image." (*We all agreed, it doesn't exist; everything is a made-up construct.*) Money is an abstraction, but its effects are fearsomely concrete: "If I long for a particular dish or want to take the mail-coach because I am not strong enough to go by foot, money fetches the dish and the mail-coach: that is, it converts my wishes from something in the realm of imagination, translates them from their meditated, imagined, or willed existence into their *sensuous, actual* existence—from imagination to life, from imagined being into real being. In effecting this mediation, money is the *truly creative power.*"[30]

We (who have money) *can invent any new possibility if we give ourselves permission.* Without the financial means, my needs and wants remain figments of my imagination. "The difference between effective demand based on money and ineffective demand based on my need, my passion, my wish, etc.," Marx continues, "is the difference between being and thinking, between the imagined which exists merely within me and the imagined as it is for me outside me as a real *object.*"[31] Take this as Marx's time-traveling caveat to Agrawal: I cannot give myself "permission" to "invent any new possibility" if I don't have the money to make it real. But, then again, if I do have unlimited wealth, what can't I do? This is a real question. What can't the wealthiest people buy, manifest, command, make, establish as normative truth? What would be beyond their commodification?

It's not just the Business of Spirituality women who make these points. Capitalist reformers make a routine of denaturalizing the money system in order to argue for its curative power—if only people would make the choice to infuse it with that energy and intention. A philanthropic-foundation manager invokes how his "indigenous worldview" has taught him that if it is infused with "a kind of mystical or spiritual power . . . money can be medicine" for a world that is convulsing from capitalism-fueled neocolonial violence. "We forget," he reminds skeptics, "that humans made money up out of thin air, as a concept, a tool for a complex society, a placeholder for aspects of

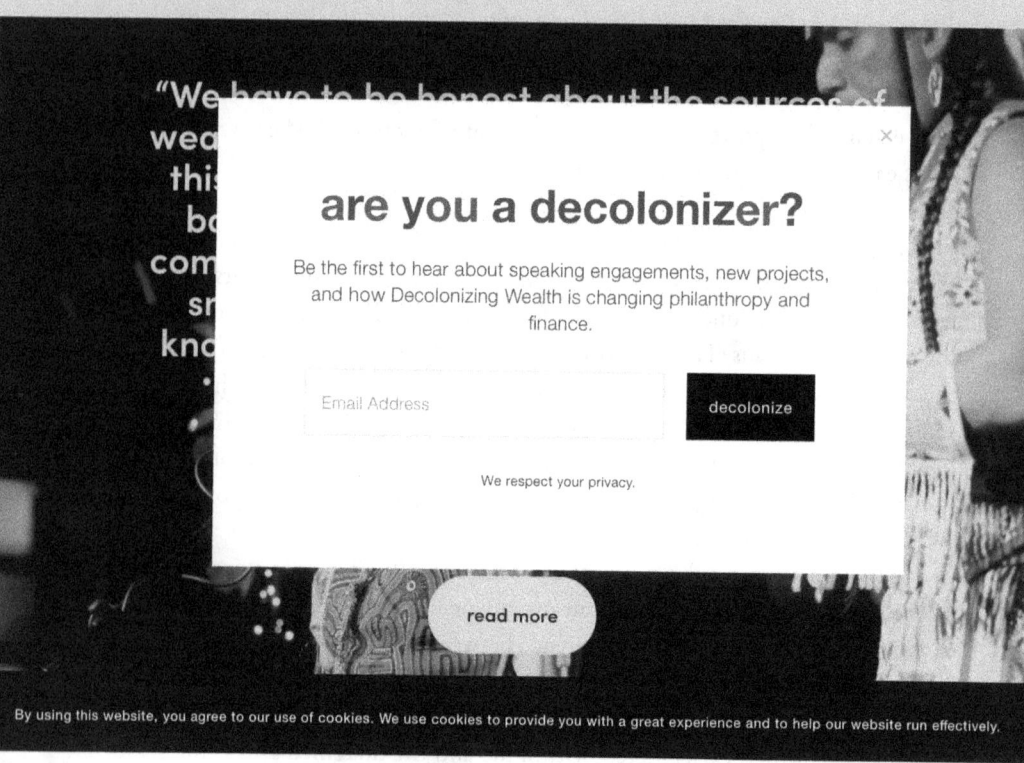

2.3 A pop-up advertisement on the Decolonizing Wealth website asks users the ultimate question.

human relations.... Money, used as medicine, can help us decolonize" (see figure 2.3).[32] The impact investor Jed Emerson conceives money as "a form of directed energy" that can "manifest the particular kind of impact its stewards intend."[33] He expounds this theory in his book *The Purpose of Capital: Elements of Impact, Financial Flows, and Natural Being*, which, among many other efforts to mine the sacred texts of world religions for wisdom on venture finance, wrestles with a strain of Christian liberation theology that castigates American-style neoliberal capitalism for having become an idolatrous church.[34] Proclaiming a "new Reformation," Emerson calls his fellow impact investors and social entrepreneurs to join the "happy heretical tribe advancing fundamental aspects of our central faith ... and pronouncing a renewed liturgy to celebrate our Eucharist." They are establishing a "Church of the New Capital" that deposes the "high priests of Wall Street" to pursue "multiple returns and a deep, sustained value creation that is part financial and in greater parts just, equitable, and regenerative." With flourish and champagne, they share their good news: "Jesus Saves. God Invests."[35]

. . . . . .

In the end, there is almost a way that these investors have landed on a similar theoretical page to none other than Karl Marx. All seek to denaturalize the money system. All say that you can manifest any fantastical vision you conjure if you have the resources to do it. All assume that capitalism makes labor an abstract quantity to be measured against and exchanged with other commodified quantities. But here's where they depart: the panelists presented an account of the modern world in which capital is no longer the final frontier of abstraction; the idea of "capital" can be further abstracted as "energy" that is equivalent to all other "made-up" substances. The spiritual and wellness entrepreneurs' theories of the commodity form inverted Marx's analogy between the commodity fetish and the "mist-enveloped region of the religious world." It's no longer that the spiritual furnishes the metaphor for Marx's theory of commodification; it's that processes of commodification now give metaphor to, and by extension become instrumental in establishing the coordinates of, the spiritual. The spiritual capitalist sheds her past vampire persona and reemerges in an opposite guise. She gave up the workers' blood and decided that she would manifest her energy into the world, catalyzing flows that began with her financial expenditures. From here, the ball rolls into the court of her employees and the consumers to whom she markets. Will I reciprocate her energetic expenditure, meet her with my own money energy and labor energy, or allow her to bleed out? And what are these categories of "capitalist" and "employee" and "consumer"? They don't really exist; they are made-up constructions; you can make your own reality. Case in point: the ones with the investor confidence just did.

. . . . . .

Meanwhile, back at my desk, I built a fortress tower of every monograph that Judith Butler has ever written or cited or inspired. *It's not true*, I muttered. *Marxist feminist social theory is* not *a stranded asset that capitalist vampires are surveying for its reinvestment potential.* I reached for my shelves for the books that I wanted to protect or that I wanted to appropriate as my talismans.

Bodies That Matter. The Cultural Politics of Emotion. The Marx-Engels Reader. Orientalism. Represent and Destroy. Dialectic of Enlightenment. Transit of Empire. Cruel Optimism. Their weight imprinted my skin and comforted me. I tried again to convince myself that even if there arose a context where "give yourself permission" didn't sound like a sexual-misconduct case waiting to happen, even if the maxim "money can be medicine" weren't a case study in neocolonial pedagogy, even if one could overlook the characterization of child-snatching border police as "people in costumes," even if it were possible to not have an ironic read of an impact investor's call to establish a "New Church of Capital," nobody could possibly read the texts they cited and follow them to those conclusions. Right? *Right?* It's not what they said. But here is the thing about a system progressively hollowed out of historical-material stakes: you can literally create any new possibility you want if you just give yourself permission.

October 2017.
No undercover cop.

You are not a real child of the Christian Left if you do not lampoon the older cohort of change makers. The preteen at the interfaith antiwar vigil who moves between pious chanting to screaming at the uncombed adults that *YOU ARE EMBARRASSING US, HIPPIES*, is living into her birthright. Her elders, if they take a moment to self-reflect, feel proud. They were the ones who taught her to distrust the powers that be. Did they expect her not to take the lesson to its logical end, to realize that the corruption implicates her mentors, too?

The impiety begins with petty taunts of adults' natural deodorants and pitchy sing-alongs at underattended antiwar vigils. These first seeds of doubt will eventually yield more pointed satire of the other generation's tactics and philosophy. My siblings and I took exception to the "peace is patriotic" yard signs (too optimistic about the US nation-state), the weekend ritual of civil disobedience and bailouts (too cavalier about jail, too reliant on the safety net of middle-class whiteness), and the bewildering faith in consensus-based dialogue (misery incarnate, a blank check for feminist-identified patriarchs to mansplain their convictions to women). We became walking bullshit detectors, sirens blaring anytime that practices contravened the ideals of egalitarianism preached at rallies and organizer meetings. We pounced on inconsistencies between content and form, principle and process. We could magnify contradictions—there were always contradictions—until they reached a crisis point. It could almost be a game, nothing off-limits to critique.

Leading up to the "Month of Action" planned by the Yale graduate union in spring 2017, Mark and I cackled about the cloying decorum that had taken over the preparations. Nobody embodied this tone more than the resident

Catholic priest of UNITE-HERE, whom the national union flew to New Haven from Los Angeles to bless our hunger strike. Or, as higher-ups kept correcting us, the *fast. It's not a hunger strike,* they nagged. *It's deeper than that.* On the eve of our organizing blitz, fresh from the West Coast and high off the history of the United Farm Workers, this leftist cleric had gathered the eight inaugural "fasters" in the sanctuary of the church that leased its basement to the union. He had arranged them in a circle, fishbowl style, at the center of the room. The rest of us there—other graduate organizers, members of the other locals, community allies—observed from the edges of the room. The priest roamed around the fasters' circle, addressing them in second person with words I now ventriloquized. *You are crossing a threshold into sacred terrain,* he cooed. *You will never be the same,* he stage-whispered, circumambulating them once more.

Mark was like *yeah that's weird, but at least you know he's not a cop, because no undercover cop, I don't care who he is, could ever pull that kind of stunt.*

I have a reverie, flashing to some street-side Hiroshima Day demonstration where seven-year-old me taught five-year-old Mark how to spot plainclothes police in crowds of what at the time we called "the granola people." I supplied him a checklist for what makes them suspect. If they have nice sunglasses that they don't take off. If they tuck in their button-down shirt, especially if that shirt has a square chest pocket for their pens. If they have a recording device and if you don't know them personally, then they are definitely a cop, and you must find me immediately. Both of us would later learn that cops are not always so easy to recognize.

. . . . . .

Three months after he died, I had disciplined my own memory enough to resume serious fieldwork, and I stepped off an airplane into a charcoal haze. My phone blinked awake; I checked the news. No evacuation order yet. Until proven otherwise, the tenth annual "Social Capitalism" conference would proceed on schedule. I had agreed to trade ten hours of free labor for a ticket to the five-day gathering convened, according to its tagline, at "the intersection of money + meaning." This year the intersection made physical residence at Presidio convention center on the San Francisco Bay. You could see Alcatraz from the parking lot. Hustling toward volunteer orientation, I squinted at the prison island and strained to fill my lungs without hacking on the smoke. *How many acres of forest did that red eye cost?* I wondered, vaguely, before my mind floated, like ash on the wind, to the more immediate concern: Would the other attendees spot me as an interloper among them?

About one hundred volunteers filed into an old-fashioned firehouse, renewed and refurbished for its second career as an upscale event venue. A silver sliding pole descended down from the ceiling, lonely without the gas masks, boots, and flame-retardant clothing of first responders who used to work here. Several dozen twenty-somethings made small talk at collapsible tables, all of us turned toward a middle-aged white woman standing at a podium in her floral blouse, bulky crucifix necklace, and white clerical collar. In her words of welcome, she identified herself as the cofounder and "executive producer" of SOCAP. But was she also an ordained priest? Her outfit suggested as much, but conference literature had mentioned nothing about sectarian allegiance. Nevertheless, here was a founding member of the senior leadership in rock clerical vestments, which signaled that she saw her involvement in the event to be both an extension of her ministry and a context of divine presence. "Our money is connected to our mission in life," she mused in an interview a few days later. "How can I say that I care about human trafficking and then buy goods and services that have a slavery footprint in them? I like to say that money is a moral and ethical extension of ourselves."

. . . . . .

It had started to seem as if for every capitalist humanitarian venture I studied, some liberal Protestant affinity would reveal itself lurking behind the curtain. Missionary-founded fair trade outposts had only been the tip of a massive iceberg. Now I'd dug up microfinance projects that had begun in the context of church-sponsored opposition to US invasions of Latin America and that had long since scrubbed ecclesial affiliation from their public image. Now, at SOCAP, not only was one of the head honchos affiliating herself with the Episcopal Church, but liberal religious groups kept popping out amid long queues of business school students and venture fund managers. A brigade from Catholic Charities had showed up, as had the Unitarian Universalists, the Jewish World Service, and the conservative evangelical parachurch organization World Vision.

Then it got personal. Posted as an usher at the opening keynote address, I met eyes with an acquaintance from another life. He had lined up at the entrance alongside two colleagues at the foundation where all three of them worked. I knew their organization well. It had an outstanding reputation for supporting students of religious and theological studies, especially divinity school students involved in social justice work and doctoral students of color. I'd received about $15,000 in scholarships during my undergraduate and master's programs. Most of this money was connected to being selected as an emerging "ministry leader" during my second year of divinity school. The fellowship included two discernment retreats with a cohort of twenty peers, almost all of whom had pursued careers in faith-based nonprofit organizing.

The luxe weekends away clarified the depth of my quasi-Calvinist, anticapitalist, queer pessimism. I liked my new friends, but I did not share their optimism about building the beloved community on Earth or their belief in natural human goodness. So pronounced was my downer role in our quasi-family system that in a slow moment before a worship service, a peer put her hands on my shoulders, locked her eyes on mine, and reassured me that I really did have spiritual gifts, even if they were irritating to others. "We need critics like you, to keep people like me on my toes," she explained. I tried to not feel like the gloom cloud over their love revival.

Now one of the foundation's vice presidents had shown up in my field site. Our recognition was simultaneous. So was our mutual demand for answers, as if in becoming the chief interrogator we could exonerate our personal presence in this den of inequity. "I'm doing research," I snapped, a little too quickly. "What brings *you* here?" One of them mumbled that the organization had pivoted. While the doctoral fellowship program would continue, the foundation would now serve primarily as "an incubator for Christian start-ups." The leadership team had come to meet investors. I wished them luck, and I even meant it. Their endowment returns must have dried up; this must have been their bid for institutional survival. Later, retreating into snark, I called my mom: "Tell Dad he is wrong. The religious Left is dead. It was replaced by a capital fund called DoGoodX."

. . . . . .

I next encountered the benefactors of my theological education at the annual meeting of the American Academy of Religion (AAR). Each year the foundation throws a reception for its alumnae, friends, and whoever else stops by to take advantage of the open bar. I sometimes duck into it because I know my parents will be somewhere else. They also attend AAR; my dad because it's part of his job and my mom to intervene if my dad gets overzealous about intervening in discussions during my panels. *If anyone here had read my book,* he declared the year that sealed my mom's decision to chaperone future gatherings, *you would know that religious Left activism was at its most vibrant in the 1980s, not in decline, as the common wisdom suggests!* I have less at stake in defending this position, but I wouldn't say it's wrong. That decade arguably marked the high tide of left Christian mobilization against US empire.[1] Still, take my advice: never suggest otherwise within his earshot unless you want the topic of Left-liberal Protestantism insinuated, or dragooned, into your subsequent interactions.

The year of Read-My-Book-Gate, I ran into him at the reception of our shared alma mater; he and his graduate school friend were talking about their trips to Central America. Apparently, every Christian leftist worth their salt went there during the years of Reagan's dirty wars. The two of them traded stories over free IPAs: my dad's hitchhiking trip through Mexico, his classmate's stint on a Nicaraguan coffee plantation, and—this story told with the protagonist absent—the trip to Nicaragua that my mom took in March 1988 while serving as associate pastor of St. Luke Presbyterian Church. The plane touched down minutes after Reagan threatened to invade the country and depose the Sandinista government from power. The group had to evacuate to Costa Rica. My father always adds that my mom was pregnant at the time, and this is the moment where I will be conscripted into the story. "Let me introduce you to my daughter," he beamed to his colleague. "She was in Nicaragua *in the womb.*" I had heard this story three dozen times. It's one of those stock lines said at every academic gathering—on par with the flexing "Lucia and I are each other's secret weapons" or the more ambivalently wistful "Soon I will be known only as *Lucia Hulsether's father.*"

My cheeks burned, and I mumbled something about dubious ascriptions of personhood to an embryo. Does he really want to endorse that politics? I cannot quite catch up to the fact that he is conjuring this infantile image for people who might one day be in a position to hire me. How many times have I gritted my teeth on a plastic cocktail stirrer and hissed *I am your professional colleague* in his direction? My reminders don't stick. They erase at least half the story. The other version would be about a miscarried protégé, turned cold toward parental expectation. He just wants to be seen, and to see me seeing him. So I again consider my obligations, this match that lights up my shelter of words.

marxists in the microbank   3
FROM SOLIDARITY MOVEMENT
TO SOLIDARITY LENDING

We have always been a solidarity organization. The words intercepted my archival revelation: the microfinance institution (MFI) hosting my summer internship had its roots in the Central American solidarity movement. A cohort of Left activists, several of them affiliated with liberal churches, had founded the Wisconsin Coordinating Committee on Nicaragua (WCCN) in 1984. Convened as a regional hub for organizers looking to fortify the embattled Central American left, at some point WCCN switched gears. Now, three decades later, it had morphed into full-fledged financier with investment portfolios in a dozen countries. The new "Working Capital for Community Needs" retained its old acronym and talked a big game about showing solidarity with the Latin American poor. They specifically were referring to "solidarity lending," in which their affiliate banks issued loans to groups of poor people who assumed liability for each other's debts. If one person reneged on their obligation, the rest were encouraged to collect the money by whatever means available, including peer pressure, public shunning, confiscating collateral from the borrower's home, or absorbing the consequences of default. How had a committee for socialists gone so far off track?

I resolved to ask the associate director, who had credited her current career path to the church-sponsored volunteer stint she'd done in Nicaragua in the 1980s. I found her in her office where, as usual, she was banging out reports beneath a portrait of a bank client tending to her flock of chickens. When I asked her about the history, she reached behind into a storage bin, retrieved a three-ring binder, and flipped it open to the inaugural WCCN newsletter, dated March 1988 with a bolded headline: *Will the U.S. Invade?* She shook her head, whether out of disgust for Reagan's coup flex or nostalgia for her more radical youth, I couldn't tell. So I paused to choose my words before I let loose the sharper version of my question. "I am thinking about how WCCN started as part of the Central America Solidarity Movement," I began, willing my end-sentence upticks to convey naive curiosity. "It just makes me wonder... how do you think that its mission has changed over the years?"

I must have botched the delivery. Her reply came out sharp, as if my allusion to a mission change insulted the organization's past and present. "*Nothing* has changed," she shot back. "We have always been a solidarity organization." Her tone told me that the conversation was closed. I returned to my desk, perplexed at clues that went nowhere: US-trained insurgencies in the global Cold War, a generation of liberal Christians who sought alliance with the Latin American Left, the 1990s microfinance boom in international development policy, and the various actors who might have crisscrossed those terrains. If there was a larger story here, I wanted to find it. Even if WCCN was a unicorn, the political stakes were too high to ignore: How does a Left solidarity activist turn into a microfinance banker? How does an organization steeped in liberation theology end up administering usurious lending schemes targeted at poor indigenous women? And, back to the director's rejoinder, how does one distinguish between a radical break in mission and a long-standing truth that is merely emerging in a new form?

. . . . . .

The affinities between microlending and the solidarity activism of leftist Christians exceed my wide-eyed moment in that MFI workspace. When the breadcrumbs added up, they led straight to two microfinance pioneers: ACCION International and FINCA International. Both of these humanitarian relief-turned-banking organizations steered Congress toward finance-based approaches to foreign aid. Both innovated lending schemes that helped open the global South to a flood of debt capital. Neither, starting out, would have expected to find an ally in the other. ACCION launched in the 1960s as a "private Peace Corps" modeled on federal programs to saturate Latin America with US soft power. Its lending arm emerged in the mid-1970s out of its efforts to thwart Left political movements with microenterprise development. FINCA owed its existence to self-avowed anticapitalists. Its pathway into microlending routed through the Central America solidarity movement; early supporters hoped to embolden peasant farmers against the free-trade agreements and privatization trends that undermined their livelihoods. Despite their apparent ideological distance, both organizations ended up as pioneers of the international finance industry.[1]

Solidarity movement, solidarity banking. They are not the same thing, but look closer and find some common principles. These articulations of "solidarity" depend on a structural power differential between the parties entering a coalition. Activist committees had money and networks, plus pained awareness of their own complicity with imperialism; they were staffed by the consumer citizens who understood before anyone else that their coffee was spiked with the blood of an oppressed farmer and that they needed to intervene in this vampire economy. They gravitated toward Central American agricultural workers to orient their own conflicted relationship to American empire. "Solidarity" named the debts owed by global North consumers to global South producers suffering on their account.

After the regional wars had ended, when the guerrillas had gone home, when aspiring allies debated where to direct resources, the leap might not have been so great after all: they could literalize their felt alliance with a solidarity loan. There was precedent for this genre of relation. Development finance had been pushing its vision for decades. Philosophers had been theorizing social solidarity in terms of debts owed for a century. Still, there remained room for new ventures to chisel out different and less predatory kinds of obligation. So that is what they aimed to do. In the process they laid the groundwork for a new model of capitalist humanitarian ethics, where being an ally to a poor person in the global South meant becoming her creditor and where "solidarity" signaled partnership forged in the context of her compounding debts.

Solidarity Organizers

On November 22, 1996, ACCION, one of the first microfinance operations in the Americas, marked its thirty-fifth anniversary. It had a lot to celebrate, from windfall deals with Citibank and Credit Suisse to a presidential leadership award. Four dinner courses into the evening, the board cochairs ascended the stage to reminisce from a script:

> The idea for ACCION dates back to 1959, when a student named Joe Blatchford embarked on a youth-to-youth goodwill tour of Latin America. Joe, a semi-professional tennis player, would play matches with the local pros and his companions would put on a jazz concert. They were known as the "Swinging Ambassadors."

Joe was deeply effected [*sic*] by the poverty he saw during the tour and he came home determined to do something. But Joe didn't want to give charity, he wanted to help people help themselves. His solution was to recruit U.S. students to spend a year in Latin America, working on community development projects. The idea was to work with residents, help build local leadership, and, eventually, work themselves out of a job.

It was a new idea—at least for a few months, until presidential candidate Jack Kennedy called for a U.S. Peace Corps. But Joe couldn't wait for the government to act. He moved ahead and by 1961, ACCION's first volunteers were already at work in the slums of Caracas, Venezuela. The rest, as they say, is history.

ACCION had not made itself redundant; it had multiplied. For this achievement, the cochairs raised a toast to project directors in Bolivia, Colombia, Nicaragua, Guatemala, and several major US cities. "It is the solidarity of this network that bridges the Americas," they bellowed, "and our ability to unite in 'one voice' that makes microenterprise such a powerful movement in this hemisphere. Muchas gracias."[2] Stage notes cued the applause.

To appreciate why debt discipline exploded in the 1990s, look first to 1960s anticommunist development initiatives and their pro-capitalist raids on the hemisphere. Blatchford built his postcollege résumé by launching privately funded copycats of federal Cold War initiatives. His first venture, the "Swinging Ambassadors," retooled the State Department program of dispatching black jazz musicians abroad as emissaries of American cultural exceptionalism.[3] Following his first musical tour of South America, Blatchford announced his intention to launch a "private Peace Corps" in Venezuela. He would call it ACCION—official shorthand for "Americans for Community Cooperation with Other Nations" and, if you caught Blatchford drunk at a party, unofficially understood to mean "Americans Concerned about Communism in Other Nations."[4] Within two years of his announcement, Blatchford had recruited twenty volunteers and raised more than $225,000 from US oil companies and Venezuelan banks, the corporate parties most keen that the political uprisings not sabotage the natural gas market.[5]

Wall Street anxieties about grassroots movements and potential nationalization peaked in the wake of the Cuban Revolution in 1959, which had persuaded huge swaths of everyday people that national and economic sovereignty went hand in hand.[6] It was with that context in mind that Blatchford staked out his territory in Venezuela, arriving just after the country's first free election in more than five decades. The president, Rómolo Betancourt of the social democratic party Acción Democrática, was caught in a tug-of-war between leftists demanding popular reforms and business interests warning of retaliation should their investments be threatened.[7] Blatchford swooped into this scene with pledges to "organize [people] to help themselves by collective democratic action."[8] Elsewhere, he referenced his "psychological plan" with respect to Latin American people.[9] "Americans, generally speaking, are good organizers," one profile of ACCION volunteers opened. "They learn the art as early as Cub Scouts and Brownies and practice it for the rest of their lives in the family, the PTA, and on the church picnic. Latin Americans are a different breed." Blatchford preached that Latin America lacked an "organizing tradition" because "they evolved under the 'patron' system of always looking to somebody above you to get things for you. The goal is to get the average man to participate in his own fate."[10] Yet Blatchford's own interventionist zeal betrayed his fear that people were already participating in their own fates, if not in the way that certain Cub Scout alumni and benefactors from Standard Oil would have preferred. Insofar as his portrayal of Venezuela's politics sounds bizarre in a period that witnessed revolutionary uprisings across Latin America, all with their own complex philosophies and praxes, it helps to remember that ACCION meant "organizing" in a very narrow and specific sense. Organizing, here, means creating an infrastructure for free enterprise and refusing the public entitlements of a socialist state.[11]

The goal was to instigate mass conversion from socialist sympathy to capitalist passion. ACCION leadership celebrated rank-and-file volunteer Rodmar Pulley, who "introduced his brand of capitalism to his Venezuelan roommate with the aid of an electric blender": "After starting a thriving milkshake business with the blender, Mr. Pulley sold his interest in the business venture to his roommate at cost. 'Now you're a capitalist,' Mr. Pulley told the Venezuelan student. Taken aback for a moment, his roommate replied, 'I guess your view of capitalism depends on who is the capitalist.'"[12] In this gold medal outcome, one volunteer instantiates a model of capitalism so delicious that when he hails his roommate with its name, the dissident assents to the label. He encounters capitalism neither as faceless ideology nor social crisis but through his friend's milky desserts. Such were the moments of personal change that ACCION members sought; they aimed for nothing less than the birth of a new frame of mind in their Venezuelan charges, until they no longer needed US twenty-somethings to guide them in the arts of self-sufficiency. Blatchford's preeminent talking point cited his aim to "train men and women of our host nation to take over the work, literally to work ourselves out of jobs."[13] This is not what happened.

What happened was that ACCION moved the goalposts from supporting volunteer service to seeding microenterprises in the "informal economy." The board—still stacked with executives from Pepsi-Cola, Exxon, and Wells Fargo—severed all formal legal ties between the original parent organization and its international satellites.[14] The newly surnamed ACCION *International* would act as an investor, lender, and networking hub for international affiliates that operated with independent charters.[15] By the time Richard Nixon appointed Blatchford director of the Peace Corps in 1969, the old volunteer service model had atrophied altogether.[16] ACCION had set its designs on annexing the global South's informal economies for American-style capitalism.

The term "informal economies" referred to income-generating practices, usually performed by poor people, that slipped the state's gaze but that, nevertheless, could be targeted for market integration. Development professionals had predicted that, if relief agencies provided poor people access to financial services and business training, they could reduce poverty while inculcating free-market values. Keen to explore this terrain, ACCION sponsored a survey of "informal" economies in the favelas of Recife, Brazil, in the early 1970s. The in-house ethnographers returned from their adventure with two big takeaways. They first observed the obvious: among Brazil's poorest population one could find a surfeit of what ACCION coined as "microenterprises." Women made extra beans and rice, aware that neighbors might pay them for it; a certain family was the go-to place if someone needed their shoes repaired; four-year-olds hawked gum and cigarettes on corners. From these findings the researchers surmised that, if the purveyors of these microenterprises could access even a small influx of capital, it would enhance their quality of life.

Executive staff approached local Brazilian banks for partnership. The resulting credit association, known as the Northeast Union of Assistance to Small Businesses (UNO), issued loans to "extremely small businesses." *Small* was a relative term. Destitute street vendors may have supplied the sparkly human-interest hook, but the beneficiaries of these loans were more likely to be up-and-running corner stores with ambitions to stock more inventory or add new staff. Eligible microenterprises could claim up to $35,000 in total assets and up to $50,000 of annual earnings; ACCION was several years away from issuing the kinds of single- and double-digit loans for which microfinance became famous. Still, the experiment spelled success. Within four years, UNO had dispensed nine hundred loans, most of which had been repaid. Its leadership decided to expand—first to other cities in Brazil (1974), then to Columbia (1977), Ecuador (1977), Mexico (1981), the Dominican Republic (1982), and Peru (1982).[17] The bank arrived in the wake of dictatorial terror sweeping through those same countries as US-backed paramilitaries massacred anyone suspected of opposition to capitalist itineraries of free trade, privatization, and deregulation.

......

One survivor of that terror was René Hurtado, forced to flee El Salvador after he refused a military commander's direct order to mutilate a dead body. The twenty-one-year-old had been serving in the national army when the voice of Oscar Romero spoke to him through the radio static. "The people you are killing are your own brothers and sisters," Romero had preached, calling on soldiers like Hurtado to lay down their weapons. The Archbishop's words triggered Hurtado's crisis in conscience, even as the dictatorship accelerated its campaign to disappear, torture, rape, and murder anyone suspected of opposing the regime—with students, teachers, farmworkers, clergy, and progressive politicians as prime targets. Case in point: soon after Hurtado's dishonorable discharge, a gunman would assassinate Romero while he performed a memorial mass. This escalation, plus mounting police raids, spurred Hurtado's flight. The danger trailed him through Mexico and across the border to the United States, where Hurtado found a second target on his back. The United States federal government had blanket-denied asylum to both Salvadoran and Guatemalan refugees. It had deputized immigration officials to deport them back to a slaughter.

While Hurtado sought relative safety in the North, ten members of St. Luke Presbyterian Church (USA) crossed the US-Mexico border without a snag. The young, wealthy, majority-white congregation in the suburban Twin Cities enjoyed a high profile within Christian social-justice circles. The church had organized protests against the Vietnam War, founded an organic food cooperative to alleviate local poverty, embraced feminist theology when many other congregations had rejected it as blasphemy, donated its backyard for the construction of a Lakota sweat lodge, and been among the first mainline congregations to enact full inclusion for women and queer people. Looking to deepen its practice as a peace church, head pastor Richard Lundy organized a trip to the Cuernavaca Center for Intercultural Dialogue on Development (CCIDD) in 1980. The Center had opened in the 1960s to provide sanctuary for radical clergy fleeing dictatorial violence at home, and over time it had emerged as a kind of intellectual hub for Latin American liberation theology. Left clergy from the United States would take their parishioners there in hopes of politicizing them.

To hear the St. Luke travelers tell it forty years later, the trip provoked a congregational transformation. Although members had already considered themselves aware and worldly, they had never seen privation like what confronted them in Mexico. Nor had they reckoned with their own complicity with its causes—what their teachers in Cuernavaca described as their collusion with structural sin that degraded Christ's image-bearers.[18] They returned home ready to act. They pledged to "resist the immoral and illegal policy" against asylum seekers and make the church "a sanctuary for refugees from El Salvador and Guatemala."[19] Their decision put them among a small and growing faction of "sanctuary churches" that had allied with the larger Central American solidarity movement.

A coatless Hurtado arrived at St. Luke in the winter of 1981. Members hustled him from the freezing night to the Sunday school room that design-savvy parishioners had converted into a bedroom. Hurtado would live there for two years, accompanied round-the-clock by members of a sanctuary committee posted to handle the regular onslaught of press and police. To pass the time and to connect with his hosts, Hurtado immersed himself in the church's everyday rhythms. Sundays found him postgaming Minnesota Timberwolves games at fellowship hour; Tuesday afternoons he dropped by social justice council meetings. Kids at biweekly potlucks counted on him for playing dolls and soccer, and he entertained rolling tour groups who came to hear his story. On any given day he might be called, again, before a judge. One step beyond the doors of the church could trigger his arrest. With his own life toggling between hemmed-in-monotony and terrifying spectacle, Hurtado's everyday presence began to radicalize the church. Congregational task forces lobbied representatives, accompanied asylum seekers to court, took arrest, went to jail, and at one point helped smuggle Hurtado's family to Costa Rica when the death threats against them escalated. "Families fleeing the bloodbath in Central America [are] being hunted and arrested and deported back to the terror," Pastor Lundy attested on the news. "We ... say 'no' to that policy of our government by saying 'yes' to what the Gospel asks of us—that we stand with the powerless and that we welcome the homeless."[20] The theology of liberation superseded the law of the state. All tactics were on the table.

. . . . . .

As St. Luke escalated its solidarity activism through the 1980s, ACCION throttled toward full-time lending. Its staff heralded a new kind of finance: "solidarity lending," which referred to the practice of issuing loans to groups of people who acted as each other's guarantors. ACCION elaborated this idea in a research project known as the Program for Investment in the Small Capital Enterprise Study (PISCES). Commissioned by the US Office of Urban Development, the final report surveyed twenty-three "programs of direct assistance to the smallest businesses within the informal sector where capital start-up is minimal, from a few dollars to one or two hundred dollars."[21] The final write-up was an unconcealed booster for finance- and enterprise-driven development. The authors noted that even small loans made a significant difference in "smoothing" revenue streams, that injections of capital created jobs, and even very poor clients tended to settle their debts. There was just one problem to lament: poor people "do not perceive themselves as entrepreneurs." Their debased self-image persisted "even when they have potentially marketable skills such as sewing or weaving." The report concluded that the people targeted by microbanks would need education not just in "enterprise development and income generation" but also in "self-worth."[22] Solidarity lending could handle both.

Was the confidence warranted? ACCION certainly believed so, and had the receipts to prove it: solidarity lending, it turned out, was a Salvadoran export. ACCION attributed both the term and the lending model to a collaboration between the country's federal government (PRIDECO) and a private credit union (FEDECREDITO). The bank issued credit to grupos solidarios of eight to twelve people who agreed to enforce one another's repayment. This model, literally branded with the same word used by activists allied against the dictator, motivated ACCION leadership to "get rid of all non-microfinance projects." All partners would be converted into MFIs; if they balked, they would be cut out of the network.[23] Within five years of the PISCES report, ACCION's lending affiliates reported more than fifteen thousand active clients and a composite loan portfolio of a million dollars.[24] "Solidarity" principles worked. Soon they would not only guide international development practices but also give language to the merger between humanitarian reform and debt-driven finance capital.

Solidarity Debts

Until I encountered these banker archives, I had associated "solidarity" with Left activism and labor organizing—not multinational financiers. The term, at least in progressive-activist contexts, usually refers to the coalitions built toward shared objectives—be it a collective-bargaining agreement, cuts to the police budget, blocks on carbon emissions, or something similar. These more-contemporary uses can overshadow a longer and more ambivalent history of the term. The word itself is derived from Roman *in solido* agreements, which were legal contracts between creditors and debtors. At stake in such contracts was not only a relationship between two parties but also the maintenance of a wider social equilibrium.[25] People who benefit from life in a community, the thinking went, should also invest in it. It was this sense of solidarity—solidarity receipt and reciprocation in the context of a collective bond—that social theorist Émile Durkheim would popularize. Writing in France at the turn of the twentieth century, Durkheim asked questions about how societies maintain collective stability and individual freedom amid drastic changes, especially those catalyzed by the Industrial Revolution. His term for social cohesion was *solidarity*. It is this valence of the term that humanitarian financiers would revive.

Would it be too extreme to characterize Durkheim as a founding capitalist humanitarian? His career blossomed on a grim question: Why had the suicide rate spiked in Europe? Countering medical consensus that attributed self-inflicted death to individual pathology, Durkheim argued in *Suicide: A Sociological Study* that the problem was social. Rising suicide rates, he showed, correlated with industrialization. Imperatives of labor and profit, combined with the flow of youth out of their homes and into city jobs, undermined forms of sociality once anchored in the state, church, and family.[26] To the extent that industrial capitalism signaled laudable evolution toward social complexity, it had ravaged the institutions most responsible for tending social bonds. For Durkheim, these bonds were everything. He considered human life literally unfathomable absent "solidarity" with the larger whole.[27] When society proves "incapable of exercising [its] influence[,] thence come the sudden rises in the curve of suicides." A "feverish" individualism had filled the social void, leaving moderns in a lonely, chaotic fugue: "Appetites, not being controlled by a public opinion become disoriented, no longer recognize the limits proper to them.... With increased prosperity desires increase. At the very moment when traditional rules have lost their authority, the richer prize offered these appetites stimulates them and makes them more exigent and impatient of control. The state of de-regulation or anomy is thus further heightened by passions being less disciplined, precisely when they need more disciplining."[28] Contrary to what certain organized socialists might have claimed, the crimes of industrial capitalism had little to do with private property. The elementary issue lay in how modern technological advances had outpaced the disciplinary traditions and religious organization necessary to maintain social equilibrium.

Durkheim recommended a course correction. Maybe industrial capitalism, a hegemonic social form, could be the ground for repairing the relationships it had wrecked. Durkheim envisioned a consortium of "worker corporations" comprised of "agents of the same industry, united and organized into a single body." Intended as hubs for social life, the associations would deepen shared interests, promote common activities, and "strengthen bonds of attachment" not only among workers but also between workers and bosses. Worker corporations were not, in other words, unions, which Durkheim classified as a "beginning of occupational organization" but ultimately deficient insofar as their emphasis on workers' material interests fomented a continuous "state of war" between labor and management.[29] The solution to class conflict—which Durkheim acknowledged as a real problem but considered to be tertiary to a more general fragmentation—was to fortify the workplace as a hub for social solidarity. If bosses got to know their employees as people, maybe they would be motivated to improve working conditions on their own—no coercion required. If workers witnessed the goodwill and humanity of the boss, this would reduce their incentive to vilify management, exercise their collective bargaining rights, or go on strike.[30] Durkheim speculated that worker corporations could emerge as "the essential organ of public life." They had potential to displace state-imposed territorial allegiances and religious sects, to awaken "profound sentiments" of identification that churches and nations no longer summoned, and even to replace the nuclear family as the privileged site of inheritance and social reproduction.[31]

A century later, Durkheim's prescriptions sound at once outlandish in their ambition and prophetic in their prediction of how the late capitalist corporate workplace orients the worker's existence. Modern corporations do refer to themselves as "families." They cultivate zealous loyalties to brand identity and to the consumer publics that congeal around them. They rival nation-states as arbiters of border-crossing mobility, social-safety-net provisions, and political speech. They capture the minds of cultural critics, including scholars of religion, who consummate Durkheim's ambitions with admission that, yes, the modern corporate form is indeed a religious form.[32] Considering these conditions, it will be unsurprising that corporate programs of finance-mediated "solidarity" accelerated in the 1980s and early 1990s heyday of neoliberal transformation.

. . . . . .

When ACCION recommended "solidarity banking" based on what its researchers found in El Salvador, it did more than just appropriate Leftist vocabulary. It also resurrected a long-standing discourse on social order and social debt. An earlier reformism echoes through the PISCES report's 1981 introduction of "solidarity banking" to development professionals:

> The idea behind the solidarity group is that the owner of the business with a need for credit will join other business owners and form a credit group to qualify for loans. The members of the group are collectively responsible for the loans of each group member. The underlying assumption is that peer pressure within the group will be strong enough to assure timely payments. Each group appoints one person to be in charge of collecting from the other members on a mutually agreed upon (often daily) schedule. The group leader is responsible for paying the FEDECREDITO collection agent who usually will collect at the home or business of the group leader each week.[33]

This founding text of microfinance not only recommended peer pressure and neighbor-on-neighbor surveillance as tactics for guaranteeing loan repayment but also did so via neutral-to-positive reference to a military dictatorship carrying out a genocide on its own people—many from the same communities still targeted for microloan programs. But the lexicon stuck. ACCION made the El Salvador model a prototype but omitted the geopolitical conditions under which it was engineered. As a report explained to investors in 1989,

> The solidarity group methodology adapts elements of the traditional model for rotating savings and credit associations (ROSCAs) that are widespread in the developing world. In ROSCAs, members contribute a regular amount each week or month, with group members rotating turns to collect the full contribution of all members. In peer group lending schemes, members receive loans, and then make regular weekly or monthly repayments with group members providing a mutual guarantee for loan repayment.[34]

Absorbing the local and the universal into one another, ACCION signals its allegiance to development policies that, in the words of anthropologist Julia Elyachar, "reconstitute the social networks and cultural practices of the poor as part of the free market."[35] ACCION nods to the prior existence of credit and debt relations in communities in order to rationalize its present intervention, not unlike how Durkheim's plan for social solidarity adapts to the industrial labor conditions that define its context. Both fuse social and economic worlds in order to maintain a degree of stability, at the same time as they accommodate a change in the conditions of production. In the canonical case of the generic ROSCA, an autonomous social body submits to the supervision of a professional credit officer to whom its members owe monthly, weekly, or daily payments.

The philosophy of group lending hit the limelight when Grameen Bank founder Muhammad Yunus won the Nobel Peace Prize for how he implemented it in Bangladesh. Yunus explained the model's rationale in his best-selling memoir *Banker to the Poor*:

> Individually, a poor person tends to feel all kinds of hazards. Group membership gives him a feeling of protection. Individually, a person tends to be erratic, uncertain in his or her behavior. But group membership creates group support and group pressure and smoothes out behavior patterns and makes the borrower more reliable.
>
> Subtle, and at times not so subtle, peer pressure keeps the group members in line with the broader objectives of the credit program.
>
> A sense of inter-group and intra-group competition helps everyone try to be an achiever. It is difficult to keep track of individual borrowers, but if he or she is a member of a group, it is much less difficult. Also, shifting the task of initial supervision to the group reduces the work of the bank worker and increases the self-reliance of the group.
>
> The group dynamic is important: because the group approves the loan request of each member, in the process it feels morally responsible for the loan.[36]

Yunus makes plain the major insight of humanitarian finance: a sense of social support yields obligation to a group that "keeps [them] in line" with the imperatives of the bank. In the decades between ACCION's introduction of group lending in El Salvador and the bestowal of the Nobel Prize on Yunus, the justifications of "solidarity" lending underwent a major transition. Initially, it was invoked as a skillful method of injecting financial services into "underdeveloped" territory, but by the late 1990s, it was an explicit technique for disciplining the "erratic" behaviors of "the poor." Although both senses of the practice were present throughout, the majoritarian valences of the concept were laid bare in the transition, as solidarity began to sound like carceral correction of those who would resist the group norm.

Echoes of Nietzsche: the debt is only as powerful as the social attachments and felt obligations that underwrite it.[37] What, if anything, is the difference between solidarity and debt? For example, I could feel that I owe something to the society that I navigate and benefit from daily. I might owe it my participation, my adherence to its norms, my volunteer service. I might call this feeling of obligation my "solidarity" with the project or people of whatever collective with which I've affiliated, but it may be more accurate to say that I feel a debt to them. When I shirk my responsibilities or cause harm to the group, I may feel as if, or be made by my comrades to feel as if, I owe some act of restitution. I can and do feel these attachments toward any of my social contexts: my union, my natal family, my alma mater, my church, my favorite basketball team, my employer, my nation-state, a stranger who returned my lost keys. My solidarity, my sense of owing a debt, pulls me back into the fold if I try to separate from it. This sense of solidarity—solidarity as attachment to a majoritarian order—is not as easy to valorize.[38] What if the normal function of the social body hinges on a prior dispossession, oppression, or terror? What if it is immobilizing or exploitative to some of its members? What does "solidarity" do for me then? What other constellations—counter-public alliances, negative affinities, bonds born in antagonism—does it keep from coming to light?

. . . . . .

One possible casualty of an idea of solidarity as cohesion is 1980s sanctuary churches. Halfway through that decade, St. Luke was knee-deep in its Central American solidarity activism. The national press reproduced images of Hurtado's bandana-obscured face alongside his testimony. Activists rallied around his image when they shuttled refugees across borders, committed civil disobedience, picketed courthouses, and went to prison.[39] Already under the spotlight, which intensified after the FBI listed one member as a coconspirator in a felony case against sanctuary activists, St. Luke still sought to deepen its solidarity work. When a parishioner's brother came through town with an chance to help Latin American farmers achieve economic autonomy, the congregation jumped to support it.

The visitor, John Hatch, explained that he had just launched the Foundation for International Community Assistance (FINCA). It aimed to eliminate poverty in Latin America by "respecting the wisdom of the peasant." In a model that Hatch later trademarked as "Village Banking," affiliates of FINCA would arrive in rural Bolivian towns with literal truckloads of cash. They offered the rough equivalent of $50 to farmers on the condition they repay the loan by the mutually agreed-upon term, plus the equivalent of $50 to replenish and double the community bank by the next harvest season. Due to outlandish inflation, people immediately invested the money in physical materials whose value would not depreciate. They would amortize the loans and replenish the town's collective fund using not cash but an equivalent sum of produce, materials, and/or livestock. Local people with a stake in the fund—anywhere from thirty to sixty people in a town—would decide together how to distribute the next round of money. To be involved in the decision and to be eligible for a second loan, however, a person had to have paid back the double initial value.[40] Hatch wanted to "help to capitalize on the most abundant resource in the

Third World—labor" while promoting community autonomy and economic independence.[41] For him, this trajectory toward independence distinguished the FINCA model from rival forms of solidarity lending.

Activated in part by the PISCES report, USAID had awarded FINCA two million dollars for its Bolivia loan fund and encouraged Hatch to seek grant support to expand into four more countries. Despite the leg up, Hatch confessed that he had been funding FINCA's administrative costs out of his own pocket. He wanted to insulate the bureaucratic aspects of the program from state funding structures. The church answered with characteristic generosity. Within just a few days, the church had raised $44,450.[42] They understood this support as an extension of their peace and justice work, and specifically their sanctuary activism. "It was natural after that point," recalled the church's account manager. "We were so into liberation theology and Romero and so on that it was a pretty easy call."

Thirteen St. Luke members traveled with John Hatch to the Bolivian highlands in May 1986. Entire towns welcomed them with feasts and dances. On a Sunday afternoon, more than thirty years later, the surviving travelers relayed their experiences to me over coffee. Lundy, now the emeritus pastor, recalled how people misrecognized the church as the source of the loans, when St. Luke's money was actually going to administrative costs:

> The people all thought we were the source of the money, because they had us dance at eight thousand feet. [Laughter and interjections from the group: "No, ten thousand feet!" "No, it was at least twelve thousand!" "I couldn't breathe!"] At the end of the trip we learned that AID was no longer going to fund small farmers, so we had a meeting with the head of USAID in La Paz in which Jean Clarke, who is a longtime member, said to the man, "I understand the plight you're in because I have a daughter who works for the State Department because she wanted to do good, and she discovered that the State Department in many cases prevents her from doing the work she wanted to do." And the dear man cried. So it was a very powerful meeting.[43]

Member Cecy Faster remembered choosing to go on the trip because she thought it would support a kind of economic development premised on groups and not individuals:

> I was intrigued by going on that trip because we sponsored villages. It was about to be an individual thing. We sponsored villages, so I think it was about to start being an individual thing, but those of us who went on

the trip had given about $10,000, which sponsored a whole village.... So it was real personal to this little village. And they did have village projects. One had a fishery, one had a greenhouse, one was doing something with a dam. The village decided how the money would be spent. And they were very, very remote. They didn't even have glasses or silverware or spoons for all of us, but the big appeal was sponsoring a whole village. But I think it was changing.[44]

And Jean Clarke, a developmental psychologist with a résumé of world travel, felt most affected by the gender dynamics of the economic system she encountered. These became apparent to her after she asked a guide why she had not seen any young girls in the towns:

> "They're *herding*," he told me. When the little girl starts to walk, they fasten the little blanket on her back because she will spend her life carrying. They don't have trucks; they have women. And so they put this little blanket on them and put a couple of things in it, like a couple of potatoes, so that they learn to get their balance with a load. And then when they are three, they start carrying another infant, because there will be another child. And they start caring for a small farm animal, and this would be a llama or a little pig, a goat. [Pause.] *And that's the family's equity.* So I spent all this time wondering how our minds and our approaches would be different if we started having a three-year-old girl handle our stock trades.[45]

These accounts may ring familiar to anyone who has listened to a church mission group or study-abroad student reminisce on their foreign travels. They plot the traveling subject in a plane of racialized economic difference and then mediate that difference through a stranger's eyes. They also embed within their recollections a latent critique of the US economic system, sometimes in counterintuitive ways.

Listen again. Lundy follows a laughing description of dancing at high altitudes with an image of a USAID staffer crying at the suggestion that his hands were tied. Faster interwove her hope to sponsor cooperative economies—as opposed to the individual ones that FINCA would later embrace—with material possessions in "very, very remote" places. Clarke conveyed horror at the idea that "they don't have trucks; they have women" before she switched to what, to me, sounded like a hopeful counterfactual to systems of wealth in the United States: what if "we started having a three-year-old girl handle our stock trades?" I heard between her lines a suggestion that the children of Bolivia modeled an alternative—less patriarchal, slower-paced, more gentle—vision for collective life, one that had stuck with her more than three decades later. But her account, like those of her friends, remained conflicted and at times contradictory. All these years later, St. Luke members were still wondering aloud what it would mean and if it was even possible to show solidarity with Bolivian farmers. The absence of clear answers made for unresolved narratives that, as they jump from one image to another, invite readings of their gaps.

There were other times, however, when the stakes demanded that they pull together a narrative and an argument about what must be done. Travelers sent a report to the US House of Representatives upon return. Congress was considering a bill that would have required allocating at least $50 million in aid funds to finance the economic activities of the "very poorest." When officials at USAID raised doubts that such populations could make constructive use of the funds, the public backlash was swift. Letters flooded in from private citizens, newspaper editorial teams, and churches like St. Luke. The blitz was coordinated by a citizens' advocacy group, RESULTS, founded five years before with the aim of recruiting newspaper editorial writers to advocate for federal policies against "child hunger."[46] In 1985 RESULTS volunteers had arranged a teleconference between Muhammad Yunus and twenty-eight US newspaper editors. The subsequent features on Grameen Bank nudged the MFI and its founder into the early limelight and persuaded wide swaths of the US public to champion microfinance as a humanitarian policy. RESULTS counted among its pillar organizational partners the mainline parachurch coalition Bread for the World, which since the 1970s had been equipping congregations to hold letter-writing campaigns for specific (and adamantly bipartisan) anti-hunger bills. When the microlending question rose to the top of the congressional docket, so did the liberal Christian voices urging its passage.[47]

John Hatch continued to make his case. "These people are totally capable of doing something productive with $50," he wrote in a public rebuttal to USAID skeptics. "They can't afford to make mistakes. They're intrinsically very resourceful, very practical. They may be ignorant of many things, but they're not stupid. They know what works in the marketplace and what doesn't. The secret is giving them a chance to show their stuff."[48] Defenders of global South farmers' dignity may not have appreciated how their words would come to augment a punitive discourse of the deserving and undeserving poor. On the eve of a catastrophic carceral overhaul to US welfare law, Hatch and a chorus of supporters argued that people should have access to basic material resources not because it is a basic need but because they are industrious workers.

· · · · · ·

ACCION continued to set the bar for innovation in microenterprise. When its client base swelled to the point that ACCION had nearly exhausted its sources of internal financing, it found a new path to growth: go commercial. If its MFI satellites shed their nonprofit status, investors would multiply overnight. Bolivia's Banco Solidario (BancoSol) lined up first. It reincorporated as the first private commercial microbank in 1992. Its monthly interest rates ballooned from 3 percent to 6 percent—with payments enforced and collected in the context of solidarity groups. Still, with its new lines of credit, the client base doubled.

Traditional banks' reticence to lend to poor Bolivians had effectively segregated the lending market into separate tracks for white and indigenous borrowers. BancoSol had a near monopoly on the latter demographic.[49] The arrangement yielded enough profit that within four years ACCION was paying out cash dividends to its private investors, in what ACCION director and BancoSol board chair Michael Chu proclaimed "a watershed in the history of microfinance" that proved once and for all "that microlending can both help the poor and yield a profit." "This is critical," he effused, "because profitability opens the door for significant private investment in microfinance, the only truly sustainable way to generate the resources needed to reach massive numbers of the poor." Cheering BancoSol's dividends, ACCION rejected programs of wealth redistribution. "Helping the poor" in a "truly sustainable way" required maximizing the value of their poverty for capital markets, Chu emphasized.[50] This shift from treating poor people as receptacles for one-way donations to hailing them as creators of capital value did alter the microfinance landscape—but this mostly was the case in retrospect, after ACCION kept pushing the issue. With renewed verve, ACCION captured its next windfall in the Mexican microbank named Compartamos ("Let's Share!").

Compartamos began as the lending arm of the health- and food-aid nonprofit Gente Nueva ("New People"), which itself was affiliated with the conservative Catholic federation Regnum Christi.[51] Per ACCION lore, the two founders of Compartamos were inspired to create the program after they encountered Mother Teresa on her trip to Mexico in 1990. Whatever its founders' motives, there is no doubt that the parent federation's preexisting resources and networks expedited its influence. The World Bank funded Compartamos to distribute microloans in Mexico's urban slums, and within the decade these loans—which carried an effective annual interest rate of 110 percent—had become so profitable that the two original founders, still at the helm, approached ACCION for help converting into a for-profit financial institution.[52] ACCION agreed and welcomed what would become its most lucrative bank into the network. With $6 million in financial backing from what was now its primary investor, Compartamos rose in influence through the early 2000s, in part on the momentum of its "solidarity group credit" programs that billed at 5 percent interest per month.[53] By 2007, the bank had amassed more than half a million clients and was perched on the edge of its initial public offering (IPO). The first MFI to ever open itself to public trading, its opening valuation exceeded $2.2 billion in shareholder wealth.[54] The majority holder? ACCION International.

From the sidelines, less rapacious microfinanciers accused ACCION of breeding the very loan sharks that microcredit had been founded to combat.[55] Meanwhile, Compartamos executives narrated their success as a happy accident: "We started doing volunteer work on health and nutrition but it all got tangled up with our entrepreneurial backgrounds and we ended up with a billion dollar company," one founder remarked.[56] If the aw-shucks tone failed to convince colleagues crying "sellout," it also constrained the field of discourse about ACCION: either ACCION was pure evil or it was pure virtue. Its exponents invested part of the IPO profits in a Center for Financial Inclusion (CFI) that churned out sympathetic research on commercial microfinance. If other MFIs took that plunge, CFI publications exclaimed, the world could achieve "full financial inclusion" by 2020. With credit doubling as a theory of history, ACCION cast its own organizational reproduction as a process of bringing more and more people into the human solidarity of financial markets.

. . . . . .

The early backers of FINCA indulged no such triumphalism. FINCA continued to grow, but without accompaniment from St. Luke. To hear the members narrate what happened in their relationship to FINCA is to witness their consternation over whether they should feel ashamed about letting the relationship drop or whether to accept that it was all for the better. Fast-forward three decades from their Bolivia trip. I sat with eight veteran church members on a chilly October Sunday, sipping Equal Exchange coffee that the church faithfully stocks, and I asked them what they remembered about those feverish days. And while I don't know what I had expected, it wasn't the answer I received. Emeritus pastor Lundy told me, and by extension the group, that he saw the FINCA years as a reflection of the church's "arrogance." To him the initial involvement, followed by a withdrawal after just two years, reflected an inconsistent quality in the church's justice commitments. The church's capriciousness came under pressure, he told the room, when the INS "tried to get rid of René [Hurtado] for twenty-five years" and left members with no option but to persist in their organizing: "We had had a tendency to be sort of faddish, to move from one thing to another. René taught us we had to stay with him; we had to support him, go to jail for him, go watch the hearings for him over all this long period, which probably pushed things like FINCA away because he was so central to what we were doing. But it kept us involved in Latin American liberation."[57]

Ultimately, it was the steadiness required to protect a friend against the carceral state that caused microfinance to fall by the wayside. As the group reminisced about their time with René, they interwove their memories with reflections about whether and how the "arrogance" charge stuck. A straight-shooting woman to my right was *absolutely sure* that FINCA was a mere stopover, and in her opinion not a very good one, on the road toward "activism" with Central American and Haitian migrants. FINCA had preceded René's arrival and, while it taught the church lessons about "the importance of community involvement" in mission work, it had not politicized them. But others begged to differ. Several people were still involved, another person retorted. They made individual donations to FINCA, even when the budget committee moved on. Someone added that St. Luke's role in Minneapolis during those years had been to "do stuff when nobody else was doing it, to plant our flag until people came and then when they did to find the next thing." She paused. "Yeah, maybe there was something arrogant about that." The rest nodded, eyes toward the windows, wondering if they did something wrong. I could not stop myself from interjecting.[58] In a cascade of words, I told them what made their arrogance, if this was even the right word for it, different. They were not trying to own any given cause; they were not trying to install themselves as a perennial fixture to their causes. I tried to make them believe, as I did, that there was something that might be, if not good, then at the very least instructive about their example. They knew when to get out.

That is, against all analytic impulses, I let my sense of solidarity overwhelm what has always been a commitment to endless, no-holds-barred critique. I tried to rescue my interlocutors from their expressions of self-critique that I should have predicted were coming. Why should I have known? Because they were engaged in a capitalist humanitarian project, and a signal quality of these projects is an idiom of self-critique—followed by a resolution of that critique in reassurances of their good work. It was out of a feeling of solidarity with the members of St. Luke that I tried to generate, for them, a historical narrative that would overcome their doubts: *You did good work, you took a wrong turn, you got out in time, you are the heroes of this history, and you did the best you could.* I imposed this redemptive narrative even though I am also the person who grimaces when someone asks me to show them the source of hope in my research, the one who savors telling certain lovers of liberation theology that the circulation of this discourse among propertied white people is precisely the problem I am talking about.

St. Luke's members' predilection for self-critique was accompanied by the fact that they were also reformed Calvinists who spoke a native language of total depravity. My interruptions tried to take that theology away from them and resolve it in a reassurance that wasn't mine to provide. I cannot recall that moment of fieldwork without trying to write my way out of having broken face. But then I return to my body at that table, palms sweaty on the bag of the fair trade chocolate I'd brought as a thank-you gift, thinking: *These people love my mother; they were there for my baptism; they knew my brother; their hearts broke with his death, too.* So I try to rescue them out of my rain cloud, to make their reflections less tough, even though I also know that these St. Luke elders would be the first to return me to what I know, or used to know: that the question is not whether violence is unfolding in any given moment, but what kind. This is the sort of thing that solidarity, in its relational allegiances, can make you forget. It is hard, if not impossible, not to want.

Solidarity Forever

What difference does it make to unearth these histories of progressives laying groundwork for finance banks? A finance bank appeals to its sanctuary origins to invest some of that countercultural virtue into its hegemonic present. A billionaire broadcasts how Mother Teresa inspired his business, as if that will cast him as an underdog success. Even memories laced with doubt do this self-framing. A skeptic of her own MFI involvement reinterprets it as a step toward radicalism or, if not that, at least a one-off tangent dropped in favor of more principled commitments. It's possible to read the memory trips of these actors as post facto attempts to say *Really, we were good. We are still good.* At the very least, they are attempts to align past action with what hindsight has revealed.

I get it: I do wish for a unified story where the people behind FINCA foresaw the role of microfinance in creeping austerity and privatization. I want them to have rejected the predations of groups like ACCION. They could have thrown their wealth behind decolonial land-back struggles or demanded the liquidation of all sovereign debt. Whether they couldn't conceive that specific agenda at the time, or whether the conditions of possibility for solidarity's neoliberal transformation were always present in some latent form, it's not what happened. The ideas and practices of solidarity managed contradictions. Its double-edged valences would be devastating to certain factions of the anticapitalist Left, as its constituents stumbled into (what they at first imagined to be) solidarity banking just as the hawks of American capitalist hegemony turned toward microfinance as their best tactic of ideological reproduction.

The microfinance pitch appealed across constituencies. You could convey its basic goals in terms of reparation, social justice, and indigenous self-determination. Or you could endorse its pedagogies of responsibility, creditworthiness, and bootstrap discipline. And for those unsure of how to practice solidarity at the proverbial end of history, microfinance held an extra advantage. It lent material quality to the kinship that activists in the global North had learned to feel with people in the global South. The loans secured these bonds so that, rather than evaporate with the geopolitical winds, they could compound through time. Humanitarian finance could even blur the lines between creditor and debtor. The investor had a chance to expiate some of his imperial guilt in a check written to the global South. The beneficiary of that foreign intervention, for once, would have a reason to be grateful.

. . . . . .

Somehow, when the tide toward microfinance pulled the strongest, St. Luke managed to maneuver elsewhere. How did they do it? It wasn't by any special political consciousness about the neoliberal gloom to which that ship was headed. The accident of their escape had everything to do with the singularity of their focus on one person, one asylum case, one twenty-five-year FBI campaign against him. The specific cause—to make a safer world for René—drew their map of the possible. Microfinance fell off the radar; their person stayed alive. It's not redemption, but, I would want to tell them, it is also not nothing.

December 2017.
Show horse of grief.

One cannot predict which distant relative will swoop into the house, poised to assist and console, after sudden loss. In our case, it was my mom's philanthropist cousins from Santa Fe. I had met them a handful of times at Thanksgiving and funerals. My mom kept in touch, but even she was floored by their generosity in the aftermath of our tragedy. "When my mother died, the first thing I did was book a cruise," Mary Amelia informed my mom, "You have to make memories." This was her preamble to a proposal: she and her husband Phil wanted to gift us a ten-day Christmas vacation at their Yucatan Peninsula mansion, tucked deep inside a rain-forest lagoon closed to almost all outsiders. The four of us (five minus the middle child) deserved a chance to create positive experiences as an altered family unit.

. . . . . .

Mary Amelia and Phil had already carved out baseline space for my brother Doug and me to survive the social scene converging on our childhood home. When the consolation calls became overwhelming, Phil body-blocked visitors before they could find us. He distracted them with stories about trying and failing to make a career in Hollywood. "I only ever got cast in low-production commercials! You know the ones where they have the sloppy 'before' guy and the hot, smooth 'after' guy? Like the old Mac and PC ads? Or ones for weight loss pills?" he'd ask, pointing to his unruly body. "I was always the BEFORE guy!"

Phil was a perfect decoy. Our downstairs had turned into a twenty-four-hour obstacle course of hands grabbing our shoulders and hors d'oeuvres breath fogging up our glasses. We shrank under the curdling gaze of matriarchs on mission to cajole the buried trauma from our affectless exteriors. Meanwhile, our mom kept reaching to touch us, like she was confirming our presence in the land of the living when we wanted to be anywhere but. Our dad kept edging in for nonconsensual hugs.

Doug broke first. *I am NOT your SHOW HORSE of GRIEF* he roared into some crowd of aunts, whose coo-cooing replies only confirmed that he was, in fact, the center of their attention. Mark's seizure of his own body had left us without claim to our own: we were the poster children of tragedy, possibly at the cusp of a long rehabilitative arc, possibly damaged goods forever. With Phil around, we did not have to be the subjects of anyone's "before" picture. He played that character across the room.

. . . . . .

They had purchased a vacation home inside a UNESCO World Heritage Site. The arrangement is not as illegal as it sounds. It's a sweepstakes for people with access to the outer stratospheres of the international real estate market. They'd netted the place through a United Nations initiative called "Man and Biosphere," which gives a small handful of buyers the right to dwell inside the Caribbean great barrier reef's most protected reserve. Fifteen years after hitting the jackpot, our cousins were in the final stages of selling the property. The buyer was a twenty-something heir to his father's hotel fortune. But the deed had not yet traded hands; the logistics of UNESCO code compliance, plus issues of staffing continuity, made for a drawn-out closing process. Our cousins still had access. They contacted the new owner, who jumped aboard the plan. Not only would he welcome us; he would treat us to an all-inclusive healing getaway. Working alongside his personal assistant, a twenty-seven-year-old retired supermodel from Germany, he intended to flip the mansion into a luxury retreat destination called "The Laboratory of Happiness." We would be its first beneficiaries.

We spent the winter break off the grid, days divided between slow mornings with the limitless horizon and afternoons shuttling through the New Age healing sessions the young heir had arranged. The week's itinerary featured sweat lodges led by feminist shamans who prayed to the goddess, kundalini yoga classes, bodywork with a masseuse who specialized past-life regressions, all-natural gluten-free vegan meals prepared by a private chef, sound and incense baths, and—the week's pinnacle, our special holiday gift from an owner whom we never actually got to thank in person—a surprise photo safari.

. . . . . .

At 8 a.m. on Christmas Eve, I looked up from breakfast as three men leaping out of a white van and charged toward the house brandishing cameras. "*Helloooo* from your *personal paparazzi!!*" howled one of them as he hustled us into their vehicle. Once we had all buckled our seatbelts, they shoved DSLR cameras into our hands and reviewed the itinerary: they were taking us on a whirlwind tour of off-the-beaten-path attractions. We swam in the crystal waters of an underground cave and rode bicycles around ruins of an unspecified civilization. We climbed a pyramid and trekked through a spider-monkey rainforest. Our guides used the transit time to rattle off mini-lectures on color saturation, shutter speed, and lens angle; we practiced a new technique of digital photography at each stop. "You will be Instagram stars!" they cheered, whenever they caught us fiddling with the buttons on our cameras. Even if the influencer life eluded us, they preached, our new aesthetic skills would empower us to create and capture our own happy memories.

That day lives forever in some desert server farm. Our paparazzo leaders amassed hundreds of images of our photogenic family (father, mother, daughter, son) living our wholesome life (swimming, biking, meal sharing, embracing, holding hands) and smiling our sweet smiles. As for the amateur photos taken by my parents and brother, they are copious enough that a few pass for professional-grade. All of my photos are failures, and I only took six of them: five repeats of a canoe whose sunset exposure I couldn't quite nail and one ironic outlier. The sixth photo shows a theme-park sign outside the entrance to the penultimate stop—the one our driver kept secret until we pulled into its sandy lot—the "Ancient Maya Village." It was less like a "village" and more like a cross between a tourist trap and a live-action role play of a bad colonial cliché. The guides described it as the "authentic household" of a family that sincerely wanted to share their "traditional way of life" with us. We entered their space through a pavilioned gift shop. Behind it, four adults and six kids milled around in an open-air wooden complex, with no closable doors or private spaces in sight. A few of them patted tortillas, others gardened, others watched toddlers, and—*oh, look, the town shaman just happened to stop in!* One of the motioned us toward the fire pit for a ceremony in which we, their honored guests, were blessed. Our guides prowled the edges, their clicks and flashes cutting through the billows of copal that had engulfed our sacred circle.

If you look at those photos, you can mistake our smirky giggles for bliss. Sometimes you wouldn't even be wrong. Diving into opal-blue water or biking under palm trees or clinking cocktail glasses in the orange-magenta light, we

4.1 A highway sign outside Tulum welcomes tourists into "Casa Maya."

glow with return to the land of the living. You might think we had managed to freeze-frame our brush with happiness—as if happiness is what our smiles conveyed, as if the landscape in the photos was not fashioned out of invisible labor, as if the fact of our bodies in the frame did not also convey the extent to which all of this was wrong.

representing inclusion 4

HUMANS OF CAPITALIST HUMANITARIANISM

Slotted into a nondescript shopping complex in the US Midwest, tucked between the headquarters of the local Junior League and a dental practice, ten staff of a microfinance institution (MFI) managed their Latin American investment portfolios. It was June 2015 and I had camped out in the lobby. The place felt almost clinical—sharp angles, big wipeable surfaces, white wallpaper, pastel green trimmings, big windows, blasting air conditioning—except for photographic prints hung around the space. No matter how I arranged my work station, a portrait of a woman grilling tortillas, harvesting coffee berries, weaving, or picking flowers loomed over me. Their smiles matched the bright foods and textiles that they held in their hands. The five senior staff of the MFI—you could tell who was senior by whose offices had doors—had claimed their favorite posters to hang on their private walls. Two interns, one regional loan officer, one technology-support employee, and I had sprawled out with the leftovers in a storage area that doubled as an open-plan workspace. Sometimes we migrated to the lobby, where the bulk of the collection was on display.

One afternoon the executive director summoned the novice staff to a surprise lecture on the organization's "theory of change." We shuffled to our seats at the big-box-store plastic table as she drew a giant triangle on a mounted dry-erase board. "This is the universe," she announced, explaining that the universe is shorthand for all of the income-earning people in the world. She drew two horizontal lines through the triangle so that it was divided into three tiers of roughly equal height. The top tier was for people who earn more

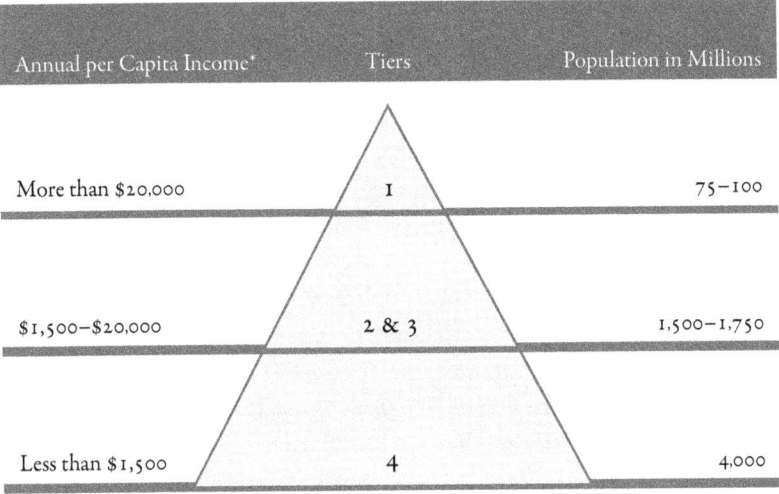

*Based on purchasing power parity in US$

4.2   This is a more detailed replica of the "World Economic Pyramid," popularized in C. K. Prahalad's book *The Fortune at the Bottom of the Pyramid.*

than $20,000 yearly. The middle tier included anyone with an annual income of between $1,500 and $20,000. The base tier represented the population of very poor people who survive on around $2 per day (see figure 4.2). This latter demographic, she continued, is of special interest to microfinanciers. By administering financial services for people who otherwise would not meet eligibility requirements, MFIs bring "financial inclusion" to the "unbanked," empowering them to "work their way out of poverty."

Geometric abstractions and stock photography in an otherwise minimalist office complex: it's a spot-on example of racial capitalism's choice optics. This, at least, was my snarky internal monologue as I willed the clock to fast forward to 5 o'clock. The modern capitalist arcade is wallpapered with the faces of people who don't have what I have but make the commodities that I want to buy: the Kenyan coffee farmer whose microenterprise paid for her children's school fees, the Bengali seamstress whose loan bought her the equipment that enabled her to create a job for an assistant, the Colombian rose grower who joined a cooperative and increased his income. As I faced down these icons in the office complex that commanded their creation, I already felt as though I knew their testimonies by heart. The triangular diagram of the universe and the effervescent photos insisted that there was life beyond war, poverty, and the migrant train. A better world was not just possible, these images announced. It was already emerging in the diagrams, algorithms, and stacks of paperwork that mapped the next economic frontiers.

I am trained to call these representations to the carpet for cynical politics and ulterior motives. A growing posse of theorists emphasizes that corporate appeals to multiculturalism function as a gloss on the raced and gendered extraction inflicted on the global South. Jodi Melamed has named this disjunction—this friction between the uneven blows of racial capitalism and the shiny appeals to diversity that supplement them—"neoliberal multiculturalism." Even as "race has continued to permeate capitalism's economic and social processes, organizing the hyper-extraction of surplus bodies and naturalizing a system of capital accumulation that grossly favors the global north over the global south, multiculturalism has portrayed neoliberal policy as the key to a post-racist world of freedom and opportunity," Melamed writes.[1] Shifting in my chair, I compiled a silent list of the diversity spectacles that could belong with these prints: the gay-pride float sponsored by Bank of America, the multilingual group of children singing "America the Beautiful" in a Coca-Cola commercial, or Wal-Mart receiving an award for its "diverse and inclusive" employment practices.[2] I imagined the portraits coming to life, detaching from the walls, shrinking, and assuming their places in the bottom tier of the "universe." Toxic waste, sweatshop labor, and predatory lending would recede behind their pluralist collage, paraded to investors whenever the next self-audit came due.

I wanted to swap out the images at the bottom of the pyramid and replace them with accounts of the neocolonial wars and profiteering adventures they scuttle from the frame. But as I set a poker face to my supervisor's elegy to "pro-poor" investing and the set pieces arranged to accessorize her enthusiasm, my rebuttal impulse was a dead end. Why should I pick a fight with this financial common sense, when smarter critics had raised the same points already? I was tired of interdisciplinary humanities scholars acceding the role of symbolic town crier—always invited to marshal another dossier on the betrayals of self-professed agents of diversity, equity, and inclusion—within systems designed to metabolize our dissent. It wasn't that the critiques were wrong. It was that the corporate addressees of my hypothetical grievances were quite eager to scout my "perspective" and incorporate it into their playbook.

Plus, those images on the MFI walls did more than simply hide violence. They also construed microfinance as way to empower communities heretofore "excluded" from free market prosperity and, in progressing toward this inclusion, to foster social justice and multicultural harmony. In this respect, they conformed to a historical pattern. When regulatory bodies have expanded access to personal credit—such as by loosening federal oversight and redefining what counts as usury—they have done so in the name of creating opportunities for "the unbanked." This invented demographic is development industry shorthand for people who lack systematic access to financial services or just prefer to stay away, but who capitalist reformers have targeted as potential recruits. The unbanked masses comprise the next frontier of neoliberal reform. These subjects have not yet achieved full economic citizenship, but if they listen to the advice of their local credit officer, they might be headed in that direction. Don't believe it? Look at this photo of the bank's newest client. Doesn't she look happy and productive?

The poster children of humanitarian finance have evolved with the geopolitical times. Some of their characteristics, however, have remained consistent. All are training for full citizen-subjectivity. All face disqualification if they do not conform to their pedagogues' prescriptions. To grasp this capitalist humanitarian discourse of citizen-subjectivity, one need only consider two turning points in its elaboration: first, an industrial-era campaign by Christian progressives who lobbied to legalize personal loans for the urban working poor; second, the early twentieth-century rise of microfinance as a star of the development industry. Separated by almost a century, these moments come together in their raced and gendered discourse of the deserving and undeserving poor. Social gospel experiments in "philanthropic lending" heralded certain regimes of credit as simultaneously an act of self-sacrificial charity (on the part of bankers) and a dry run in the disciplines of normative heteropatriarchal citizenship (on the part of borrowers). The tactic, whereby interest-bearing loans were used to goad racialized poor people into performances of assimilated citizen-subjectivity, eventually wended its way into mainstream secular financial reform paradigms. As US policy influencers welcomed microfinance as a panacea against poverty, they reified racist typologies that pitted the modest, responsible, dignified subject of international microloans against the lazy, irresponsible, philandering subject of domestic welfare programs.

The valorized half of this pair—the figural woman micro-entrepreneur plastered on so many capitalist humanitarian billboards—ascended the Nobel-winning pedestal just in time for international derivatives markets to crash. From there she could survey her unluckier counterpart—the over-indebted black borrower of a postindustrial wasteland—taking the fall for the speculators who landed them in their current situations. Still, this uplifted paragon kept flashing that grin, kept speaking her conversion: from lost to found, from parochial to universal, from excluded to banked, and, if luck went her way, from the nonsubject of debt to the subject of credit.

Philanthropic Banking, Racial Capitalism, and Christian Kinship

I've seen it happen a million times. When financial adventurers enter new territory, they break the ice with a sign of their own generosity: *Congratulations, our firm has chosen to include you.* One day *you* will become a new normative center, the role model to which an excluded population can aspire. Up to the 1920s, most credit options were reserved for wealthy businessmen, and working-class people had to make do on their own. But when a confluence of railroad shipping monopolies and extreme speculation on agricultural goods tanked crop prices and, with them, farmer income, the center would not hold. An industrial-era coalition of agrarian populists demanded reprisal. Specifically, they sought a systemic fix in the form of a federal "subtreasury" tasked with issuing cheap, crop-backed loans to rural producers and regulating an explicitly cooperative market.[3] Their massive organizing effort did not escape the radar of the Progressive Era reformers looking to persuade business interests to invest in wider social welfare. A cohort of Christian philanthropists in New York City seized the baton of affordable credit, but not by extending the populist campaign for central regulatory structures. They instead advocated for the repeal of the usury laws that prevented banks from lending to the working poor at sustainable interest rates. These progressive reformers' tactics of public persuasion, combined with their regimes of private surveillance of borrowers themselves, preview the practices of microfinanciers more than a century later. Residing in a Manhattan tenement building at the turn of the twentieth century, we meet the forebears of the iconic global South entrepreneur who, the official story goes, would be destitute and writhing in the clutches of a predatory lender if not for the mercy of the philanthropic bank.

Picture a mother. She crouches at her child's sickbed while her spouse paces in the background. Their daughter lies inert. She will die without medical care, but her parents can't afford it. Their rent is due. Desperate, they open their newspaper to the classified section, where a headline jumps off the page: CHEAP MONEY! They just need to put up their furniture as collateral, and they can get $25 "within an hour." The relief is instant. The girl gets the medicine she needs. She has finally sat up to play with her dolls when, at that exact moment, the loan officer bursts in. Brandishing his half-smoked cigar, he orders the father to cough up the $7.50 monthly interest payment. But the family doesn't have the money. The scene repeats the next month, until the incensed lender dispatches a young woman to the man's workplace to demand the cash. His office mates assume he is having an affair; the boss fires him on the spot. And the debt only compounds as the desperate father searches for his next job—which, in a miraculous turn of events, he finds. His new "enlightened employer" marches him straight to the "Cooperative Saving and Loan Association," which issues him $25 loan with a six-month term and a 6 percent interest rate. The new boss also alerts the district attorney that his worker is "in the clutches of a loan shark." But it is too late. The man returns home to goons storming into his home and removing its heirloom furnishings, down to the bed from underneath the fragile child.

The Russell Sage Foundation (RSF) coproduced the silent short film *The Usurer's Grip* in 1912 as part of a public education campaign about "the loan shark evil" preying on a full third of working families in New York City.[4] The RSF also proposed a solution: raise legal interest ceilings. Its lead staffer Arthur Ham had drafted a model "Uniform Small Loans Law" that proposed maximum interest rates of 3 percent monthly and 43 percent annually. The model legislation also imposed a certification system for small lenders, with penalties for doing business without a license.[5] Amid dramatic clashes between organized labor and capital interests, moderate finance-reform campaigns carved out a middle ground for liberal reformers: the state could intervene on behalf of finance capitalism and, in so doing, allow private bankers to uplift the masses without jeopardizing their returns.

It was an aesthetic pitch as much as an economic one. Reformers imagined their main beneficiaries as urban white ethnic men with families. A sentimental portraiture of these families' productive and reproductive labor—as well as the public threat posed by their potential moral erosion—took center stage in reformers' pitches. For the RSF, the white ethnic poor stood at a crossroads between two possible futures. They could embrace the normative disciplines of heteronormative upwardly mobile citizenship, or they could spiral into the destitute, racialized urban mass. The hope was that financial institutions, with an assist from the state, could secure the correct trajectory of this unbanked population.

Margaret Olivia Sage, widow of the railroad baron Russell Sage, launched her husband's namesake foundation in 1907 to cultivate "improvement of the social and living conditions in the United States of America" through a mix of social scientific research and humanitarian intervention.[6] The foundation's biblical motto—"Inasmuch as ye have done for the least of these my brethren, ye have done for me"—framed its reform efforts in terms of the Christian kinship networks it could foster.[7] Olivia Sage valued her programs in child welfare and women's industrial work, but it was the campaign to legalize personal loans that distinguished the RSF from other progressive philanthropies. Leaders of the RSF shared the broader social gospel certainty that all people should have access to good schools, good playgrounds, good health care, and good jobs. But the RSF was unique in its insistence that if working-class people could get access to dependable financial services, then solutions to the other issues would follow.[8]

The RSF used a combination of sociological research and public narrative to drum up support for the Uniform Small Loans law. Olivia Sage commissioned a team of researchers, led by staffer Arthur Ham, to investigate informal lending outfits in the city. Fanning out into urban tenements and seedy brokering agencies, the team discovered that New York workers in financial straits were paying between 60 and 480 percent annual interest to underground lenders.[9] They likewise reported that most victims were first- or second-generation white ethnic immigrants.[10] These demographic details paired well with stories about the consequences that ensued when family breadwinners, facing emergency, turned to predatory lenders as a last resort. In his stock address to commerce associations, titled "Remedial Loans as Factors in Family Rehabilitation," Arthur Ham chronicled these victims. There was the "sober and industrious" police officer who, after the death of his wife and the sudden illness of his children, took out a $300 loan at 10 percent monthly interest. He lost everything when he defaulted. There was "a woman in a Southern city" who borrowed $4 on an agreement to pay $1.60 monthly interest. Seven years later, with the debt still compounding even though she had paid back the original sum many times over, the lender confiscated all of her furniture. There was the "young man holding a responsible position in the New York office of a Western corporation" who endorsed a friend's $50 note from a loan shark. He was subsequently extorted for over $250 in excess of the original check. All of these borrowers met tragic ends: the cop "turned to drink and is now an inmate of a county home"; the southern woman "came under the care of a relief society" and lost custody of her children; the cosigning buddy disappeared and, his family feared, had killed himself. Every story held a double moral, which celebrated subjects' civic potential at the same time as it fearmongered as to the causes of their fall.

Typecast representations of "responsible" borrowers dovetailed with the explosion of poverty photography and human-interest stories during the industrial period. Artist Jacob Riis's exposés of New York tenement life, catalogued in books and theatricalized with new projection technologies, animated the reality of slums for wealthier audiences. The new photographic realism constructed the urban poor, and particularly urban poor children, as Christological types. Audiences who beheld images of tenement dwellers, depicted as angelic and suffering, destitute and transcendent, were initiated into what historian Gregory Jackson has termed a "spectral kinship" revealed in "photography's power to render visible the invisible web of religious obligation that united Christians in the new covenant of the urban community." The photographs operated as "heuristic guides for action" that motivated audiences to ameliorative action against poverty—not just on behalf of the poor, but on behalf of the viewer's own potential transformation into the sacrificial type that social-gospel aesthetics depicted. These ways of seeing and looking announced a "national family and broader humanity"—exactly the ethic of spiritual kinship that Progressive reformers sought to proliferate.[11]

What would happen to this kinship if predatory lending spiraled out of control? The philanthropic financiers at the RSF feared the worst. "Once infected with the borrowing germ a man will borrow from every possible source...his family suffering and he himself finally becoming a veritable slave," Ham warned. The contagion risk extended to society. "This business inevitably leads to the social deterioration of the borrowers and accentuates the bad social effects of poverty," one RSF researcher explained. "The general welfare is thereby detrimentally affected."[12] Desperate debtors might cheat on their wives, force their children into the workforce, revert to labor militancy, or become a public charge. These possibilities justified the screening processes that reformers exacted on clients of an industry designed for their rehabilitation.

To guide interactions with its potential clients, the RSF lifted from early twentieth-century social work playbooks. It required that all credit assessments occur inside loan applicants' homes. For each case, the appointed "investigator" should review receipts for household items, discuss the applicant's reliability with neighborhood merchants, and collect the bill of sale for any furniture offered up as collateral. He also should note any subjective "opinions on [an applicant's] other qualities" not captured in the standard surveys. Sound judgments about a credit risk can occur only after the investigator "has had an opportunity to observe what kind of housekeeper the wife is, and whether her grocery and meat bills have been extravagant or economical. He knows how much rent the family is paying, and he has been able to judge how much teamwork exists between husband and wife."[13]

The guidelines communicate the premium placed on privatized domesticity as an indicator of one's capacity for assimilation into the whiteness of US citizenship; they also hint at a future in which women will become the prime targets of the remedial finance, and simply the supporting cast for the husband.[14] As the credit officer transitions from the household to the office, from realm of sentimentality to center of bureaucratic decision, the investigator translates the aesthetic quality of the house into a gut criterion for either issuing or denying credit. That is, Olivia Sage and the barons who emulated her wanted something more than basic income for families, calories for children, and leisure time after work. On the contrary, they were equally convinced that good work happens when parents spend their assembly-line shift dreaming of their children's future, balanced nutrition takes place at a tastefully set table that teaches appropriate manners, and well-used leisure time masters the domestic creations of an upwardly mobile class. These philanthrocapitalists knew that there could be no economic impact without a sentimental posture.[15]

They were holding their charges to an impossible ideal. Reformers expected their loan clients to make their homes into private domestic sanctuaries but also claimed the right to enter and evaluate their housekeeping at any moment they pleased. The fact of this continual access dramatizes the gap between reformers' subjective standards and the borrowers' lived realities. How can a person keep a stable home if they don't know when a social worker or debt collector will come knocking? It put borrowers in an impossible bind, but, then again, maybe that was the point: applicants for small loans did not yet have the self-possessive qualities of full citizens, but one day, with appropriate surveillance and coaching, they could get there.

For Russell Sage researchers, the steady expansion of credit systems encapsulated nothing less than the long arc of human historical triumph. The concluding volume of the foundation's in-house series on small-scale lending explained why: "Lending presupposes ownership, and since private property, in one form or another, seems to have existed in the most primitive human societies as well as among many of the lower animals, the history of lending probably coincides with the history of human society."[16]

The rest unfolds as a bird's-eye view of credit's conquering spirit. Credit and debt, the text proclaims, originated as a "duty" of life in "communal" hunter-gatherer societies that relied on sharing to survive. The evolution of settled agricultural lifestyles brought the conception of land as "private property," and with it, early forms of debt collateral. Ancient Israelite traditions, according to Deuteronomy and Leviticus, protected private property and forbade usury on loans, even as they preserved "primitive" traditions of jubilee and resource sharing. A few centuries later, the ancient Greeks and Romans charged interest on loans and condemned bounced debtors to slavery, even as Catholic and "Mohammadan" traditions remained faithful to their ancestors' prohibitions on usury. This changed in the thirteenth century, when the Catholic Church permitted feudal *monts-de-piété* to issue credit to peasants. Meanwhile, the combination of anti-Semitic job discrimination and the exemption of Jews from canon restrictions on usury meant that "Jews became moneylenders" across Europe. Jewish bankers remained dominant until the Protestant Reformation severed canon law from state law. No longer answerable to the Catholic Church, established merchants could seek loans from low-interest lenders. But moneylenders continued to circulate among the peasant poor in Europe and, now, in the United States. The US situation began to shift, very slightly, when states relaxed usury laws in their bids to attract commerce following the civil war.[17] And finally—in the heyday of industrialization and baron capitalist philanthropy—the Russell Sage Foundation entered the scene with its campaign to use the market against usurers, repeatedly coded as Jewish, in the express service of Protestant human kinship actualized through finance.[18]

This official history defined the most evolved version of the human being as an owner. It did so on the heels of a sabotaged reconstruction, at the height of Jim Crow law, and as the US military invaded and colonized new territories in the name of bringing new populations into the circle of modern, possessive humanity. Spoken as a universal, this theory of the human has roots in the early twentieth-century regimes of domestic racial terror and foreign empire building, in which US banks were central players.[19] When financial history is revalued as salvation history, commercial lending is configured as a spiritual practice that transcends any singular context, even as the enlightened Christian creditor can step up as the most evolved iteration of humanity. This subject has overcome the primitive, the Muslim, the Catholic, and the Jew.[20] Their next task is to prepare others to join this circle of evolved humanity. Who else shows capacity to settle their own debts? Who is approaching their ideal actualized state of self-possessed ownership?

The operative ontology is thinkable only in the afterlife of slavery, with its founding conflation of whiteness with the human and blackness with its negation.[21] Between the two structural positions, and at the same time as social scientists busied themselves "proving" scientific links between blackness and criminality, financial reformers discovered the white ethnic immigrant worker on the brink of social belonging. They diagnosed his marginally outsider status not as a problem of constitutional deficiency but as an accident of access and environment.[22] Under the tutelage of banks, he could learn the racial, religious, and gender norms required for entry into the community of propertied selves.

The forward march of this history could even sweep "Shylock" toward respectable "philanthropic competition." Reformers boasted that their interventions had inspired moneylenders to abandon covert businesses and operate in the licensed light of day.[23] One reporter lauded the "rehabilitation" of the industry and claimed that "it was not until the problems [of moneylending] were attacked by economists and financiers from the Russell Sage Foundation... that the responsible and legitimate moneylender came into his own."[24] Another journalist analogized modern anti-usury statues to the "dead letter" of Mosaic law. He then praised RSF for rooting out these "anachronistic" polices while also taking aim at the real problem of "moral usury" among the business class.[25] At stake was as much the soul of the (Christlike) tenement dweller as of the (Jewish) banker. Maybe one day the latter would see himself reflected in the former, and realize that he, too, had debts that needed to be forgiven. As ever, this reconciled image of Christian kinship remains parasitic on an image of the life it supersedes.

The respective historiographies of progressive movements and late industrial capitalism recall this dynamic when they maintain a separation between humanitarian ends and villainous exploitation. There is a tendency in the history of US religion to treat the social gospel as a sincere and valiant, if limited, counterpoint to the runaway profit impulse that surrounded it.[26] Meanwhile, the growth of finance appears as either the one-dimensionally nefarious global designs of profiteers or the unintended consequences of good-faith reformers. Proceeding from a Russell Sage origin point at the beginning of the twentieth century, the broad strokes of our accounts are something like the following: as personal loans became part of US everyday financial practice, automobile companies such as General Motors and Ford pushed for the legalization of installment credit, opening a pathway to membership in the consumer republic for people who lacked the up-front cash. The crash of 1929 and the resultant Great Depression sparked the normalization of long-term loans as the Federal Housing Authority (FHA) offered loans to help people avoid bankruptcy by refinancing their homes. Consumer financing flourished after World War II, with the heyday of federally subsidized home loans for beneficiaries of the 1945 GI Bill and the 1947 introduction of revolving credit cards in department stores. Use of consumer credit expanded even as the US economy stalled and companies embraced cheap offshore labor in the 1960s and 1970s; citizens could bridge the gap between their consumer needs and their stagnating or absent wages by charging the difference to plastic. Meanwhile, the Federal Housing Authority and the Federal Home Loan Mortgage Corporation found ways to grow their profit margins amid economic stress. They introduced a debt-securities trade that enabled them to lend to "risky" borrowers without incurring the costs of default. These were the first subprime loans, defended by their champions as instruments to help integrate new populations into home ownership even as critics of capitalism memorialized them as a symbol of excess and exploitation.[27]

Each one of these turns could be studied in terms of the illustrations of good and bad, responsible and irresponsible, patriotic and dangerous, creditworthy and uncreditworthy, new citizen and never-citizen that they produce and presuppose. There is always a humanitarian impulse within them—not just in terms of the basic question of finding ways to feed the hungry and care for the sick, but also in routing these efforts through the question of who is (or who could be) sufficiently human to participate in a global community of entrepreneurial labor and financial credit. The exercise of imagining someone's eligibility for credit is a process of reading her relationship to humanity: her potential as a postured self, her possible reconstruction as a subject for finance, her racial horizon.

Financial Inclusion, Micro-Entrepreneurs, and the Racist Subprime

Corporate microfinance had a major coming-out party in 1997. Following a decade of momentum building in scattered initiatives, First Lady Hillary Clinton called a World Summit on Microfinance to unify the efforts. Just under three thousand people converged on Washington, DC, for a weekend of workshops and plenaries held toward a commitment to "reach 100 million of the poorest families, especially the women of those families, with credit" by December 31, 2005. Grameen Bank progenitor Muhammad Yunus opened the festivities. "Just like food," he intoned from the podium, "credit is a human right" on which the equality of the "human family" depends.[28] How appropriate, then, that tonight's ceremony would celebrate the four inaugural recipients of the Presidential Awards for Excellence in Microenterprise Development.

ACCION International waited in the wings to be recognized for "Excellence in Providing Access to Credit."[29] The award honored ACCION's nascent program for US borrowers. Although its board had been brainstorming ideas for a domestic affiliate since the mid-1980s—on the rationale that "microentrepreneurs are important role models for youth and those on public assistance"—it had not launched its Bronx pilot program until 1991. Over the next three years it added branches in Chicago, San Antonio, San Diego, and Albuquerque.[30] "Our programs charge the highest rates allowable by current usury laws," an internal document reassured staff when some predicted that the high costs of lending in the United States would undermine the project's long-term viability.[31] Now, in the Clinton Era of slashed welfare, their poverty-track model of "economic enfranchisement" and "self-reliance" could enjoy its flowers.³² "CONGRATULATIONS TO YOU ALL," screamed the email from ACCION's vice president for communications. "And now I have to get down to business."³³ Regional program directors should send, immediately, press-ready client profiles. For their convenience, she laid out a suggested formula:

> ACCION's clients in ____ are seamstresses working out of their homes, taxi drivers, foodstand operators (TAKE OUT OR EMBELLISH HERE AS APPROPRIATE). They may be single mothers who need to work out of their homes, former employees of down-sized businesses, part time wage earners, or first generation immigrants serving their communities. They all see self-employment as a means to improve the economic prospects of their families and their communities. As expressed by _____, an ACCION _____ client, "QUOTE HERE FROM ONE OF YOUR CLIENTS ABOUT WHAT ACCION MEANS TO THEM."³⁴

The Mad Lib for writing about the deserving poor knows what its subjects look like. They are families, workers, and law-abiders. They are down on their luck but reluctant to make use of the social safety net that is their entitlement. They are the "role models" to another class of poor people at which the fill-in-the-blanks worksheet can only dog whistle: black moms on welfare, undocumented immigrants, the unhoused, and the incarcerated.³⁵ Just as "philanthropic banking" hinged on the racist differentiation of the deserving and undeserving poor, the millennial advent of microfinance relied on the tacit expulsion of racialized welfare recipients from the circle of economic and social citizenship. This trend accelerated in the wake of the financial crash and subprime crisis of 2008.

ACCION discontinued its US-based lending programs only a few years after their White House fete, but calls for financial inclusion of "the poorest" continued to enchant. "Why can't we make capitalism inclusive?" asked C. K. Prahalad in his multi-award-winning book *Fortune at the Bottom of the Pyramid: Eradicating Poverty through Profits*. He counseled executives to prioritize the "bottom of the pyramid" (BOP) in their business strategies. As with the diagram drawn on that microfinance office whiteboard fifteen years later, the bottom of the pyramid is how some capitalist humanitarians refer to the four billion people in the world who scrape by on less than $1,500 annually.³⁶ Prahalad and the economists who emulated him argued that if investors approached the BOP "not as victims or as a burden" but rather "start recognizing them as resilient and creative entrepreneurs and value-conscious consumers... a whole new world of opportunity will open up." He meant, first, business opportunity to the tune of $13 trillion in purchasing power that "the poorest" wield in aggregate. "A billion people living on a dollar a day," I once witnessed a Yale School of Management professor intone to his class, "is a billion dollars a day!" Prahalad also predicted a humanitarian upside to his intervention. When businesses hail the BOP as a viable segment of the consumer market, they "create opportunity for the poor by offering [them] choices and encouraging self-esteem."[37] How can capitalism be inclusive? How can capitalism promote human dignity? Prahalad's answer concurred with the one favored by progressive reformers and early microfinanciers: through blowing open who is "recognized" as a creator of capital for a global economy and, the implied flip side, curtailing the scope of public entitlements.

In the early 2000s the introduction of the BOP to development discourse gave shorthand to an accelerating merger between humanitarian and capitalist notions of freedom. Its message brought good news to Wall Street: the emancipation of the global South from poverty required the emancipation of multinational corporations from checks on their power.[38] Just as the repeal of usury prohibitions empowered "philanthropic lenders" to make kin with the urban working class, now the contemporary financial analyst had a chance to reconcile their profits with social purpose. They need only "recognize" the expectant faces smiling out from the triangle on the wall: resilient in adversity, resource-prudent with their tiny margins, creative about problem-solving, and unjustly abandoned by the elite economic bodies that wrote them off without a second look. Missing is any critique of the crisis ordinary that has made qualities such as "resilience" and "creativity" life-or-death necessities. Prahalad is silent on the environmental meltdowns and endless wars of neoliberal order; even less does he account for the sweatshop metropolises, austerity measures, and bootstrap gospels that play the second act to so many disasters.[39]

. . . . . .

Banker to the Poor won the Nobel Prize on the eve of the international mortgage-backed securities market nosedive. Six months later, in April 2007, ACCION toasted having once again etched its name into the history books: its MFI affiliate, the Mexico-based Compartamos Bank, had unleashed an initial public offering (IPO). No other MFI had crossed the threshold into the open market. Now, with stock trending upward from starting valuation of $2.2 billion, the board claimed that the cascading capital would allow Compartamos to serve populations otherwise excluded from financial services. The bullish entry of a microfinance bank into the stock charts would also, according to a Harvard Business School case study, yield new points of contact between the

BOP and the TOP.[40] Yet the ostentatious wealth that was being generated from other people's poverty begged the question of who, exactly, the bank intended to address in its titular enjoinment to "share." Who was doing the sharing? What were they sharing, and with whom? And what, if anything, did the skyrocketing profile of Compartamos and of the microfinance field broadly have to do with a spiraling housing market? As MFIs basked in unprecedented public admiration and private returns, the mortgage-backed securities market finally collapsed during the summer of 2007. A million foreclosures followed. The United States entered recession in 2008, the same year that *The Fortune at the Bottom of the Pyramid* went into its second printing and the US federal government shelled out more than $700 billion to buy out distressed subprime mortgages.[41]

Swift blowback against predatory banks upended the enthusiasm with which finance professionals had endorsed the subprime as a social equalizer. Federal Reserve governor Edward Gramlich had commended the model as merely "lending that involves elevated credit risk," and that, in embracing those risks, set off a "democratizing effect" in access to financial services. "Millions of lower-income and minority households now have a chance to own homes and build wealth," he gushed in the 2004 speech, before praising the subprime for its positive effect on both banking practice and property ownership.[42] When Gramlich later proposed stricter federal oversight of subprime deals, his Federal Reserve colleagues outvoted him.[43] Even in the wake of the crash, Reserve chairman Ben Bernanke showed conscious optimism about subprime democracy: "Minority households and households in lower-income census tracts have recorded some of the largest gains [in home-ownership]," he remarked, before predicting that the upturn would "strengthen neighborhoods" by motivating people to "maintain their properties and participate in civic organizations."[44] For Bernanke, a real estate mortgage was a central rung on the ladder toward full inclusion in civil society—never mind that the same banks approving those mortgages were taking out short-run bets against borrowers' ability to pay them off or reap their future rewards. These spokespeople swore by the axiom that democracy needs banks; they agreed that projects of financial inclusion require tools for managing the "risks" that "risky" borrowers pose to lending institutions. Within the descriptions offered by finance chiefs, "risk" codes for black, brown, and low-income. Every risk is also an opportunity for reform, and thus for profit.[45]

Be clear about this simultaneity: a model of finance that targets women of color in the global South emerged as a star of humanitarian dreams just as Wall Street buckled under. Paula Chakravartty and Denise Ferreira da Silva contend that lenders targeted poor black and brown people "because they are not constructed as referents of either the relationship between persons presumed in commerce... or the capacity that according to Karl Marx ultimately determines their value of exchange."[46] Financial institutions treated these populations as always and already expelled from the forms value presupposed in neoliberal capitalism—values such as possessive and sovereign individualism, respect for contracts, and a trajectory toward productive citizenship. Subprime debtors navigated a field that had already produced them as existing in a state of moral and social debt. Banks offered credit as a means of personal reform: build your credit score, acquire assets, achieve the American dream or promise its possibility to others. It was a trap. Subprime schemes enjoined borrowers to practices of financial responsibility in a system stacked against them, which guaranteed profits to investors while denying borrowers access to reciprocal exchange.[47]

The advance of microfinance into Latin America, Asia, and Africa both presupposed and perpetuated the symbolic and material expulsion of US subprime borrowers from social life. In graphic representations of the global South community of modern financial citizens, inclusive banking produced the upwardly mobile micro-entrepreneur as foil to the figure of the discredited and stagnant, but still profitable by virtue of her compounding debts, feminized black borrower. As everyday people were thrown onto the streets of US cities and as Wall Street floated on its $700 billion parachute, Prahalad's writings on the BOP offered conscious capitalists reassurance by way of an old piety of development economics: the way to honor the personhood of the poorest people was to expand free markets with these populations in mind. Redistributive and regulatory interventions—from direct aid to investments in the social safety net to consumer protections—replayed the racist paternalism of past development strategies.[48] What poor people needed was a chance to step into their purchasing power and grow their businesses. Whereas the subprime borrower had fumbled her chance at upward mobility and damaged the reputation of debt capital, the global South microentrepreneur would rise to the occasion: inclusive finance would have another run.

. . . . . .

Who can embody the promise of inclusive capitalism? The Center for Financial Inclusion (CFI), established by ACCION with the spoils of the IPO, has engineered the basic prototype. I met her the same summer 2016 day that my BOP-drawing supervisor sent me from her lobby presentation and back to my desk to read the CFI's latest "state of the field" report. She thought it would bring me up to speed on the "values" of the microfinance industry. I paced back to the room with stacks of boxes and early 2000s Dell desktop computers and, while the website loaded, stepped out one more time to refill the United Church of Christ–branded "God is still speaking!" coffee mug I'd borrowed from my aunt that morning. I was raiding the kitchen for half-and-half when the sound of a syncopated marimba at maximum volume exploded into the suite. *Shit*, I gasped, sprinting back with hands over my ears, *that's my computer!* I slammed the mute button and investigated the noise. It had come from a video animation entitled "Constance Considers Financial Inclusion," now rolling along silently on the CFI homepage.[49] Subtitles introduced Constance as a "young woman, mother, and wife" in the process of discerning whether she would benefit from financial services. The proprietor of a local market stand that sold baby clothes, Constance wore a floor-length embroidered dress and a wrap to tie up her frizzy hair. Her chalkboard-style cartoon waved at me from beside a thatched hut. Captions ventriloquized her dialogue: "Why do I need financial services?" It is just the question that the CFI hoped that she would ask.

The four-minute animation toured me through Constance's life, glossed as a frame-by-frame list of her desires. Each item was stalked by a hovering, disembodied script that dispensed advice about how Constance could survive and thrive. To pay her son's school fees, the captions advised in the second person, "A savings account would help with that, or you might need a loan." Regarding her goal to purchase a bigger house, "That's a big dream. It will take a lot of savings and probably a loan." With respect to her microenterprise, "Businesses use payments, savings, and loans to work better." Anticipating future health-care costs, Constance should consider "a pension, savings or insurance." The compendium of needs and wants, and the one-track route to their fulfillment, created false equivalence among the items. The challenge of affording an elderly parent's medical care was comparable with the question of how to pay for a child's schooling was comparable with the desire for a new couch. It wasn't just the commodities with an exchange value. Constance's desires had an exchange value, too, in the interest leveraged on the loans she would use to pay for them. These monetary debts would create moral credit for Constance, proving her eligibility as a future free market subject. Viewers could regard the protagonist as if she were their own mirror image. Constance, like me, had wants; she, like me, worked to achieve them; she, like me, hoped for a better future; she, like me, needed access to a bank. The invisible credit officer, pounding out captions in the second person, could just as well be talking about me, or you, or anyone.

"Constance represents just one of the 2.5 billion people around the world who are financially excluded," the floating script declared, before a photocollage of brown and black people engaged in manual labor covered it over. Constance was these workers. But she was also more than just one of these workers. Her allure lay in how she was scripted to share the commodity desires of a global elite whose comfortable lives depended not just on global proletarianized labor but also on the idea that these laborers shared Constance's outlook on life. As her body made the bridge between a deterritorialized labor force and the cosmopolitan citizen subject, her name spoke her vocation: faithful, perseverant, and stable in her work to surrogate the world that capitalist humanitarianism brings to life.

The Human of Capitalist Humanitarianism

After enough encounters with prototypes like Constance—whether on cardboard cutouts at the supermarket, corporate Mad Libs, jejune films on philanthropic credit, or online lending platforms laid out to resemble personals ads—one might suspect that capitalist humanitarians choose their ambassadors the way that United Colors of Benetton chooses its models. Their stylized diversity signals a boundless inclusion but, at the end of the day, makes for a fairly uniform lifestyle. Benetton celebrates "all the colors in the world" while pushing the value of thin bodies, clear skin, cosmopolitan mobility, and the disposable income necessary for seasonal wardrobe renovations. The multicultural poster children invoke an inclusion whose tacit premise is docile citizenship, bootstrapping responsibility, and optimistic labor toward self-reform: inclusion, too, becomes a system of credit.

Luckily for Constance, she makes the cut. Where would she go if she didn't? Is there an outside to inclusion's closed system? Suppose that capitalist humanitarian poster children decide that they do not want to be legible in the way that corporate scripts prescribe. Suppose that financial governance stripped autonomy and self-determination away from their community. Maybe they will decide to keep their savings under a mattress or ask neighbors for loans rather than entrust them to a financial institution. Suppose that they live in a surveillance state. Maybe they have reasons to avoid electronic transactions. Suppose that the schools teach a redacted and nationalist version of history. Maybe they would rather educate their children closer to home, under the direction of neighbors who have earned their trust, and spend the school fees on other needs. Suppose that the ruling administration has repealed voting rights, stockpiled weapons of war, and criminalized popular dissent. They might be wary when this same power invites them to be included in its community, and they might be suspicious of assurances that all has been reformed for the better. Why should they trust humanitarian overtures extended by their oppressors?

Go too far down that track, and the financial counselor will intervene. He will pay a visit to Constance's house. Is her child still enrolled at school? Is the house tidy? Is her husband working? He might pay a call to Constance's neighbors. Have you seen Constance lately? Has she paid her grocery bills on time? What's her political involvement like? Has she been contacted by any radical groups? The financial counselor hopes that these casual reminders of the bank's presence will inspire Constance to resume her mandatory classes in financial literacy and to be a positive role model to her solidarity group. Her personal testimony will be more compelling now that she's experienced doubts and overcome them. The financial counselor tries not to dwell on what happens should Constance not get back on track. She can be a prototype of the inspiring laborer only if she brackets a political-economic analysis of her situation; she fits the mold of a poster child only when she is keeping her anger and critique at bay. Without this restraint, the exemplars of capitalist humanitarianism morph into monstrous negatives of their public images. She becomes disposable. She is a body to be contained or expelled before she sabotages the inclusive society that rejected her. She has only herself to blame; another emissary will step into the role.

That is the thing about financial inclusion. Across generations, it speaks the language of universality and performs its regard for each one of the populations it ushers into global citizenship, even as its itineraries of progressive reform are premised on the expulsion of whomever failed to accede to a profile of creditworthiness. The circulation of multicultural poster children and upwardly mobile diagrams of global poverty is more than a deceptive branding scheme. The prototypes of capitalist humanitarian success write the expansion of financial markets in terms of a world-historical advance of what it means to be a human person; they model the poses that subjects must strike to be "included" among those who are worthy to claim, in the words of Muhammad Yunus, "credit [as] a human right." The issue is not so much what evils they cover up as it is what notions of being, value, and difference they reify.

. . . . . .

Three years into my fieldwork, two summers after my encounter with the "world economic pyramid," I traveled to a different office, this one outside of Guatemala City, for a day visit to a small-scale MFI. By this point, I considered myself inured to the production of good and bad financial subjects, and I didn't think I would be thrown by another example of the discourse. Then, on the tail end of the requisite tour of the headquarters, my hosts insisted that I look at one last thing. They wanted to show me how they taught women in their loan programs to distinguish between good and bad *lenders*. The four of us squeezed around a plastic folding table. They slipped a DVD into a beat-up ThinkPad and cued up video footage of a recent training for current and prospective clients.

The screen filled, pixel by pixel, to reveal rows of women seated in folding chairs with their backs to the camera. They faced a presentation area where two members of the MFI's administrative staff mimed the process of making tortillas. They were playing women in need of credit—that is, versions of the people in their audience—and wore identical polo shirts with the MFI's logo. On stage left, the first woman patted invisible masa between her hands and mumbled to herself about how she could use some capital to grow her business. On stage right, the second woman petitioned her brother—acted by the MFI's director of finance—to float her another cash loan. He refused, his awkward loudness mismatched to the other characters' inside pitch. The room howled in laughter as the scene devolved into a slapstick screaming match—interrupted, finally, when three more MFI staff took the stage. They approached each of the women in turn with a pitch for their gateway credit program. The women would attend two educational seminars, after which they were eligible to apply for a loan that came with monthly capacity trainings and regular advisory support. Woman 1, pensive, said she would consider and get back to them. Woman 2, agitated, clapped back. Mandatory classes? Absolutely not. She needed the money *now*.

Next scene. A voice vroomed and growled as if to summon a motorcycle. Two middle-aged men sprinted into the frame, one after the other. I recognized the person in front as the MFI's head accounting officer. The second man, trailing his boss, brandished a rolled-up poster-board gun and copycatted his companion's movements on a split second delay. The audience thundered with laughter as the two actors mimed a bike dismount and, still in near sync, approached the two women with a deal. Did they want 200 quetzales in cash? The money could be theirs today, no waiting required, with a quick signature. To qualify, one needed only to pledge to make the Q25 interest payments for every subsequent day that they maintained a balance on their account. The first woman chased the men off her porch—*Sharks! Thieves!*—and strode away to call the original, legitimate loan officer. The second signed the predatory lenders' paperwork without a flinch.

Next scene. A handwritten pasteboard cued our jump to "One Month Later." On stage left, the first woman sat with a credit officer. He reviewed her account book and praised her for her climbing profit margins: "Your discipline and patience are paying off!" Meanwhile, on stage right, the second woman begged her brother to resolve her debt. She was desperate. A pounding at the door cut her off. The miming motorcyclists had returned. They mime-kicked through the front entryway as the woman dove behind a chair, where the men found her. They dragged their blubbering victim into the open and shoved the poster-board gun into her forehead. "WHERE IS THE MONEY?" they screamed. "HAND IT OVER!" The woman sobbed her excuses, to which the men barked their guarantee to return the next morning, and the next after that, for the compounding payment. "I have to get out of here! Tonight!" the woman cried to her brother as the loan sharks exited the stage.

Cut. The staff actors returned and bowed, and the screen faded to black.

"We just have to show them," said the MFI director as she packed up the computer. "This is real life." Poor women could join an established financial institution or capitulate to a predatory lender. Within the logic of the skit, the two options correlated to inner virtues: some people indulge short-term desires that portend long-term ruin; others cultivate a discipline of delayed gratification and reap the rewards. That the happy ending involved a woman passing an account book to the man who was her business adviser—a fiction not far off from the everyday fact that this was also a lower-tier employee passing an account book to a senior supervisor—suggested that at least one of the women had attained creditworthy subjectivity. She had been financially prudent, responsive to authority, self-disciplined, and optimistic about her future prospects. Likewise, the worthy creditor collected the debts with civility. That final scene contained zero intrigue. The triumphant characters were exactly who the literature on financial subjects predicted they would be; the borrower's life was everything that her creditors hoped it would become.

The second woman, foil to her neighbor's entrepreneurial paragon, was not so fortunate. An indebted woman cowered under the gun of a loan shark. Again, this is a lower-level staff person bent under a supervisor's would-be weapon. The man urges the woman and her potential doubles in the audience to take out a loan with the organization that employed both of them. How can I not read this scene as a psychic fantasy, where the finance director and head of accounting punish a woman who, in her overindulgence, betrayed her creditors' good faith?

The director of accounting played the loan shark. Or the loan shark played the head of accounting. Either way, he retaliated when the woman—cast as his client but also there in the capacity of his employee—expressed the wrong kind of consent. She said yes to the informal lender and no to a neoliberal structure of extraction, *yes* to immediacy and *no* to responsibility. The loan shark dragged her out of her hiding place, not to capture her for an inclusive capitalist commons but to disqualify her with redoubled force. Her disposability, narrated as a self-inflicted consequence, gave negative exemplar to the question asked of the women in the audience: What structure of extraction will you choose? The woman in the skit took the best option on the table. She ran.

February 2018.
Delusions of reference.

"Anybody have some sage?" I cackled to my graduate cohort. "That's item one. Saging this room. Bad vibes." A friend mounted an upholstered chair and conjured an invisible smudge stick. She leapt from seat to seat in mime-cleanse of the seminar room on the ground floor of the Yale Graduate School of Arts and Sciences (GSAS) administrative fortress, where a cabal of deans and provosts kept their offices. I had anticipated a sleeker interior. Instead, marbled busts and musty atlases cluttered the shelves; the place was a dead ringer for the parlor in *Django Unchained*. "Actually," a first-year student mused, "how about an exorcism? Who here can do an exorcism?"

On February 12, graduate union organizers awoke to news of another ending: our lawyers had withdrawn our petition from the National Labor Relations Board (NLRB) appeals process. Just over a year ago, graduate teachers had voted to affiliate as UNITE-HERE Local 33, our ecstatic sobs reverberating from the auditorium where federal officials counted the ballots, through the sleepy campus quads and into the streets downtown.

These celebrations were premature. Yale refused to bargain until the stalling left the union no option but to file an official unfair labor practices complaint with the NLRB. We knew that the law favored our case; the state had already certified the bargaining unit. All that the university could really do, at this point, was attempt to exhaust our financial and moral resources and hope that we would retreat. The win felt imminent—until Yale hit a windfall in the results of the 2016 presidential election. With a far-right executive on the brink of inauguration, the university's "union avoidance" law firm only needed to stall the appeals process until the new administration stacked the courts with conservative judges. If Local 33's petition landed in front of the reconstituted

NLRB, the new appointees were likely not only to torpedo our specific campaign but also to use our case to overturn the precedent that allowed graduate students to unionize at all. We couldn't drag other schools down with us. The fight was over, and we had lost.

It did not matter that we had anticipated the outcome. I trudged through muddy snow to campus, same route as ever, perturbed that I had chosen today, of all days, to present a chapter at our doctoral colloquium and apoplectic that the session had been moved to Warner House at the last minute. Graduate students were not welcome in this building. Most of us only ever came as close as the union rallies held on its front steps, where we danced to whatever song that fit the mood of the day. *Bitch better have my money! Pay me what you owe me!* Just a few weeks ago Rihanna's voice had pulsed through portable speakers into the offices where university officials and a cartel of their millionaire attorneys discussed strategy. In fact, I felt certain that today the American religious history students had been summoned to the literal room where those conversations happened.

Was the venue-change some kind of taunt? It hadn't been intended that way—our faculty had reserved it because our regular room was double-booked—but this knowledge had little effect on our spirits. Our antics with the sage were the kind of absurdist humor born in defeat. For months, informational emails from department chairs had warned doctoral students that unions poisoned mentoring relationships and sabotaged academic freedom. What we heard: there will be no mental health care, no recourse for harassment, no pay equity, and it is naïve and greedy to ask for these things. In my mind we had two options. Option 1, expel demons. Option 2, bust into the provost's office and charge him, and anyone else craven enough to have earned a desk in the building, with manslaughter.

. . . . . .

The call center where Mark worked during the final year of his life sold itself as a socially responsible business. According to its official literature, the company provided voice-based communications technology for people with hearing loss. Unlike typical call centers that answer customer service requests or place solicitation calls, this company generated live transcriptions of personal phone calls. Subscribers paid to have a third-party human listener present, silently and in real time, on every phone call and voice message. The call center's low-wage eavesdroppers transcribed the interactions as they happened—or, more accurately, they would translate between the voices on the phone and machines that relayed the words back to subscribers via live text.

On any given day, Mark would enter the warehouse and scan his ID card into the automated system that parceled his work, bathroom, and lunch time into milliseconds. He would settle into a cubicle among the hundreds of others in this windowless open-floor wasteland. Logged into the network, he would wait for the computer to beep. This was his signal to join a conversation as its invisible ghosting party. Then that split second of suspense: What kind of call would it be?

Debt collectors and phishing expeditions were the most common. Almost as frequent were communications in and out of other call centers, probably based somewhere overseas, and too often involving a *do-you-even-speak-English-bitch-where-are-you-anyway* tirade from the person on the receiving line. Sometimes the transcribers played the mediating third during phone sex. Rarest of all were the casual catch-ups or I-was-just-thinking-of-you sweetheart rings. Life was worst during national election cycles, when politicians eager to win Wisconsin blew up the lines with automated get-out-the-vote pitches. These calls might elicit noises of agreement with the far-right's dog-whistling white supremacy or tirades against the organizer for daring to call during those particular hours, or—a mercy—just a hang-up.

All Mark heard, he had to reproduce, verbatim, into a microphone. His job was to absorb the lulling, cresting cadences of everyday communication and repeat the sounds back in a staccato monotone appropriate to the auto-transcription machine standing by. This artificial-intelligence setup, mediated by cyborgs, generated a text stream of each phone conversation as it progressed. A task that used to require typing fingers happened through voice transcription. But to ensure accurate inputs, Mark had to ransack sentences of their timbre and cadence, making his call-center voice into a dystopian musical instrument. He transposed everyday exposition—rising, falling, inflected, muffled, sharp, loud, whispered, hateful, caressing—into random info units that just happened to stumble into proximity. The software handled it from there.

On good days, Mark would go home and jam with friends in his hip-hop collective or compose new beat tracks for his art-rap duo. On bad days, his brain never left work. And although his bandmates also had jobs at the call center, only Mark seemed to get hung up on what happened there. Alone in a bedroom furnished with a mattress and nothing else, he rewound the day's calls in his head, a chorus of voices synthesized in expressionless mimicry of conversations that didn't belong to them.

. . . . . .

The same summer that Mark moved to Milwaukee, I was shadowing microfinance bankers in Guatemala. A week into my trip, a "director of social impact" had offered me an unpaid internship in her offices. She wanted my help on a specific issue: using robo-calls to survey loan program clients on their "customer satisfaction." The MFI cared about this kind of assessment, she told me, as a part of its mission to "empower women's voices." Until now, the organization had deputized credit officers to collect client feedback at the same time they collected their monthly payments. But the staff suspected that the women were "not being fully honest" in their replies—which were uniformly glowing. The shortage of negative feedback made it look like the MFI was lying about its own performance. And how could they grow their market share if they lacked a sense of where to improve? The director hoped to glean more "honest" (read: variable) feedback by divorcing the moment of feedback solicitation from the moment of debt collection. She asked me to contact several Guatemala-based call centers to learn about their services and price points. I would then write a report that assessed the product landscape, compared the top options, and recommended next steps.

Anything else I could say about this project was subject to an NDA. Still, I wrote Mark. Subject: EVIL. He replied four days later. The email contained very few of his own words. He had copied a link to a lecture by a cultural theorist he had started to follow. "Maybe this is useful, who knows!" he opened, then transcribed the passage on his mind:

> What's the ethos of the NGO? It's not "we're here to speak for those people." Precisely the opposite. The NGO's ethos is "we want to allow these people to speak for themselves, to enunciate their interests." The moment that social life steps forward in that form and says "here are our interests," makes them discrete, makes them available, makes them visible, in that process of governance, is also the moment that they can be captured.[1]

Revisiting the message four years later, I notice how he withheld comment about my choice to help a financial institution cut a deal with an employer much like the one that was torturing him. I notice how, in the off-hours of a job that required his decumbent echo of the hegemonic American phone call, he deconstructed the fantasy that it is possible or good to represent oneself. I notice that, whether one empties their words of meaning or speaks on their own behalf, they are still trapped. "If that's what your research amounts to," he signed off, "that is sort of scary."

. . . . . .

Interlude five

"Your chapter is the sage." A voice interrupted our theater. Our adviser, recently ascended to an associate deanship, had arrived. "You know, a thorn is going through my heart right now," she said. "A lot has happened in this room. Today you become a part of its history. Why *can't* this chapter change this room? Why *can't* you create a new university?"

I narrowed my eyes. *Of course she said that.* She had been on a kick about insider-driven institutional change. She wanted me to believe, with her, that the right people, with the right set of tools and techniques, could bend this place toward good. This, at least, was what the available evidence had led me to conclude.

It wasn't like I hadn't wrestled with the same issue. My militating negativity toward reform sprang from how frequently I revisited this exact question, hating myself each time I was tempted toward an affirmative answer. Could one person's maverick presence in a glorified hedge fund do much more than offer a commodified token to its managerial toleration? I doubted it. More likely, the aspiring change agent will find herself transformed into something that she would not have liked when she started out. She is sage, lauded and waved around, and the room is purer for her self-immolating presence. But if my chapter was sage, it had given itself up: its point was to not confuse inclusion with emancipation, to not mistake broken silence for any kind of freedom. Commit them to text, and the words are already snitching on themselves.

· · · · · ·

Once I joked that Mark actually worked for the NSA, wiretapping people. He stayed silent for a long time before his voice broke: "It's literally the worst of humanity." I had to guess. Did he mean subscribers who berated customer-service workers? The Republican propaganda that plagued Wisconsin that summer? The scammers who targeted hearing-impaired elders? The collections agencies? He wouldn't say more. There were NDAs. All I knew for sure was that what he heard he had to repeat back, flat and cold, and he had heard everything: the words, the words beneath the words, and—at the end—the secret memos insinuated into the range of tonal variation that the computer tolerated. There was some leeway, in the end. He could perceive the secret messages in how neighboring workers repeated *Hello, I am Donald Trump Jr.!* in that subtly clowning way or growled *I am calling to collect a debt* with their head cocked toward the left or promised that *We care about you* with a maternal lilt. He knew that they were speaking to him; every word to the computer transmitted a subliminal code.

· · · · · ·

Here is the question that I am always asked in colloquia like the one in Warner House: *What comes after deconstruction?* It happened again that day with the sage, this demand to do something other than showcase complicity. A philosopher predicted that my book would be "a pamphlet, not literature" if it failed to elevate some principled intention that these call centers and debt collectors betrayed and to which they could return. *There is no way out of complicity*, I replied, my tired refrain. Next time I will scream until my vocal cords collapse.

. . . . . .

Months too late, a psychiatrist described my brother's sensing as "delusions of reference." It is a classic feature of mania in bipolar 1. People with this structure of mind discover cosmic significance in random utterances, movements, and images. Scattered data points, through their eyes, are infused with spiraling meaning, both personal and collective.

I want to see him as a sonic cartographer sailing through a parallel galaxy, unfurling his maps in yet-to-be-discovered colors and shapes. There is glory in the image until I turn again to encounter the rest. No matter how far he goes or what messages he transmits, the walls close in. The manager listens. Show me the delusion.

the hunt for yes 5

ARCHIVAL MANAGEMENT AND
MANUFACTURED CONSENT

A man in a suit slid a consent form toward the teenage girl across from him. She was the youngest member of her weaving cooperative; he was the regional director of a microfinance institution (MFI) looking to add to its portfolio. The director had come to her town in central Guatemala to assess whether a community development center—which sponsored the women's textile arts co-op as well as an eco-friendly carpentry business—qualified for financing. I was present for the interaction, having gained the MFI's permission to do fieldwork alongside its due-diligence trip. To reciprocate for my access I assisted with small number-crunching and paper-pushing tasks. Today my colleague asked me to help identify candidates for the "client profiles" on the MFI's revamped website. Only three days had passed, but already our supervisors in the US office were nagging us for photos.

These profiles went beyond simply snapping a picture. Before a photo could be matched to someone's identifying information, the MFI needed to secure the subject's permission to use it in whatever venue, in perpetuity. To that end, the regional director and I had already secured the signatures of five or six others. So far, the bureaucratic finagling had posed no issue. The people we surveyed would have had a hard time refusing, given that the person making the request wielded determinant influence over their future income stream. As I watched my colleague push the form across the table, it seemed doubtful that consent—with its constitutive elements of willing, equitable parties developing a contractual agreement—meant much in this context. What is "consent" when routed through itineraries of poverty assessment? Or was I being too dismissive of the subject's capacity to use the document to her own end? Maybe the MFI director was relinquishing power when he paused to ask upfront: Yes or no? On this day, the young artist's quiet demurral surfaced conflicts that nobody on this trip had acknowledged out loud. What if the people whom capitalist humanitarians sought to serve did not acquiesce? What if they preferred not to be cast as the next mass-produced stars of neocolonial development?[1]

The scene unfolded at the home of the weaving cooperative's president. My colleague had selected her place as the most comfortable option for a get-to-know-you lunch and monthly members' meeting. Remittances from the woman's husband in the United States had paid for a tiled outdoor terrace and new concrete walls, notable upgrades in comparison to the earthen floors and corrugated metal ceilings more typical of the area. Fourteen women, plus a handful of children running around in the yard, had gathered at an outdoor table for an afternoon meal. Co-op members had prepared it for us on top of their child-care obligations, textile production quotas, and mandatory afternoon interviews with my colleague and me.

Our surveys adapted an open-source assessment instrument known as the Progress Out of Poverty Index (PPI). The Grameen Foundation commissioned the tool as part of a bid to promote longitudinal research by "organizations and businesses with a mission to serve the poor." The PPI identifies populations "likely to be poor or vulnerable to poverty" and, in tracking changes to their quality of life over time, enables development inverventionists to "integrat[e] poverty data into their assessments and strategic decision-making."[2] Tailored for sixty countries and counting, the PPI assesses standard of living through a "poverty scorecard" comprising ten multiple-choice questions about "directly observable household characteristics."[3] The sum of the answers is their "poverty score." The average poverty score in a predetermined demographic—such as the clients of a certain MFI or residents of a certain geographic area—predicts the likelihood that any given person in that group lives in poverty. The PPI guidelines tell development groups to first establish a baseline and then to return every few years to track its changes over time.[4]

The staff of the MFI whom I shadowed saw the PPI as a means to two ends. They first needed an aggregate poverty score to determine whether the co-op's members were "poor enough" to merit assistance. Then they needed to generate a reference from which to measure changes in the local standard of living. When everyone had finished lunch, the women bused the plates to the sink and then sat down to socialize and weave under trees on the opposite side of the yard. The regional director and I remained at the table. One by one, the women came forward to be interviewed. Ticking off questions about household composition, personal possessions, and income, we remained mindful of the adjacent task: finding candidates for the MFI's online human interest features.

My colleague kept soliciting my opinion on who would make a "good" profile. I denied having an opinion. I reasoned that he had already set his criteria and decided whom he wanted. He didn't need my help. But I was aware that my internal debate over how to navigate the ethics of his request proved that I, too, could picture what he wanted and believed he could find.

We interviewed the youngest member of the cooperative last. The ten core questions remained the same as with every previous encounter (see table 5.1). How many people in your household are thirteen years old or younger? *Five.* Are all of the children between the ages of seven and thirteen enrolled in school? *No.* Does the head of the household know how to read and write? *No.* Does anyone in the house work as a hired agricultural or domestic worker? *No.* What material are your floors made out of? *Dirt.* Do you have a refrigerator? *No.* Do you have a gas stove? *No.* Do you have a stone mill? *Yes.* Do you have an electric griddle? *No.* If anyone in the household works in agriculture, do you have any cows, horses, or mules? *Nobody works in agriculture.* When my colleague inquired about how the family generates income, we learned that the girl's father had migrated to the United States three years ago and never gotten back in touch. At this point, my colleague turned the survey to its blank reverse side and began to compose a first-person narrative in longhand: *I am sixteen years old. My father left for the US three years ago. I haven't heard from him since. I support my siblings, mother, and grandmother by working in the weaving cooperative. I am the primary source of income for my family. I dream of returning to school and starting my own business.* He passed her a consent form and explained that her signature would grant us permission to post her story and picture on the MFI's website.

The girl hesitated. "Where are you putting my photo?" My colleague repeated that he wanted to put her story on his company's website. "*Es inspirador.*" It's inspiring, he said. When her brow remained furrowed, he suddenly guessed, correctly, that she was unfamiliar with the term *sitio red*. "Oh!" With overanimated gestures he explained that a website was "like a billboard" except for that it was "on a computer." "Millions of people" could see it—"people in Guatemala City, in Mexico, in China, in the United States! Your father might even see it!" The girl didn't reply. The financier added that there were computers at the local development group's offices and that she really should get one of the staff to show her how to use the internet. She still did not respond. He

Table 5.1. A Simple Poverty Scorecard for Guatemala

Entity	Name	ID	Date (DD/MM/YY)
Member:	_____	_____	Joined: _____
Loan officer:	_____	_____	Today: _____
Branch:			Household size:

Indicator	Possible Response	Points	Total
1. How many household members are aged 13 or younger?	A. Five or more B. Four C. Three D. Two E. One F. None	0 10 12 17 23 33	
2. Did all children ages 7 to 13 enroll for the current school year?	A. No B. No children ages 7 to 13 C. Yes	0 2 6	
3. Can the female head/spouse read and write?	A. No B. Yes C. No female head/spouse	0 6 9	
4. Do any household members work mainly as casual laborers or domestic workers?	A. Yes B. No	0 5	
5. What is the main construction material of the residence's floors?	A. Earth, sand, wood, parquet, or other B. Mud bricks or cement slab C. Formed cement bricks D. Granite or ceramic	0 3 9 15	
6. Does the household have a refrigerator?	A. No B. Yes	0 9	
7. Does the household have a gas or electric stove?	A. No B. Yes	0 8	
8. Does the household have a stone mill?	A. No B. Yes	0 3	
9. Does the household have an electric iron?	A. No B. Yes	0 8	
10. If any household member works mainly in agriculture, animal husbandry, hunting, or fishing, does the household have any cows, bulls, calves, pigs, horses, burros, or mules?	A. No B. Yes C. No one works mainly in agriculture	0 3 4	

Microfinance Risk Management, L.L.C., http://www.microfinance.com   Total score:

persisted. Technological literacy would be important to her long-term success as an entrepreneur. She stared at the sheet of paper.

I witnessed all of this in silence. I felt awkward: awkward because of his lust for her signature, awkward because she was on the spot, awkward because I was colluding with these interactions. The pause between the request and the expected response had put all of us in a zone of irresolution. What would happen? Up to this point, the geopolitical facts of our presence in this community had all but guaranteed that, for interviewees, a "no" to our request was off the table. Everyone knew that the MFI can make or break the financial stability of the cooperative. Everyone knew that it was economically unwise for co-op members to deny the financier what he asked. Still, I found myself willing the girl to read my mind: *Say no. Say no because this guy is skeevy and so is how he uses that camera. Say no because you clearly are not amped about being on a "billboard." Don't do it.* I said none of this out loud. I convinced myself that I was on her side.

The young woman finally shook her head. She would not sign.

It took a beat for my colleague to register her answer. He clenched his teeth and his voice came out an octive higher than usual: "You don't want to be photographed?" When she repeated herself, he snapped. He lurched from his chair and snatched the blank form. *VALE. NO HAY PROBLEMO.* He tore the paper in half, then in quarters. *NO PROBLEM*, he snarled, tearing it into even smaller pieces. *We WON'T take your photo. We WON'T go to your house.* With each new rip of the sheet: *NO . . . PROBLEM . . . NO . . . PROBLEM.*

Except that there clearly was a problem. When I think about it now, I remember him yelling. Was he yelling? He definitely was standing up. His voice was raised. I wish I knew how the girl would have narrated the situation: Did she experience him as screaming? Was our presence there just one long scream? Did the scene faze her at all? The discernment of anger, and also the discernment of abuse, can be so straightforward and also so contingent on whatever one imagines as reasonable.[5] What I can offer is clarity that something was off; it was a tantrum in response to no provocation at all. The fragments of the consent form floated away on the breeze and across the yard. The girl drifted back toward the others. My colleague packed up our paperwork, and ordered our driver to ferry us back to the hotel. The place charged as much per night as an average member of the cooperative earns in three months.

I have circled back to this interaction many times. What was my colleague trying to obliterate when he ripped up the form? What relationship was she refusing when she said no and then, a few minutes later, when she walked away? However singular the financier's outburst, and however singular my silence in the midst of it, the intensity of this event had everything to do with the relations that scaffolded it. The financier's outburst was enabled by the routines of intimate surveillance that structure capitalist humanitarian practice—where for every "no" there are dozens more "yes" answers. Nevertheless the home office is calling to say that they need more: more consent to the order already being imposed, more paperwork on the rationale for this bureaucracy, more proof of good works. To be a capitalist humanitarian is to be always running toward some reassurance that your target populations agree to your structures of extraction, even if that agreement is secured through conditions of compulsion. So the hunt for yes will keep advancing—from the headquarters that order the assent to communities where agreements are uttered and ticked off and back to the offices innovating new bureaucracies to manage the information that, no matter what else it might reveal, keeps adding up to that recurrent word: yes.

Contract, Survey, Desire

The hunt for yes has a counterintuitive quality. It splices an ends-oriented production of populations as aggregate data points with the acknowledgment of these same subjects as autonomous, individuated, choosing agents. I aggregate you as a plot point; I recognize you as a voluntary willing subject. I data-crunch your life; I pass you a consent form. I care not at all about your yes; I need your yes.

My colleague had seized power as assessor of life under precarity. He had also asked, via the consent form, that subjects of his evaluation enter into a relationship of free exchange with him. The literature on the history of contract theory helps explain the contradiction. Amy Dru Stanley describes the contract not simply as a genre of document but as something akin to a "worldview" premised on the "idealized ownership of the self and voluntary exchange between individuals who were formally equal and free." Within a contract framework, the wider social order derives its legitimacy from agreements made by free subjects and premised on "principles of self-ownership, consent, and exchange."[6] The legitimacy of the liberal state derives from its citizens' free *consent* to be governed; the legitimacy of a marriage derives from the free *consent* of parties to enter it; the legitimacy of a boss's directive derives from the worker's free *consent* to an employment contract. These relations would, in theory, be void if established under conditions of coercion.

When the MFI representative passed the weaver a contract, he recognized her as the sovereign captain of her own will. Her hypothetical signature would signal her free choice to transfer power over her image and story to the bank. It would indicate that she *wanted* this relation. On some level I can appreciate the historical appeal of contract liberalism. The blueprint for liberalism's self-owning, rational, consenting subject emerged as a critique of, and alternative to, feudalism.[7] Under the principles of contract worldview, the former subjects of a paternalism and its status birthrights can now claim ownership over their bodies and futures. They can submit, or not, to being governed. Liberal political orders are hypothetically illegitimate sans the consent of the people.[8] Now the bank's paperwork also presents participation in finance discipline as a free choice for liberal modern subjects. The credit officer awaits the answer: Would you rather be property or owner? Bound to the status of your birth or member of a contracting equals? Indentured or entrepreneurial?

The options do not have to be so limited.[9] Political theorists have exposed the roots of enlightenment liberalism in heteropatriarchy, colonialism, and white supremacy. These entanglements manifest in who has historically wielded political-economic social power in liberal modern orders—but this is nowhere near the core of the critique. Most troubling are the ramifications of liberal philosophical anthropology for how collectives are able to imagine, desire, and pursue intersubjective freedom. When the normative definition of the human is one of possessive individual self-mastery, the horizons of political struggle will atrophy accordingly. The expansion of freedom becomes a matter of continually expanding the circle of liberal rights-bearing subjectivity to previously excluded populations: women, brown people, black people, indigenous people, queers, immigrants, children, disabled people, the so-called unbanked.[10] There is always another frontier; each new gesture of inclusion remains premised on a prior expulsion.

A massive flight in the critical humanities toward alternative frames for considering human subjectivity, or dispensing with its strictures altogether, indicates one thing above all: the liberal subject, whoever and wherever she is, has earned her bad reputation. Resist how she hails you. Go somewhere else. There are other ways to be. Try queer relationality, in its infinite becoming.[11] Try the death drive.[12] Try fugitivity of spirit, of breath.[13] Heed the wisdom of sea mammals.[14] Write poetry.[15] Engage in workplace sabotage.[16] Organize.[17] Whatever you do, do not get pulled into the liberal subject's carceral orbit.

Inclined to imagine the life otherwise, I am tempted to elaborate the weaver's response as a revolutionary break in script. Her *no*, her walk away from the table, would herald her refusal to be hailed as a possessive individual subject. I could elaborate the financier's retaliation as the disinterment of an interpellating violence. I would read the financier's explosion as how he punished her for not recognizing her subjection as her freedom. It would see her refusal as fugitivity from his neocolonial demand. I would speculate that her walk away from his scene leads to alternative possibilities for human relationality and subjectivity. Where would she lead? What would she show? What alternative world exists where she is going? We could imagine that her trail went to the secret escape route from secular modernity's hell-bent project to incorporate every difference into its sinister totality. If the financier situated the girl as a step in his scheme of world-historical development, critics of the financier produced her as emblem of their own retort. This girl is the possibility before, after, and beyond the imposition of Western man as universal subject.[18] We could follow her.

These gestures do not resolve the problem of her subjection. They might circle back to the position they sought to escape: in the invocation of an out-of-secular-time life against which the subject of modernity develops along her historical arc.[19] Meanwhile, nowhere in the interaction did the weaver refuse liberal contract relations. On the contrary, she accepted at face value their acknowledgment of her equal standing in the negotiation. She said "no." If anyone betrayed the promise of liberalism—or dramatized its underlying authoritarian current—it was the credit officer when he ripped up the document in protest of an answer to a question he himself had asked. He was irate that when she refused, the girl withheld not only her photograph but also her participation in what the assessment-photojournalism tour tried to install as common sense: the notion that this capitalist humanitarian knowledge regime could count on adjunct performances of reciprocal desire so that words like *submission* and *obedience* and *coercion* would remain foreign to the microfinance bank's self-image. When the weaver used the sliver of yes-no space extended to her, she mobilized the contract against its own incorporative project.

The two documents—assessment survey and consent form—elicited synchronous and conflicting performances of relation within the bureaucracy that framed them. First was the coerced imposition of a capitalist humanitarian hunt for information, which then helped to plan future projects. The PPI survey collected impersonal data to be channeled into financial algorithms that would then determine resource distribution for the global South. It stripped subjects of specificity and wrote their lives as raw data to be crunched by experts.[20] The consent form then entered, post facto, to hail those subjects as sovereign agents of their own selves and futures. Each document had a pedagogical role in relation to the other. The survey did not just collect preexisting data; it also forced economic interests into speech.[21] The contract did not merely involve an agreement between parties; it was more like a final survey question, except with higher stakes. The yes or no of the contract tested the survey's pedagogical effect. If you were in the hot seat, you would now rehearse the jobs your family members don't have. You would slog through the commodity items you do not own.[22] And there is one more thing: *Do you WANT to own? That is, do you want to be the kind of subject who owns?* You may not possess a refrigerator, but you can possess your desire for one and your will to get it. Sign on the dotted line. *Yes.*

Archivists of Capitalist Humanitarianism

The hunt for the yes is an exercise of archive creation, and the capitalist humanitarian paperwork keeps piling higher. There are documents generated by funding organizations: grant proposals, annual reports, budget statements, educational curricula for subjects of intervention, historical archives of the organization, donor pledges, strategic plans, directions for evaluating credit risk, spreadsheets of demographic data, spreadsheets of repayment rates, spreadsheets of loan types, spreadsheets of future price projections. There are documents produced by the subjects of intervention and filed by the funder: booklets to track monthly budgets, quarterly reports for every funder, documents to prove that you are not using pesticide on the crops that you market as organic, contracts for timely repayments, contracts to show up to a monthly financial-literacy workshop, contracts to complete the product order by a certain date. The capitalist humanitarian archival marvel rides on the proliferation of its contracts. As the contracts go, so goes the rest of the paperwork.

I have never encountered a humanitarian-finance institution that is not consumed with the expansion of its archive, the refinement of its data-management protocols, and its pedagogies of self-surveillance. These qualities manifest not only in the words that people say to me but also in how operations run. Business schools and social-entrepreneurship conferences feature whole tracks on how to deal with all of the data. Software companies compete to invent the best new platform to digitize and aggregate information into server farms. The MFIs that I visit are nearly always crammed with file cabinets. Sometimes there are whole rooms dedicated to file cabinets. I once visited a microfinance office in which the brassy cabinets had displaced staff desks. Storage units doubled as standing desks for staff thrown out of their own cubicles. A station of ten file cabinets had been set up, like a kitchen island in a McMansion, at the center of a coworking room. It served as a group standing desk. Potted plants and photos of microloan recipients decorated the file cabinet complex that literally propped up the staff-member bodies crunching the data that would also, one day, be part of the furniture.

The majority of this data focuses on the populations that capitalist humanitarian reform chooses as its primary focus: women and girls in the global South. The kinds of accounting that subjects are asked to perform—not only to disclose their employment and income but also to quantify their domestic life and their aspirations for it—reiterate a bond between their intimate lives and their potential capital value. It is not just that household possessions and family size translate to "poverty score," and thus rationale for financial reform. It is also that the expansion of capitalist humanitarian archives, via data-collection missions, produces the household as both a sphere of economic value and the site of a truth that requires constant maintenance. Every document occasions a future document. A due-diligence trip is also a mission to make a narrative profile. A new mission tagline is also a donor-appeal strategy. An annual report is also a financial calculation. A personal account book is also an index of the health of one's marriage. A survey is also the occasion for a return trip to the field, that wellspring of data and desire. Sometimes I wonder if there is a point to all this paperwork, but then I remember the main purpose of archives: they don't just store random data. Their work is to place each dissonant thing, to fold every display of difference and each out-of-joint object back into a principle of unity. It can happen with paper, but sometimes the paper is just the alibi for this ongoing search for living additions to the humanizing archive that is global capital.[23]

. . . . . .

Another day, another capitalist humanitarian data system. It was July 2016, and I had come to Amity Assets, a small MFI outside of Guatemala City, at the invitation of one of their senior staff. The executive director, Regina, had already toured me through the building. Now I waited in a common area while her colleague, Clara, tinkered with a projection screen. A tarp hung lopsided off an exposed pipe behind her, in a droopy denotation of the constituents whom the agency meant to serve: FOR WOMEN WITH A BUSINESS DREAM.

The staff would repeat that motto many more times throughout the day—first, in a private presentation that I surmised they had given to more than one visiting researcher. It opened with a collage of flowers, volcanoes, fiber art, market produce stands, and other national scenery. "These are the colors of Guatemala. We are a happy country," Regina beamed. The panorama was the preamble to a cascade of demographic and financial data, occasionally augmented with personal stories. I learned that the average woman in the program was forty-one years old, had just four years of primary education, supported a large dependent family, and made $1–$2.08 per day. I learned that Amity issued loans with 25 percent APR on a nine-month cycle, and only in the context of solidarity groups. Women were eligible only when they enrolled in group business classes and accepted one-on-one "advisory support" from Amity's staff. The money brings the women to the program, Regina explained, but the real value lay in the educational components: "If someone does not accept all three parts, we do not accept them into the program," she assured me. For Amity, a better future for Guatemala rested on these women's agreement to a pedagogical project. "Women do not know about debt. They do not know what it can do to their lives," Regina concluded. "Our goal is for them to be out of debt." She paused. "To be free."

Borrowers achieved freedom by becoming archivists of themselves. They were required to keep double-entry account books that business advisers reviewed at biweekly home visits. This constituted the foundation of Amity's education program. Obligatory classes covered accounting, cash-flow management, marketing strategy, savings, and other topics in financial literacy. Amity required its clients to pay 140 quetzales, or about 19 USD, per session. "You don't appreciate things unless you pay for them," Regina quipped. The assumed correlation between monetary investment and feelings of gratitude did more than justify a mandatory "donation" for mandatory classes—it also voiced an endemic capitalist humanitarian virtue ethic. Microfinance officers supervised clients in the cultivation of self-forming habits. Routine exercises, such as paying for an activity they were required to attend, were intended to form them as particular subjects: namely, ones who were grateful because they knew that nothing in life is free.

Fidgeting in my plastic chair, I struggled to hear their truisms as much other than genteel warnings against redistributing wealth to people who had not explicitly earned it, whether on an individual or systemic front. I thought of how many times I'd watched MFI employees wring their hands over whether clients would blow the money on consumer commodities rather than invest it in their microenterprise.[24] They see this prospect as a problem for two reasons. It is a problem, first, because it probably sinks the borrower further into debt. It is a problem, second, because it reflects failed empowerment on the part of the borrower and the MFI cultivating her as a financially disciplined subject. The borrower who spends her profits on leisure items, or even everyday staples like groceries or hygiene products, has not internalized financial responsibility. Her failure of learning is evident from her capitulation to personal desires, her ostensible confusion about how those desires add to her debt, and her reticence to sacrifice her urges in service of her "future" goal. Or, in Regina's words: "Women need to know that if they take eggs from their own store, they need to pay for them, or else they are losing money."

Only once I had returned to my rented bedroom and begun to jot down notes from the day was I able to take in the full strangeness of her quip. Who exactly is losing money? The woman? The store? The commodities in the store? In that moment the imperial reach of MFI information culture coexisted with the selective insistence that the subjects of that information divide themselves into pieces: personal and business. These categories were divisible insofar as the "personal" had a consequence for the microenterprise. Until a woman could monitor and withstand "personal" cravings, and thus perform an emergent capacity to invest in her "business" future, near and present dangers would plague her life. She would be food insecure. Her children would get a substandard education. Loan sharks would line up at her door. She would be vulnerable to intimate partner violence. Capitalist humanitarian empowerment continually finds the solution to patriarchy, wealth inequality, and colonialism in the global woman's initiative to overcome these problems through her own self-organization.

The pitch rang familiar to me until Regina mentioned that Amity also mandated that women receive instruction on proper hygiene, parenting, self-esteem, and family planning. She told me three separate times that the bank teaches women how to do self-checks for breast cancer. I scribbled notes: *What is the principle of archival unity that puts double-entry bookkeeping alongside workshops about feeling for breast tissue irregularities?!* But I had heard about the physical health units of financial literacy pedagogy enough times to have a hypothesis: both are encapsulated in the capitalist humanitarian commitment to an amorphous "empowerment." This buzzword dissolved the constructed barrier between home and work, between what was intimate and what was professional, between the number of children in a household and that household's poverty score. Within capitalist humanitarian discourse, *empowerment* can name both this encompassing reach and the pedagogies it takes to actualize it. Still, the word is as vague as it is ubiquitous. When I ask capitalist humanitarians what it means to them, the answer inevitably is about gaining a capacity to determine your own future. Yet the fact that this term gets appended to the lives most exposed to systemic violence—here, poor indigenous women in the global South—raises a flag. Empowered to do what and toward what future? To say a person is "empowered" might be to say that she sees and combats patriarchy, and against which she is empowered. An "empowered woman" could also be someone who has gained power within patriarchy, through which she has gained relative power. The directionality of empowerment makes all the difference, which is why it is significant that it usually languishes in an unspecified zone.[25] Above all, the assumption is that women needed to curate capacities in all parts of life to reach their goals; their future is a work of constant vigilance and self-accounting.

Then, as if on cue, Regina jolted me from my own thoughts. "Now let me show you something I think you'll *really* be interested in," she teased. "We thought you might like to see our data-management system." Two clicks brought Regina out of the PowerPoint and into a software platform where Amity stored data on every woman who had ever been through their program, on every topic that the trainings encompassed, no matter how vulnerable.

. . . . . .

The software loaded, and I recalled the summer before. I had spent a little under a month at the MFI with the file cabinets turned into standing desks, doing unpaid administrative work in exchange for access to the organization's archives. Keen to take advantage, and possibly misinformed about my skill-set, the director requested that I perform an "audit of gender equity" among the MFI's partner organizations. I should do so, she said, by developing an "algorithm to measure women's empowerment." This algorithm did not yet exist; I needed to invent it. Per the director, my work would involve counting the number of women employed by the smaller development groups and companies to which the MFI lent funds. I would plug these numbers into an electronic spreadsheet and activate my algorithm to rate them. The math itself was up to me, so long as it resulted in numbers that could be plotted on a graph. After several days of trying to reteach myself statistics and algebra, my nerves had frayed. There were so many documents to go through, so much information to process. The paperwork brewed an emotional state of boredom and anxiety. I would never master Excel! I would never get through the documents! I knew a lot of researchers who would kill for access like mine, but I still couldn't wait for my workday to end.

I understand in retrospect that my internal dialogue bore an unflattering resemblance to the privatization hawks whom I thought I had come to critique. That is, rallying cries to eliminate "bureaucracy" are standard among venture capitalist "disrupters" of industries that don't move at their preferred speed. A discourse of neoliberal reform, humanitarian or otherwise, has been about the need to remove and replace ostensibly inefficient systems of regulation with "efficient" and "flexible" ones. Why dial a taxi or wait for mass transit when you could just order a faster ride with a click? Why purchase a record when you could use an app to stream whatever you want on demand? Why absorb the infrastructure costs of maintaining a company office when your staff could just work from home and pay their own electricity bills? Start-up gurus, corporate union busters, and masters of the gig economy criticize "bureaucracy" and its paperwork albatrosses when they brand their ventures as better alternatives to, among other liberal inheritances, the public social safety net, collective-bargaining agreements, and even contract-based employment. This accelerationist propensity wends its way into everyday structures of feeling and speech. Case in point: me at the file-cabinet desk, draining the last of the stale coffee, staring through the spreadsheet boxes that had blurred into a single pinkish blob, indulging my twee resentment.

Were I to do it again, I would have checked myself. Wasn't I the one who had told my peers in untenable employment situations to document everything? Didn't I have several folders to this effect on my laptop? The problem is not in the paperwork itself but in the process of its production. Just because something is privatized does not mean that the bureaucratic structures shrink. It simply moves those processes out of view, behind NDAs, with underpaid or outsourced labor performing the main work, all to feed it into a surveillance data lockbox that is controlled not by the public but by a select few with an ownership claim. In the case of humanitarian finance, the in-office paperwork is the tip of the iceberg. The real pressure is on borrowers who must perform constant self-assessment and self-accounting in order to keep the cash flow coming.

Still: I was glad to escape that office for the Guatemala countryside, where my host family introduced me to one of the cooperatives that I'd read about back in those stacks of documents. The grandfather of the family was the cooperative's former president; we drank its coffee and poured its honey on toast each morning at breakfast. On a Friday evening, about three weeks into the trip, I had wrapped up a day of shadowing beekeepers at their mountainside hives and begun the two-mile twilight trek back to town when a younger member of the co-op, who also had been moonlighting as its part-time accountant, slowed his motorcycle to offer me a ride. Grateful, I hoisted myself onto the back. We took off down the hill, swinging around curves made treacherous and thrilling in the rainy season's mud. *WHAT ARE YOUR WEEKEND PLANS?* I screamed over his unmuffled engine. He was a regular at pickup soccer games, which his crew would cap with beers at the local sports bars. The NBA semifinals were on. *END... OF... THE... MONTH*, he answered. *WHAT?* I yelled back, not following. *SO... MANY... FORMS*, he shouted through the wind. When we got off the bike, he explained further. His cooperative relied on small pots of funding from about a dozen benefactors and buyers, all of which obligated their global South partners to complete either monthly or quarterly self-audit reports. There was no standard form. Each organization had special questions, based on their mission statements and what their own donors want to hear. For the cooperative to stay afloat, its members had to generate anywhere between 24 and 144 reports per year—and that didn't even factor in extra proposals for grants, product orders, tax documents, and so on. Their forms would go to some other office, where some other worker would punch their data into a spreadsheet or cram it into a filing drawer. There was so much paperwork. As soon as they collected the information, it was already going out of date. Something had escaped the archive, and they had to go get it. *End of the month*: it meant that you couldn't get away.

. . . . . .

Now, a year later, I contemplated Amity's database for filing, categorizing, and tracking borrower information across every conceivable metric. Regina demonstrated its operation through a single client case file. "V-I-L-M-A," she typed into the search field, pulling up four people with this first name. She chose one of these Vilmas at random. I squinted to see a clutter of tiny text boxes projected onto the wall, the lines of bricks colliding with the print on screen. This grid, Regina explained, summarized aspects of Vilma's life. It logged data about her business (textile crafts), the number of loan cycles she'd completed with Amity (2), her record of repayment (100%), her attendance at meetings (good), and "average wage" for the months that she'd participated the loan program (calculated by dividing overall cash flow by amount spent on the business). There were records that counted her children (8), logged recent medical emergencies (none), and indicated her completion of birth control and breast exam training (yes). A final tab stored qualitative descriptions of her interactions with Amity staff. This database, Regina assured me, is the basic foundation for all the other documentation of client outcomes—like all the handwritten files and the separate statistical modeling software that "cannot be manipulated." The data came from personal relationships between Amity's staff and borrowers themselves, she said. Now we would witness one of these relationships in action.

It was time for a home visit. The two staff and I drove a beat-up Toyota twenty minutes out of the city, until the car could no longer muster the steep hills. We unloaded and hiked another two hundred meters to the house. Along the way, Regina and Clara radiated praise for today's chosen borrower, Sindy. They counted her as among a handful of "exceptional" women admitted into a lower-interest, longer-cycle loan program reserved for four-year veteran borrowers who "dream really big." Sindy met the criteria because of her repayment record and because of the impressive number of businesses she ran. She made tamales, tortillas, cakes, and almuerzos (lunches) for day laborers. The staff strained to remember if she had other businesses—"we can check when we are back at the office"—when the three of us walked into a cloud of smoke billowing out of Sindy's front door. We batted through it to find her with her mother, both of them at work between two open-fire-fueled stoves. Sindy held tamales steaming in what must have been a twenty-gallon pot, and her mom tended a skillet loaded with tortillas. There was hardly enough room for the two women, yet somehow a polo-shirt-clad business adviser had crammed himself onto a plastic stool in a corner. Now three more people had arrived. Our bodies were sardines in the doorframe, all of us looking on as the adviser flipped through the pages of Sindy's account book. He narrowed his eyes, and I gathered that we had shown up at a tense time. "How could you have made 125Q last week?" he asked, "These numbers don't add up. What is the real number?" Sindy worked the masa and shrugged. "I was sick last week...?" Her reply landed as a guess, not an assertion. Unimpressed by the dangling afterthought, the credit officer asked her, if she really had been sick and out of work, what sales the numbers indexed. She mumbled something that I couldn't hear and continued cooking with her back to him. His patience frayed, "*Well?*"

Amity sought a set performance of financial subjectivity and humanitarian worth: someone personally responsible, self-scrutinizing, submissive to the bank's authority, and full of future aspirations.[26] Sindy's apparently deficient bookkeeping had disappointed the standard. I heard the semi-inquisition as rising action to a reckoning over the account book. It didn't seem coincidental that Clara chose this moment to invite me outside and away from the fumes. "We try to make it as easy for the women as possible," she reassured me in the fresh air. "That's why we go to their houses. Since most of them work from home, we don't have to make them interrupt their work." The one issue with the visitation system, she continued, was that it suppressed Amity's total number of women staff. She was aware of, and apparently harbored some anxiety about, the fact that her organization would not have stacked up well if ever subjected to another MFI's empowerment algorithm. The problem, she explained, was that women couldn't travel alone in the countryside, much less in a uniform that bore the insignia of a financial institution. Gangs and drug traffickers would target them. "Loan sharks travel with bodyguards, but we don't have that...," she observed, trailing off. We fell into silence, both contemplating the dirt road, and Clara passed me some almonds as three stray dogs milled at our feet. Eventually we returned indoors and found the rest of the group small-talking about Sindy's children. They must have resolved the conflict. We said our good-byes and headed back to the office.

The Hunt for No

If capitalist humanitarian reform can be conceived as an extended exercise in archive creation, then a way to describe the shape of its intervention might be as the creation of subjects who curate and manage archives. The paperwork communicates information, but the self is the true repository of knowledge. You have to know yourself, your desires, your bank account, your demographic flaws. You are the steward of the knowledge that you possess about the world and that you reflect back to the world. And if you don't manage your own archive responsibly, you are fucked. Like an archivist, you have to make decisions about what merits preservation for future history and what can be shredded. Archives are collections of items that somebody decided were worth incorporating into a whole: the whole of history, the whole of religion, the whole of the university, and the whole of the self. Some, probably most, candidates for inclusion in an archival unity will get thrown out on the way there. That document is deemed irrelevant. That woman does not fit our client profile. That attachment is not entrepreneurial. Archives are as much about elimination as they are about accrual. It is the former that makes possible the latter. Cut this thing to make room for something else. Cut that quality and allow your better self to emerge. Archival curation—with its slashing, accumulating, cutting, and adding, with its regard for remaking the whole—is a reformation.

A month after my day trip to Amity and exactly a year after the consent form meltdown, I found myself in the offices of another MFI, Hope Connection (HC), staring down at a different contract. This time I was the one on the spot, having been asked by the senior staff to sign it before proceeding with the call-center research that they had assigned me. The project was the following: I would assist the "director of social impact" in identifying effective methods for collecting client feedback. As is common among MFIs, HC expects its loan officers to collect not only payments but also measures of client satisfaction. When I began my research, the HC data-gathering process involved surveys delivered in person, by the loan officer, at certain times during the course of the loan cycle. By all accounts, the client feedback glowed: clients adored their loan officers, they felt great about the quality of services they were receiving, they felt hopeful about their future as entrepreneurs and as holders of credit, and they were grateful for the funds. But the feedback was so affirmative, said the director of social impact, that there was no real way to take action on it. So as HC sought to expand its commitment to client protection, it wanted to create more avenues for clients to speak their experiences fully, honestly, and assertively. They were, in a word, hunting for negative answers. *No, I am not fully satisfied. No, all of my needs are not being met.*

The project of "empowering the client voice" permeated every organizational initiative at Hope Connection. "The client voice"—almost always in the singular—was the what staff cultivated in leadership trainings and financial-literacy classes that were a condition of membership. Loan officers were to respect it. Social-impact officers should be guided by it. The idea was that indigenous women's financial stability would emerge in proportion to their capacities not just to identify *but also to speak to* their own interests.

It disturbed the social impact team that, in the words of one staff member, "clients may not be being fully honest" with their credit officers. Were cultural barriers getting in the way of clients' candor? Were power dynamics compromising the exchange between clients and the staff? Were they not asking the right questions? Whatever the issue, they needed to figure out a better—more discreet, more probing, more revelatory—feedback mechanism. Recent industry research pointed toward a potential fix. Studies indicated that clients expressed more-forthcoming criticisms via automated phone surveys delivered by third-party contractors, and they tended to demur when their credit officers solicited their comments in person.[27] Now HC wanted to explore interactive-voice-response (IVR) technology as an alternative to live surveys. A computer would call randomly selected HC clients with prerecorded multiple-choice questions. Clients would punch answers into a keypad. This method would preserve client anonymity while making the assessment process more efficient and, in the long term, scalable.

The social impact team hoped to subcontract a Guatemala-based call center to handle the operation. This was where I came in. My job was to call the sales departments—and, in a few cases, to place direct calls to top-level executives known to HC leadership—to explore options. The HC staff had drafted preliminary list of questions: about cost, about range of services, and about whether employees speak indigenous languages. I was also to inquire about whether the service package could include an independent complaint line for clients who wanted to convey their qualitative concerns to someone other than their credit officer. Finally, I would compile a ten- to twenty-page report that compared the options and recommended next steps.

. . . . . .

Hope Connection could not have proposed a more ideologically loaded research project if it had tried. Call centers have multiplied in Guatemala over the last two decades, to the point that the region is now the primary hemispheric hub for multinational corporations seeking to offshore their customer service labor. The companies that subcontract with call centers headquartered in Central America enjoy the expected advantages of lax regulation and tax breaks, but—unlike what they would find in India or the Philippines—they net these benefits from a location and time zone more accessible to US markets. Call centers in Guatemala also have a constantly replenished supply of bilingual workers. The United States Immigration and Customs Enforcement (ICE) policy toward Guatemalans—it deported nearly 55,000 Guatemalans in 2019 alone—might as well moonlight as an employment service for euphemistically named offshore "contact centers" looking to hire English speakers.[28] Every day undocumented young people embark "removal flights" destined for Guatemala City, often after spending the majority of their lives in the United States. No small thanks to this deportation economy, the influx of call-center business to Guatemala threatens to outpace itself. To keep up with hiring trends, the Guatemalan Alliance of Exporters (AGEXPORT) has collaborated with the Guatemalan Ministry of Education to prepare high school graduates to enter this workforce. Young adults in their twenties who speak intermediate English can enroll in a government-subsidized ten-week program—named "Finishing School"—that trains them to converse at call-center standard, emphasis on ostensibly neutral pronunciation. They then complete guaranteed internships with participating business process outsourcing (BPO) firms. Interns promoted into formal jobs will earn pay at double to triple the country's official minimum wage.[29] Pitched to underemployed young adult deportees, the line is this: you could make $1,000 per month. Pitched to multinational corporations, the line is this: you could have a full-time employee for $1,000 per month. Yes.[30]

If you are searching for the ground zero of neoliberal service economies, look no further than the multinational call center.[31] Try to imagine yourself working in a cubicle somewhere ten and twelve hours per day, required—at pain of your lost income—to consistently address angry, abusive strangers in a tone of polite deference. Many of the people to whom you are required to defer will interrogate you about your country of origin and spew venom at you when, reading from a script, you chirp back that you are so very sorry but your company's parent company's return policy does not cover that particular item. This is not even the worst thing. The worst thing is that you will spend your days on the phone with people who have the things you cannot have, who live in the place you cannot live, and whose police may have arrested, jailed, and ultimately expelled you to a country whose global-entry-passport-holding elites tell you that you are lucky to work inside this living dystopia of the network service economy. This is a great job: you should be happy about it. You should say yes to it. You should express your agreement even with the customers who subject you to verbal abuse because, after all, their business is your income. So now, in the folksy accent that you worked so hard to hone, you know what to say: Is there anything else I can help you with, sir? No? Well, we appreciate your business. Have a great day!

. . . . . .

My interlocutors at Hope Connection had devised a research project with what looked like an opposite motive to the one that is typical of capitalist humanitarian reform. They hunted not for yes but for no. *No, I do not feel fully satisfied with the service I am currently receiving. No, I do not feel that my loan officer respects me. No, I do not feel that my life has improved since entering the loan program.* That they sought these statements, to the extent that they were considering adding contact center fees to their budget, indicated the value of the nos. What was that value?

Recall the director's fear: there was an honesty problem. Her concern rested on the credulity of women in the loan programs, as opposed to the larger credibility of the financial institution itself. To the extent that clients might have been hiding their possible grievances from the accounting staff, the social impact team worried that this trend spelled trouble for the whole organization. HC has premised its entire institutional identity on supporting women's empowerment. When they went after new market shares, it was in the name of empowering women. When they rolled out a new financial literacy module, it was with that goal in mind. Where did this empowerment reside if not in their clients' capacity to identify and articulate their own interests? What did it mean that they might be hiding their true thoughts from the very people who believed so much in their voice?

Try again. A battery of questions extracts a self-accounting. The account must always be of what you lack. This recitation of what you do not have— household appliances, electricity, indoor plumbing, a job, a feeling of satisfaction toward the bank, a gratifying relationship with your creditor—is the prerequisite for knowing and saying what you do want. No, I do not have a refrigerator. Yes, I want a refrigerator. No, I do not like my credit officer. Yes, I want a credit officer whom I like. Or, better: yes, I *want* to like my credit officer. I want an attachment to him. Always him. The first question incites internal consternation and brings it to enunciation; the second question turns the first into an affective bind between you and the institution that promises to correct your problem and fill the empty space within you.

......

Where is the hunt for yes? It is anywhere that anyone is learning to want the conditions of her compulsion and anywhere that this desire is being transmuted into the newest positive addition to the archive of capital. Which is to say: it is after you, and it is in you.

You are the target of the hunt for yes. You crunch data in an open-platform shop furnished with beanbags, round-the-clock snacks, and in-house yoga, amenities that sustain your ninety-hour-per-week grind. You sign up for the flex plan and accept the grant to trick out your own home office. You inventory your values on a political constituent survey and, when the election rolls around a few months later, you choose your favorite Wall Street candidate. You leave the wildcat building occupation and accept an invitation to serve on your institution's special committee on diversity and inclusion, from which you now address your proposals to the governing board. You let your commodity indulgences be led by how likely they are to spark incremental improvements in someone else's plantation existence. You bristle at the alternatives: the hundred-hour-per-week job without snacks, no vote at all, no option to work from your couch, open institutional hostility to diversity, overtly exploitative products. You are critical but grateful to your governing institutions' efforts. What you have is not a bad existence. You are learning to love its freedom.

You are on the hunt for yes. You urge a disaffected colleague to document each instance of harassment and file the dossier with the same bureaucracy that empowers her tormenters. You announce bonuses for the firm's hourly employees while crossing your fingers that they'll tolerate you and your colleagues' bullshit for another twelve months. You order a ride share, guiltily aware of the company's horrific labor record, and ask your driver friendly questions about her day. You know that none of this is enough. This does not stop you from seeking some assurance of your goodness amid the violence that you cannot help but keep inflicting.

You think: maybe I should just get out. I will find radical, queer, fugitive freedom. The hunt for yes follows you there. You articulate your no to the institution that governs you: the bank, the school, the prison, the development agency, the family, the corporation, the hospital, the city—and at this very moment your protest becomes eligible for addition to its archive. You think that you have evaded capture, but the reply comes too fast: *Pursue your freedom here. No? You said no? We thought you would say that. Everybody says that. No problem. Over-compliance concerns us. We prefer honesty. You said no. It's as good as yes. You didn't mean it that way? No problem. You identified your interests. Or we extracted them. Whatever. No problem. They're on our list of acquisitions. They're on their way to our archive. Our archive is here to include.*

Ongoing.
She created humans.

Sometimes I resent my brother for taking the out first. Add that to the list of lost things. Even if I wanted that end, I couldn't do it. "I can't die," I told my mechanic after my brakes gave out last week. "My mother would never recover." She told me to say that, acting as if I don't already know that she won't recover.

Sometimes she asks me when I am going to fall in love and "give" her babies. This is the actual wording. She became more persistent after Mark died. Less than forty-eight hours after his body had been shipped to the Waukesha County morgue, my aunt walked in on my mom draped over the kitchen counter, wailing that she had just lost one out of her three chances for grandchildren. "You have to have babies," she sobbed to me later that week, "and name the first-born Mark." I gazed over her head at two paintings of dancing vegetables, the first prints my parents had bought for themselves, back when we were a young family transplanted from Minnesota and Mark thought that adults were teasing us when they spoke in southern accents. "Or if it's a girl," she considered, "Maria."

I left the room. Was she really going to respond to my brother's death by telling me to have children? Not only was it way too early for this sort of healing impulse, but the entire conceit assumed the reparative value of childbirth. I could already see the paint-by-numbers narrative coming together: a bereft mother grieves her lost child; she experiences his death as her failure as a caregiver and a person (because those are the same); she descends into a masochistic spiral, refusing food, comfort, and care; she revisits prayers and hymns that she knows by heart; she finds within them the trace of a resurrection promise; and—now—she witnesses grace in the form of a new life that opens a new chapter for the once-broken family. It wasn't that this sequence was conscious; it was that it was the overwhelming script for articulating feminine grief. It was that it would kill her.

......

She brought up grandchildren again in December 2017. The phone rang as I was walking to a book-launch celebration on the other side of campus. The author had graduated from the Yale doctoral program in American religious history about seven years earlier. Then, two years after that, she killed herself. Her colleagues had shepherded her incomplete, and by all accounts brilliant, manuscript to press. Topic: evangelical Christian business tycoons during the Great Depression.

I expected that the event would throw off whatever footing I'd established in the months since my brother died. But when the night came, I second-guessed my plan to skip. It would look unprofessional to miss an event this relevant to my research. At some point my legs drifted from my alcove in the stacks, across the campus green, toward the Hall of Graduate Studies, and into the familiar second-floor room, less by choice than by magnetic pull. The drill-sergeant alibis for why I "had" to go didn't extinguish the truth I had yet to recognize, which is that I had a stake in her memory.

Not that I'd ever met her. She died the same year I'd wrapped up my master's degree. The loss registered as a news item on the small subfield-specific blogs I read, set to become one more quickly sublimated red flag about the casualties of academic precarity. But my mind circled back to her once I arrived in New Haven. The more I learned about the graduate program, the more elaborate my attachment became to who this alumna might have been. I wished I knew what had driven her to such a hopeless place. There was a lot I wanted to ask her. How did she interface with the union? What was her take on mentoring conventions in our department? Did she let herself cry at writing group? Did she go to the karaoke parties, and, if so, how much alcohol did she allow herself once she was there? To what extent did her emotional stability ride on attention from the charismatic geniuses who supervised us? Did she ever want to be them? Contemplating these questions now, I realize how her figure was my projection screen for working out the desires of which I felt most ashamed, these competitive and self-hating instincts that I usually attributed to the institution's manufactured scarcity but feared had been inside me all along. What could a place like this do to a person like her?

I made my way up the stairs, half-listening to my mother as she continued to talk: "When are you going to give me grandbabies?" Five years steeped in queer theory had primed me against the implicit Christian theological tropes attached to secular conventions around reproductive natality. The Christian story features a teenager becoming non-consensually pregnant with God's child, who grows up to be crucified at the hands of an imperial state. God resurrects his son in a sign of divine grace strong enough to overcome death's so-called curse. Christians will detect this template everywhere. They will envision rebirth when the dark cold gives way to a blooming spring. Liberation theologians have construed murdered revolutionaries as martyrs resurrected in a spirit of resistance against injustice. Some evangelicals crucify their sinful natures to be reborn into a redeemed family of God. Then there are philosophical and literary works that reiterate this plot structure in less conscious ways, so baked into the grammar of Western modernity is the death-and-redemption telos. Once you notice the pattern, it's hard to unsee. Needless to say, I was not enthused about becoming the figural vessel for my brother's symbolic rebirth. And insofar as it would be unfair to portray my mom's grandchild aspiration as a literal replacement theory, I still didn't consider my potential reproductivity a valid answer to our grief.

I bit my tongue, said good-bye, and slipped into a wood-paneled room with green and maroon carpet. The panelists were midway through a game of academic inside baseball. One of them had questioned the utility of another historical study of the affinities between evangelical Christianity and American capitalism. Hadn't their relationship been established? Was this historical research worth doing at all? Maybe the author's meticulous archival culling was "Like placing / pebbles exactly / where they were / already. The / steadiness it / takes . . . and / to what end?"[1] These words, harsh and generous and addressed to the author's grieving friends and octogenarian ex-teachers, might as well have been a blowtorch hurled into the crowd. I took my seat just as the factions began to close ranks—read: endowed chairs rising to spit laments to lost historicist rigor—when the author's cohort mate intervened. "If she were here," this colleague cried, "we would all be *laughing*. Because *she* was someone who *laughed*."

It takes only one person to open the floodgates. The mother spilled next: her girl had been a genius, the most unique person, smiling all the time, the literal incarnation of compassion. One of the emeritus historians waxed poetic about the scholar's fascination with a certain Yale-specific fraternity game named after a part of the urinary tract. Did we realize that *he* had actually played bladderball as a Yale undergraduate, back in the male-only days? Could we believe that he, an avowed emissary of "Old Yale," would attract interest from a *person like her*? When the author's adviser tried to interject—*hold up, her project was about critiquing Yale's elitist culture of masculinity that marginalized her as a quee*—she got drowned out in the ramble of a law professor who had hired the deceased historian as a research assistant. "Amid all the tribalism we are living in today," this juris doctor decreed, "she created HUMANS out of the archives she found" and showed "empathy for the other despite how those others *stood in relation to her.*" I gaped at the mascara-smeared faces of so many young scholars who had known her and wished we could make bets on how many times somebody would allude to the author's queerness without naming it. "AND I JUST WANT TO ADD!" shouted the bladderball man, who had not yet taken his seat, "she was a SPARKLY PERSON. Just SPARKLY." The mother, still sobbing in the front row, collapsed into the arms of her companion.

. . . . . .

Empathy, happiness, sparkle: the qualities rang a bell. This was also how many of us in Mark's biological family counted our loss or—this is more accurate— managed not to see it coming and failed to admit its cause.

It wasn't all wrong. *Depressed* does not capture the ten-year-old practicing bebop riffs on his trumpet from the backseat on the fourteen-hour family road trip. *Psychotic* misses the pensive transfer student in the oversized wool sweater who carries mugs of ginger-lemon tea to class and logs every encounter in a micro-notebook so that he can greet people by name when they crossed paths again. *Manic* can't sum up the liberal arts graduate on track to become a nurse, the perfect mobile gig for a sensitive guy hoping to follow his hip-hop collaborators wherever the scene seemed most promising. Yes, he bottomed out of his Plan A college, but that was an elitist cesspool with a substandard student affairs division. Yes, he'd floundered in his prerequisite biology coursework, but what artist doesn't take detours? Yes, there was concern that he was experiencing some delusions, but this was probably because he'd overdone it on the weed last night. Don't say suicide. Say accident. Don't say we knew. Say family heals. Say it was all good until, in a flash, it wasn't.

"No! He was my happy boy! He was my happy boy!" Seventy-two hours after Mark's death and twenty-four hours after my mother had inveigled me to make him my firstborn's namesake, I wandered into our living room to find her wailing into the landline. *Fuck*, I breathed. On the other end of that line was either a telemarketer who had no clue what she'd just opened up, or a police investigator who did. Nobody else used the house number. I snatched the phone from my mom's hand, stormed back upstairs, and snarled into the receiver: *What do you want?*

A deputy sighed back at me, like she'd endured this same scene a thousand times. "We need to rule out foul play, and we can't do that until we have a motive," she apologized. "Was your brother... depressed? Your mom..."

I understood my role: myth-bust his happy normativity. If I answered the right way, they would release the body to our family, close the file on whatever unlucky trucker had been behind that wheel, and leave my mother alone. I didn't even have to lie. Yes, he was depressed. Yes, it was a suicide. Yes, there were signs. Yes, I am sure.

......

I know I'm not supposed to judge the grieving for their processes. Everyone has their own experience of loss. That's what the loveliest of humans, the ones who baked us casseroles and who remember the anniversary year after year, always say. But I do fault people for how they grieve, and I think you should, too, if not for the feelings themselves then for how the causes and consequences of those feelings tend to get a political pass, how they insulate lived experience from critique and underwrite dubious recovery projects whether or not they're conscious of it.

I inherit my standards from my mom (this is a compliment to her). After Mark died, she announced a race for what we called the "Consolation Prize." It involved ranking the most gratuitously bad attempts at comfort. The third-place prize, awarded in part on the basis of its repetition, went to the colleague who on a near-daily basis harangued her, "You can't walk around sad forever! You have to reclaim your *joy*!" The second-place prize was clinched by the man who approached mom at a meeting of Presbyterian clergy, rested his hands on her shoulders, and said, "Mark lived exactly the perfect amount of days. Not a day longer or shorter than he should have. He died precisely at the right time. I want you to believe that." The same guy went on to use the figure of speech, "I'd rather get run over by a truck," multiple times over the course of a day in her presence. The grand prize went to the person who, after he overheard my mom say something about her boy being at peace now, felt moved to inform her that she, a minister, should know better. It was possible, after all, that Jesus had remanded her boy to Hell. "Whatever the Lord's judgment, we trust in its righteousness," he boomed, patting her back. "The Lord is always righteous."

The Lord's judgment has nothing on mine. Neither does my mother's. I am making an inventory of all of the worst ways to express grief. Where do you even start? There was Achilles, who responded to the death of his boyfriend by slaughtering thousands of people on the battlefield, then revenge-murdering the perpetrator and dragging his corpse around Troy on the back of a chariot.

There was God, whose grief at the scale of sin prompted him to commit genocide on the planet, except for Noah and his cherry-picked companions, with a catastrophic flood. Then there are the less mythical examples. I'd nominate anyone who ever cited the death of John McCain or Ronald Reagan or any other war-criminal statesman to silence popular dissent or valorize "civility." I'd dedicate a whole category to the generational traumas used to justify military occupation, apartheid, and racist state-building. I'd file it next to the bracket that tracks the mass-commodification of loss: breast-cancer ribbons and the tyrannical optimism they inflict on the sick, designer T-shirts emblazoned with the latest victim of police murder, rainforest-certified products by companies that dump tons of wildlife-murdering carbon into the air. Any grief memoir that effaces its political context. Any grief memoir that is the preface to an advice manual for corporate executives. Any grief memoir that ends in a nationalist credo. Any grief memoir that derives closure from new babies. Any and all grief that imposes normativity on the most endangered of the dead: the queer, the mad, the disconsolate, the extreme, the uncompromising, the lost.

hope for the future 6

REPRODUCTIVE LABOR IN THE
NEOLIBERAL MULTICULTURAL FAMILY

What qualifies a person for credit? The question preoccupies people who seek to broaden the reach of financial infrastructure to populations without prior exposure to its audit and qualification processes. Put in bureaucratic terms: How should bankers assess individual risk in the absence of formal rating agencies? The first time I heard someone raise this issue, it was for the purposes of instructing non-experts in alternative evaluation techniques. Imperious at the front of a hotel meeting room in western Guatemala, the executive director of microfinance institution Capital for Change (CFC) held court over an audience of ten international travelers. We had come there as part of what CFC advertised interchangeably as a "poverty tour" and a "social-action adventure tour" of the region, its privation, and the finance-based solutions to the latter.

It was day 3. I'd spent the night awake with a low-grade fever and a body spangled in itchy red sores, I assumed from a bedbug infestation in either this hotel or our previous one. It didn't seem worth mentioning. As far as I was concerned, the single rooms, decent internet, and made-to-order breakfasts were already extravagant perks on a trip to a region where 70 percent of the population lived below the national poverty line.[1] I'd asked the front-desk attendant about who typically stays in this hotel. "People like you," he'd answered, "they come to do business with the bank." He thought for a moment. "Also missionaries." I despised the idea that I could be compared with either of these groups—and then was repelled by my instinct to disassociate—so I shrugged off the bites. I popped an antihistamine and headed downstairs for chilaquiles. No need to hold up our day, which I had been told would be jam-packed with home visits to local beneficiaries of CFC financing.

I arrived in our eat-and-meet boardroom just as the executive director interrupted the small talk to deliver an unsolicited diagnosis: our group demonstrated a weak grasp of the nuts and bolts of "pro-poor investing." We required an "orientation to microfinance" before we saw it in action. Microcredit, she explained while the rest of us ate, refers to the practice of issuing small, short-cycle loans to people who otherwise would be ineligible for financial services. She reviewed major keystones in its rise as a development strategy, including the lionization of Grameen Bank founder Muhammad Yunus and the budding revelation among aid organizations that poor people needed financing to "smooth" their income over the course of a business cycle. Then she arrived at today's puzzle: "How do we know the credit risk of someone who has never had a bank account and doesn't even know what a credit score *is*? What qualifies them for credit?"

One dramatic pause later, she was answering on our behalf. "There are three criteria," she announced. "First, talent. Does the person have a marketable skill that they can use to start a business? Second, social support and accountability. Does the person have a community that will pressure her to pay back the loan? Third, and most important, positive attitude. Does the person believe that she can overcome poverty? Does she have hope for the future?" Converted into quantities by the bank, these characteristics become the basis for determining an alternative credit score.

. . . . . .

Talent, accountability, and positive attitude: it's a convenient summary of what capitalist humanitarian reform looks to cultivate in target populations across scales of intervention. So resonant is this speech-act with the background din of late capitalism that I could almost pass it over as one more instance of the prosperity grit preached everywhere, from employee handbooks to self-help literature for single women to fitness magazines to manuals on overcoming addiction to every TED Talk ever performed. But I want to argue that the prosaic quality of the director's remarks that merits scrutiny. Over just a few sentences, she managed to sum up the biopolitical disciplines of late capitalism in terms of an aspirational mandate to anyone who seeks status within its domain. The question, "What qualifies a person for credit?" unfurled into the yes-or-no litmus test, "Does she have hope for the future?" A discussion of abstract geopolitical development strategy became a prescription for pointillist surveillance of people's everyday lives and labors.

The command to hope can be a tall order when poverty, vigilante violence, environmental catastrophe, and a selectively absent state are the stuff of everyday life. Against this bleak backdrop, capitalist humanitarianism holds out a cure for the suffering body: the next generation of laboring subjects. Scholars of gender and sexuality will be unsurprised to hear that conscripted performances of "hope for the future" coagulate around the bodies of children and families. One does not have to spend much time cruising the literature of humanitarian finance programs to observe that, when the hope question comes knocking, there is a surefire formula for response, and it involves invoking the "next generation" as the motive for pursuing greater prosperity.[2] By trafficking in the symbolic power and material labors of children, a pedagogy of neoliberal hope attempts to annex intimate practices of care and kinship for their untapped wells of monetized value.

The association of credit, future, and the next generation recasts institutions of capital production and labor expropriation as a ground zero of social reproduction. When capitalist humanitarian pedagogies of the future take hold in their various institutional locales—the bank, the home, the factory, the hotel, the tour vans shuttling between them—they test the limits of theories that describe neoliberalism as the subjection of all social demands to a bare economic calculus. From the window of the tour bus, I could almost see the inverse of what Michelle Murphy has termed "the economization of life" and what Wendy Brown has described as the figuration of "human beings... as 'human capital' across all spheres of life."[3] On display was less the creep of finance capital into the fabric of a formerly autonomous social than the revaluation of finance capital and offshoring ventures as sites of reproductive care. Capitalist humanitarian reform imposes on the burned-over present an interpretive scheme in which the children of the global South are fostered by and then adopted into the family of neoliberal labor. The social-action adventure tour exhibited this discourse at three sites of its concentration: the articulation of genealogical inheritance as a principle of inheriting labor, the figuration of the off-shored workplace as an alternative maternal caregiver, and the celebration of the racialized and suffering child as the body through which the present's broken promises may yet be redeemed.

Care, Maintenance, and Reproduction

First stop: the bank. We drove two blocks up the street to a two-story concrete building that from the front resembled a shoebox blown up and turned on its side. A fleet of company-owned motorcycles crowded the front parking lot, ready for the credit officers who would ride them to clients' homes that day. Winding the bikes' maze to the door, we entered a cream-colored lobby where women waited in bright plastic chairs for service. Nearly every surface, from the windows to the notepads, displayed what I recognized as one of the twenty glyphs from the Maya astrological calendar. Projected onto a mounted screen in a conference room upstairs, its neon greens, reds, and yellows cast a tint onto our bodies as we settled in for a presentation from the bank's vice president who, by way of welcome, informed us that this sign was the official company logo. The founders selected it to honor the bank's indigenous clients and their unique cosmovision. The ceremonial component of the calendar, he told us, is divided into twenty periods of thirteen days, each of which corresponds to a set of character traits, an energetic tone, and an elemental or animal spiritual guide. The bank chose to honor the calendar's eighth cycle because of its associations with "fertility, wealth, and abundance." Under the sign of the Q'anil, or seed, the bank nurtured the agricultural economy and harvested prosperity from native ground.

The vice president walked us through typical MFI practices used to achieve these goals: targeting women, filtering transactions through sex-segregated "solidarity groups," and mandating financial literacy lessons for all clients. But this bank added another, rarer, perk of participation and compliance. Not only did clients receive training in budgeting and marketing—they also had exclusive access to the MFI's medical clinic, which was equipped to treat all manner of minor illnesses and which specialized in family planning. "They can deposit into their savings accounts and pick up a prescription right here in the bank," the vice president boasted. "It's important for women to know about the consequences of childbirth. How are you going to get out of poverty if you have ten children to feed?" His quip sat awkwardly alongside their next program of focus: the youth entrepreneurship program, which, in exchange for a fee, trained borrowers' children in budgeting and business-development skills. The slide show ended with testimonials from the women clients. They smiled out from their photos, posing with their kids or their work materials, and gave testimonies: *Because of microcredit, I can give my children a better life; my investments in my business have improved life for my family; I hope one day to send my children to university.* Over and over, these slides framed social impact in terms of how clients were now able to imagine future upward mobility for their children.

Alone at the corner of the table, mindlessly picking at my inflamed skin, I was still wrapping my head around the clinic: the *bank* ran it? Who in this room would choose to have their finances and health care bound up in the same institution, in the same building? I dragged my fingernails through one of my welts and registered blood streaming down my leg. *Shit*, I mumbled, adjusting my jacket to hide the gore.

......

It was my first but by no means last encounter with a microfinance program that invested in the clinical management of women's reproductive lives, even as it mobilized rhetorics of children in "the next generation" for feel-good blurbs and proof of creditworthiness. These two discourses sound contradictory. Mothers hear that their children are hope for the future, but their children are also the chain that keeps them bound to the present situation. A child is a potential credit until and unless that child becomes an actually existing debt. One could almost read it as two kinds of strategic messaging, with the child-as-hope line used to pull external support and the child-as-debt line a means of internal discipline of the actual clients. But the messages are more connected than that. They converge in how they manage the reproductive lives of women and girls.

Capitalist humanitarian organizations use health care as both an incentive for engagement and a means of intimate surveillance.[4] From the common obligation to attend parenting and birth control seminars to the free checkups for loan program enrollees to medical clinics literally run out of microbanks, these initiatives have been multiplying ever since Muhammad Yunus's Grameen Bank required loan-program borrowers to "keep our families small" and use contraceptives.[5]

No doubt, medical programs respond to a need. Accessible health care is tough to come by in Guatemala. Navigating a stratified and privatized system, people seeking medical support choose between two bad options: to roll the dice on a perpetually broken public hospital system or to absorb the fees levied by private doctors. Nonprofit mission and development organizations have long tried to fill some of these gaps with lower-fee mobile clinics, medical mission trips, and preventive health education in underserved areas. These programs are increasingly housed under the auspices of financial institutions.

One of the country's largest MFIs, which lends exclusively to women, dispenses pap smears to active borrowers. The bank collaborates with a US-based health humanitarian agency to dispatch a traveling nurse on an annual trip to each town that has a solidarity group or bank branch. Once there, the nurse offers group instruction on sexual health, followed by individual cervical cancer screenings with women. All of this takes place in one of the borrower's homes. An outgoing employee disclosed that the MFI had launched the program as a cheap client-retention tool. Women became eligible for medical care only after they complete two nine- to twelve-month loan cycles, in which month-by-month interest payments added up to approximately 35 percent APR. This was not the only reason that the pap smear program was all but guaranteed to pay for itself. The MFI expected that it would draw women into its new credit product: one for medical debt.[6]

Insofar as these programs fill a demonstrated void in care, it's important to remember that this demand was never inevitable. It was created in large part by decades of International Monetary Fund austerity measures and neocolonial governance that annihilated any semblance of a social safety net, leaving foreign finance capital to step in.[7] Capitalist humanitarian pedagogies that would instill personal resilience and the will to "overcome" poverty exacerbate the problem insofar as they transfer responsibility for health outcomes to individual persons enduring baseline untenable material conditions. The message is this: check yourself for breast cancer (your bank taught you how, and it has a credit program for treatment if you test positive), reduce your sugar consumption (disregard the contamination of local water supplies and the widespread availability of carbonated sugar), schedule regular checkups (at the clinic housed in your bank), and limit your family size (while performing hope in your children). Health care can be attached to the bank insofar as health itself can be articulated as personal asset and future investment.

Women's reproductive lives are in the crosshairs of these reforms because of how their reproductive lives matter for future labor pools. Michelle Murphy has detailed how neoliberal development turns reproduction into a frontier of capital optimization, which operates on the biopolitical mandate that "some lives must not be born so that future others may live more abundantly/consumptively."[8] Thwarted births are considered imperative to the survival of the family and the dreams of its children. The message from capitalist humanitarians in Guatemala is that indigenous women should have enough children to support the family's relative social mobility, but not so many or so few that ratio of labor to capital tilts too far out of balance. Women are to optimize their childbearing in a way that prefigures their, and their children's, smoothest adoption into the regimes of production that will sustain their current lives. Thus, whereas it is common to claim that neoliberalism transforms the biological family—as well as friendships, civic service, and education—into sites of calculated investment and return, it is equally the case that capitalist humanitarianism, as one expression of neoliberalism, transforms the boundaries of the social. Not only does it remake the biological family as a site of economic activity,[9] it also, and more pointedly, revalues indebted labor as the foundation of social reproduction and cultural endurance.[10] It is not just that women are instructed to imagine family as a domain of investment. It is that, because of the bank's intervention into maternal life, children can be adopted as subjects of its capitalist care.

. . . . . .

"Are you bleeding?" A tour mate, the teen daughter of a CFC board member, had spotted my mangled leg. I whispered something about bug bites that look uglier than they feel, and our local host overheard. "You should go to our clinic!" he exclaimed, rushing over. He was serious; their in-house clinician could see me right away. My protests were ignored. The CFC executive director endorsed the plan—I assume she wanted to see the clinic herself—and pressed her hand to my shoulder. They marched me back through the motorcycles and into another lobby, which copycatted the earlier one: bare registration desk, line of chairs for women waiting to be seen, and walls decked with posters, in this case of the FDA food pyramid. I glared at the floor while the small crowd of patients sized up our little brigade; I imagined they were curious why one of the bank's top dogs was escorting a random white foreigner to the front of their line. The doctor waved me into her consult room and handed me a gown as I tried to convey in broken medical Spanish that I didn't feel that sick, I didn't need to take away time from other people, and bedbugs are not a big deal. When my attempts went nowhere—I was probably not communicating well—I altered my strategy. It seemed clear that objections would add to the spectacle; I just needed to get through this so that we could all continue with the day. So I undressed and submitted to her exam. She was businesslike, quick. Then I noticed the syringe. "This will help you," she stated, dabbing my thigh with an alcohol-soaked cotton ball. The needle pinched my leg before I could ask what the vial contained. "Bueno," the doctor approved, slapping a bandage on me, "Que te sientas mejor." She waved me out.

It took five years for me to mention this experience to anyone. I still feel residual mortification when I remember it—the way I'd taken the spotlight, sucked up scarce medical resources, failed to set a firm boundary. I also persuaded myself that the visit was irrelevant to the rest of what I saw on the tour that day. So many other people had it worse than I did. Still, it bears asking: if I could find myself wrapped up in this scene, from a position of relative power, how vulnerable were others to medical intrusions that they neither asked for nor understood? I'm certain that I wasn't the only person in that waiting room with rocky Spanish. But it is possible that I was the only one whose reproductive health was not under the financial institution's clinical surveillance.

Inheritance, Genealogy, Labor

Finally, we were back in the van. Our guide announced from the passenger seat that our next stop would be the home of a borrower who had used working-capital loans to grow his weaving business. We drove an hour over bumpy, washed-out terrain, parked on the side of a dirt road, and walked single file up a side path to a door. One of the financiers knocked. No answer. The financier knocked again. We waited a few more minutes. A man in jeans and a faded polo finally cracked the door, eyes widening as he registered our crowd of capris-clad gringos loitering in his front garden. His credit officer introduced us as supporters of the bank who had come to Guatemala to learn about microfinance and who were very interested in seeing his handiwork. The weaver shook his head, "Ah, well, this isn't a good day for that," he apologized, "I just sent off a big order, so there isn't anything to show you." It wasn't the right answer for the creditor. "There isn't *anything* you can show us?" They argued back and forth, and although I could hear only snippets, the fact of our ongoing presence in the yard indicated that the credit officer did not intend to take "no" for an answer. After a few minutes, they settled something. The weaver reentered his house, closed the door, and a few beats later swung it back open. He stepped backward to let the thirteen of us inside.

A foot loom dominated the room. Its wooden skeleton stood a half meter taller than the tallest man on the tour. Threads snaked through vertical and horizontal rods attached to the frame. To weave, a person would press a foot pedal, adjust the position of the rods and the thread, and then repeat the motion. In this case, the person working the loom was a child who I guessed was eleven or twelve years old. It was fast, whole body labor. She extended her leg for the pedal, stretched to adjust a rod, pumped the pedal again, moved another rod, on infinite replay. The man introduced this child as his daughter. I surveyed the rest of the space—the terrace where a woman cooked on an open fire, the suspended bedsheet that separated the family's sleeping space from the living area—and wondered how many US nationals had imposed on this home before us.

Someone in our group requested a tour of the house, so our reluctant host led us into a side room taken up by two more foot looms that were occupied by two more kids. Our questions tumbled out. We had been encouraged to ask whatever came to mind, but the morning orientation gave coordinates to our inquiries: *When did you enter the loan program? How have you applied the money? How has it changed your life? How many loan cycles have you completed? Do you pay on time? Do you have hope for the future?* The substance of our interrogation had been reverse-engineered from the answers we already expected this field trip to confirm—answers that reflected his gratitude for the business opportunity, his compliance with the bank's accounting mechanisms, and his desire to share his traditions with us and to pass them to his children. There had been ample opportunities to revise this script; the man under our microscope had made a formidable bid to temper our presumptions when he wavered at the door. But the bank officer balked, and when we didn't just walk away, our tour group conspired in blocking the man's attempt to say no. The tiny bump in the day didn't redirect the arc of the story, at least not in any immediate sense. We got inside the house; we asked our questions. Our expectations retained their freight even against the explicit assertion they were misplaced. *I have nothing to show you*, he'd said.

His protest, in retrospect, was kind of a weak one. We were not primarily there to buy anything or even to look at his textiles. The main commodity we were after was the spectacle of the loan recipient and his hopeful self-narration. The weaver, in any case, withheld his full participation. He attempted to control access to his house. The credit officer tacitly reminded him that his sovereignty over his space was contingent on his good standing with the bank. The retort *I have nothing to show you* rang as an indictment of the rotten exchange that our group offered him, as in *I'm not about to perform for you if there is no chance of you actually buying something from me*. The banker's impatient *You really don't have anything?* could be a perturbed *What are you doing that you don't have anything?* It could be a stressed middle manager's *Please, dude, just do me this favor, my US boss is here supervising me, and I can't fuck it up*. It might just as well have been *I'm your credit officer*.

Now the slam, swish, slam, swish of the children's movements played background music as their father, the weaver, entertained our curiosity about his business. "Who taught you to weave?" the executive director asked once everyone else had finished their turn. "My father," the man answered. "Your father?" she responded, sounding incredulous. "Yes, my father," he repeated. She asked him who had taught his father to weave. "His father," he answered. Again, it was not the answer she expected. "His *father*?" I dug my fingernails into my bicep, willing her to back off. He affirmed that, yes, his grandfather taught his father to weave. "And who taught *his* father?" the director goaded. The answer remained the same. "Will you teach your sons?" He said yes. "The craft is passed down through the men in the family, then?" she confirmed. His one-word answer was still yes. She finally suspended the interrogation. She grinned, a bit maniacally I thought, at the man.

I strained to imagine why she would be so captivated by this pedagogical lineage. Maybe she was under the impression that men don't weave? On the contrary, men typically operate the foot loom. Women tend to work on the smaller and more mobile back-strap loom. If the director wanted to extract a testimony of gender transgression, she should have asked more sensible—although no less invasive—questions about how the man's daughter came to the skill. Nobody bothered to correct the misunderstanding. I had already concluded, maybe prematurely but nevertheless, that our group had come to find a story with a prefabbed plot. In the familiar capitalist humanitarian fable, the advent of finance capitalism catalyzes modern gender equality in countries that are ostensibly behind the liberal feminist ball. Examples of this rhetoric abound. Among the endorsements I've heard: microloans elevate women from a "traditional" sequestration in the home into "public" leadership within the community. When women earn a profit, they reinvest it in their business or spend it on their kids' schooling, whereas men blow it on liquor and gambling. "Gender lens" investment strategies, by isolating women as loan recipients, can shame shiftless men into economic productivity because they don't want their wives or sisters to outdo them.[11] I interpreted the executive director's grin as an extension of a discourse that counts reformed masculinity as positive collateral to women's empowerment. Or maybe it's not even that the men are collateral; maybe the empowered women were the means to their end. It wouldn't have to be intentional to be true.

Either way, the characterization of microfinance as a panacea for liberal gender norms relies on a creepy premise: women in the global South are a passive monolith who live in historical anachronism and who are whipped around by the whims of incompetent men, until a financial institution's white horse comes to rescue them into a more enlightened system of gender parity. Besides the fact that capitalist humanitarian appeals to women's "empowerment" tend to ignore local feminist and queer movements, they also reify the heteropatriarchal nuclear family as the telos of development intervention.[12] The goal of these interventions is not, say, to abolish the neocolonial family form or smash the capitalist system that blackmails the privatized family into acting as a substitute social safety net. The goal is to trigger the patriarch such that he returns to a provider role in a more disciplined and inclusive way. If he cooperates, then both women *and* men will be free to participate in the reproduction of surplus value for the bank. Both will be empowered to pass their labor to the children that they bear in just the right numbers.[13]

. . . . . .

The director's performance of confusion about gender roles was the minor note in her interaction with the weaver; the major element was when she asked him to rehearse his labor, and the labor of his children, as a matter of genealogical inheritance. It is significant that she stripped her words of any economic terminology. She asked not who taught the kids to *work* or about the pedagogies of *credit* but about the propagation of artisanal knowledge among the children who could carry it on. With generational inheritance as the governing lens, immediate and ongoing histories of colonial expropriation, financial austerity, and genocidal dictatorship could fade from focus. They could be overwhelmed by sentimental fawning over an "ancestral tradition" that the bank not only put on exhibit but also took credit for preserving, from the nuclear family unit to the global marketplace.

The director's line of questioning did not merely elide geopolitical context; it also formulated a practical theory of late capitalist kinship and care work. Her valorization of labor passed down through generations held uncanny resonance with a Christian theological discourse that figures salvation as a special inheritance set aside for the children of God.[14] In the theological narrative, to become a Christian is to be adopted out of one's family of birth and into a priestly lineage descending from (and returning to) a divine origin. *Yes, my father taught me.* One's position within the universal family of God overwrites previous social, national, racial, or gender designations and replaces them with the singular identity of *heir. Yes, I will teach my sons.* Thus, the historical arc of salvation is marked not in terms of years or months, not in terms of biological descent, but rather in terms of divine descent from adoptive fathers to adopted sons. The birth of the child to one parent or another might as well be irrelevant; what matters is that the child will be adopted into a universal family that supersedes her parochial and limiting family of origin.

If it feels as if we have ventured far into the weeds of biblical exegesis and that this is not the book you thought you were reading, hear me out: politicaltheological tropes of divine adoption are recurrent in capitalist humanitarian discourse. Instead of a Christian adoption out of ethnic particularity into the universal and redeemed family of God, now it is adoption out of historicalmaterial difference into the care of transnational, transcultural capital. The pivotal quality to notice is the symbolic supersession of local forms of kinship and collective organization—ones that, if riven with their own contradictions and conflicts, nevertheless might have tried to evade financial capture—by the free market's universal, multicultural, inclusive family. Now the finance bank doles out self-care advice for girls and guidance for new mothers. Now the factory provides after-school care. Now the universal family is the corporation, comprising any and all comers who accept the promise: no nation but your debit card.

Whether conceived as a sectarian road map to redemption or as a political-theological plot structure whose specific nouns can be traded in and out, this discourse of adoption and salvation rests on a questionable politics of gender and sexuality. When salvation is figured in terms of an adoptive family, as scholars of feminist and queer theology have shown, it is made unavailable to those outside of the patriarchal lineage.[15] The maternal—understood not only in a filial sense but also in the broader sense of socialization and interdependence—is denied any claim to property, power, and kin. If she bears a son, he'll be stolen away from her into a different line of patriarchal heirs. If she bears a daughter, that daughter eventually will be enfolded into the work of producing new subjects for the family of God—a family that depends on women's reproductive labor even as it remains invested in a different register of ritual reproduction.[16]

Humanitarian finance acknowledges that the household is a site for the production of surplus value. The crucial product, and the most sensitive to manage, is the future work force: human capital. Again: financial counselors encourage people to bear children in quantities that will maintain equilibrium in the labor market. These same credit officers then score parents on how convincingly they perform hope that the next generation can have a better—meaning more consumptive and credit-driven—life than what was previously available to them. Or if the material circumstances don't change, then at least there will be one thing left to hold onto: the cruel faith in that better horizon, even as it recedes again and again and again.

Generation, Children, Future

The final stop on the day's social-action adventure tour was a footwear factory. Our banker guides regaled us with its backstory on an hour-long journey through the most elevated, bumpy terrain yet. The owner of the enterprise launched it as a solo start-up with a $150 loan and, less than four years later, had grown it into a shoe-manufacturing business with forty employees. Unlike other microenterprises, which were run out of their founders' homes, this one had acquired commercial property near the center of town. One side of the street ran along a mountain's razor edge, which plunged downward to the farm plots and houses below. On the other side, a few children milled outside of a primary school, and sleepy bodegas advertised discounted sodas. We pulled to the side, unloaded, approached the door of the unmarked two-story building, and filed into a dim downstairs cluttered with furniture and tables. A staircase—more like a glorified ladder jutting out from a hole in the ceiling—descended into the middle of the room. Beneath those stairs, a woman hunched over a Bunsen burner. We passed her on our way to the steps, which led to a brighter room where about twenty people worked on a haphazard assembly line. Fabrics, shoe molds, and various cutting and measuring tools had spilled from crisscrossed tables onto a floor so cluttered with detritus that only about half of it was visible. I calibrated every step to avoid tripping, not least near the table with more open flames. Torn-out pages from an old swimsuit magazine issue decorated a segment of the wall. "Stressed?" asked a newsprint caption glued near one of the beach photos, "Masturbate! It will relax you." Less than a minute in, my surroundings had turned blurry. Were the glue fumes affecting my balance? Why were there no windows in here? I began a countdown for how long I could hold my breath, and only then did I register the youth of the workers themselves.

"They can go to school in the morning and then come to work to earn money," the founder explained over the noise. Their families needed the income, so they came here to paste together shoe parts, melt down globs of plastic, sew canvas, and thread laces through tiny holes. They also showed up to talk and laugh with their friends. The sounds of chatter clanged off the concrete walls. Two older men circled the room in apparent supervision of the production process, directing workers back to their tasks with a spoken reprimand or a physical touch on the shoulder. Our group fanned out to the extent that we could. The board member snapped photos. At no point did our group actually talk to the workers, except in those instances when certain tourists half-requested a person's consent to a photo and half-announced their intention to take one. They would nod, or sometimes giggle or make eye contact, and then return to whatever they had been doing before. I loitered by the exit and inhaled through my T-shirt. If I was heaving for breath, how were these workers faring? How were they working? And how would one even begin to describe this scene without sensationalizing it? Our leaders had prepared us to encounter a prize microenterprise developed by a guy who had started fixing shoes as a side gig out of his house and then grown into the biggest employer in town. They had brought us to a sweatshop.

Now, back in the van, my tour mates buzzed. "He's employing the youth of the community!" the board member said, scrolling through her trove of digital photos while her daughter peeked at them over her shoulder. "What a great opportunity for them," added another longtime donor to CFC.

I swallowed hard, trying not to unleash a tirade, and interjected with all the diplomacy I could muster, "I don't know. They looked pretty young. Did anyone have concerns about the air quality?" When my seat mate replied that

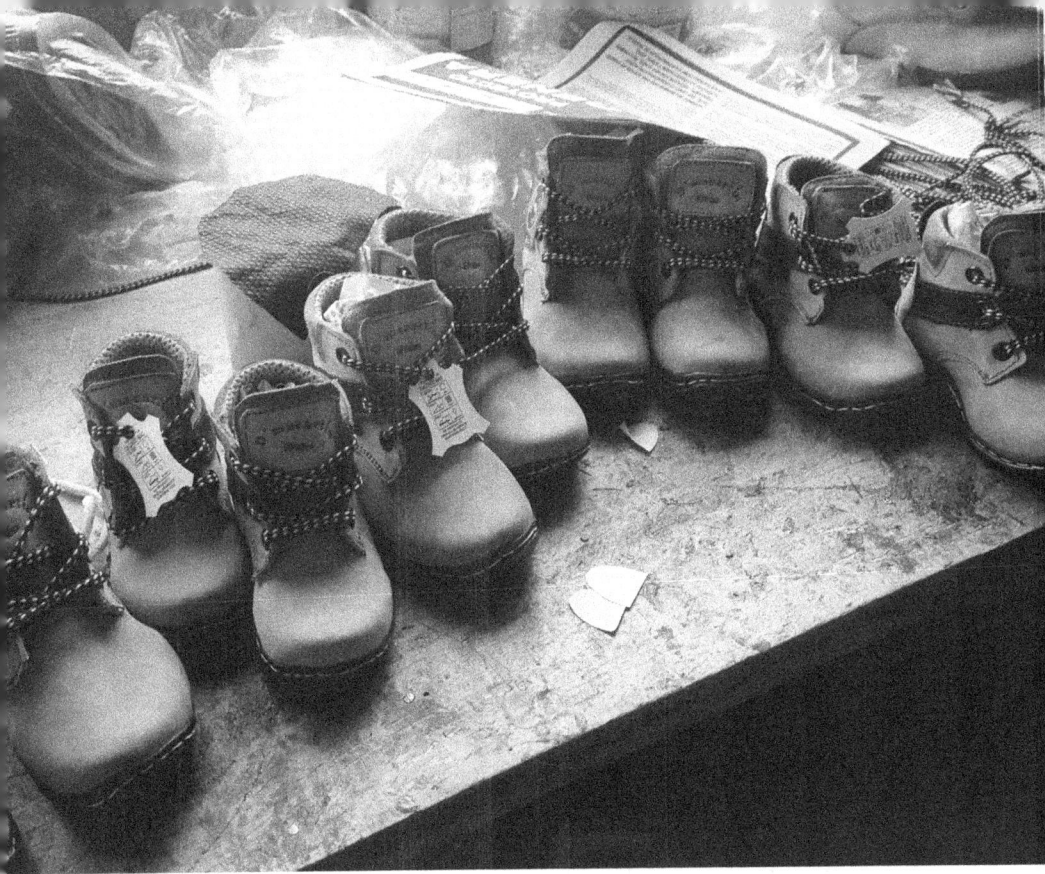

6.1 These shoes, sewn by child workers at the maquiladora that was the last stop on a commercial tour of microfinance initiatives in Guatemala, await their final product packaging.

it was messy and stuffy but seemed fine otherwise, I showed her the photo I'd taken of the masturbation quip. At the time I was confident that it would prove something about the bad working conditions. My neighbor, the adult daughter of the donor, raised her eyebrows and agreed that the display was "weird," but the director interrupted before any discussion could get traction. She told us that the factory was the best option that these kids had—not least because they were building skills and a record of work that would help them land more lucrative jobs in the future. It was like parallel universes. I saw sweatshop labor; she saw empowerment.

. . . . . .

Then it happened again. One year after the trip to the shoe factory, outside a café on a block of pastel-colored storefronts, I absorbed the testimony of a self-avowed "impact investor." He had left behind his job at a Wall Street brokerage firm and moved to Antigua to build a venture capital fund for Central American start-up companies. One by one, he had ticked off the current investments, until he arrived at his most recent partnership. "We are very excited," he shared between sips of his drink, "We just made a seed investment in a socially responsible maquiladora." I thought, first, that I had misheard. I liked this guy. From the moment we shook hands, he had regaled me with observations about new books on the history of capitalism. Had I read *Freaks of Fortune* by Jonathan Levy?[17] What about Bethany Moreton's monograph on the evangelical Christians behind Walmart?[18] He wanted to understand my intervention in the academic literature. When I told him what had been true at the time, that I want to know why "social investing" had boomed at the same time as the 2008 financial crash, he mused that it was probably because all the stockbrokers got laid off and needed another option: "Maybe you don't need a complex description! Ockham's razor!" I enjoyed him in spite of myself. So when he dropped the phrase *socially responsible maquiladora* as casually as he'd said *I'll have the strawberry-mango smoothie* half an hour ago, I assumed that it was a mistake. I'd seen a million enterprises slapped with the tagline "responsible," but never had I heard this term modify the word *sweatshop*.

Earlier I had asked the investor how he measured "impact," and he had reflected on how broad that definition can be. "Job creation" can be a form of social impact if the community is in poverty, he said. When I retorted that the current Republican Party construes the ultra-wealthy as "job creators" in order to justify cutting taxes for the rich and defunding public programs, he clarified that he wouldn't invest in "just any job." Simply having a job was not the same as having a good job, the kind of job that could support a decent standard of living for a person and their family. On this principle, at least, we sort of agreed.

Now he had raised the idea of a "socially responsible sweatshop," and I was again wary. "I know!" he exclaimed, still jocular in his bid to intercept my doubt. "How can a maquila be socially responsible?" To explain, he described his encounter with the founder during a conference in which regional entrepreneurs mixed with prowling investors. Her pitch evinced the radical improvements she had made over most maquilas. The working conditions were healthy and humane. For example, the space boasted natural light and good ventilation. Workers had access to a company store stocked with everyday necessities, which they could purchase on credit. Best of all, the business sponsored a youth employment program, in which unemployed minors were shepherded into open jobs. When my raised eyebrow betrayed an unspoken comeback that "company store" and "child labor" were generally not signs of ethical business practice, the investor assured me that the store priced its commodities fairly. Moreover, he continued, the factory staffed only young people who had no better options. The founder had headquartered her business—her *woman-owned* business—in a "severely underdeveloped" area of Honduras with these youth in mind. "These aren't kids in school," the investor clarified. "These are kids on the street, sniffing glue. Now they have a place to go." He wanted them to have that place.

. . . . . .

The figure of the laboring child has played a recurring role in debates over the best approach to economic regulation and social provision. Gilded Era progressives made soot-faced waifs toiling on assembly lines into the mascots of campaigns for workplace safety measures and minimum-age-of-employment laws. Cold War propaganda vested American national identity and moral exceptionalism in the private nuclear family, whose children went to school (instead of suffering in a Soviet labor camp) and returned home to cookies baked by their own mothers (instead of surviving on Moscow's rationed gruel). A distorted echo of these figures—industrial era urchin and communist child tragedy—carried over into the 1990s high tide of anti-NAFTA activism. From workshops at the World Social Forum to Students Against Sweatshops (SAS) chapters popping up on campuses around the world, Left organizers demanded that wider consumer publics confront the glassy-eyed, dirt-faced child laborers suffering for the sake of the global North's cheap luxuries. I cannot forget a middle-school social studies teacher who dedicated a day to studying the child labor scandal at Nike. We filled out a reading comprehension worksheet about a journalist who had paid $50 for his sneakers to be embroidered with a customized "tag." He had filled out the standard order form with his select phrase: *sweatshop*. But Nike refused to fill the request. It was "inappropriate slang," a spokesperson claimed.[19] Over a decade later, the director of Capital for Change used this same term to reprimand me for voicing concern about labor conditions at the shoe factory. "What you said was inappropriate," she admonished behind a closed door. "There are donors on this trip who *really care about women's empowerment*. Do not make them question our commitment to that." At some point the criticism of child labor had become more offensive than actual child labor.

The scandal was never what labor the children were or were not doing but what political formation their stylized images were being used to support. Lauren Berlant has written that the late twentieth-century fixation on rescuing the suffering child indexes an antipolitical fantasy that "a nation can be built across fields of social difference through affective identification and empathy." Against a notion of public life as a terrain of struggle and conflict, the difficult-to-oppose "movements" to save children "white out marks of hierarchy, taxonomy, and violence... central to public struggle over who should possess the material and cultural resources of contemporary national life."[20] Insofar as the iconized child laborer is a central totem of this "sentimental public sphere," she is also joined by a cast of figural dependents awaiting their own empowerment: the victim of sex-trafficking, the breast-cancer patient, the self-harming teenage girl, the global South entrepreneur who needs a microloan.[21] To criticize campaigns to liberate or at least help these subjects can feel almost unthinkable. Even if I tilt my head at the absence of historical or materialist analysis in branded movements to end sex trafficking or fund cancer research or raise awareness about suicide, I feel hesitant to be that jerk who disses them out loud. Are they really doing that much damage? What kind of person would be against these public projects?

Critique may be most necessary in circumstances that are most impervious to it. The traumatized child, says Berlant, is a powerful avatar for "expanding class unconsciousness" that looks and feels like political awareness and activation. "The scene of pain and its eradication"—not only the rescue of the suffering child from harm, but the conversion from ignorance to awareness and helplessness to activation—has been converted into "the scene of the political itself."[22] When interior sentiment is transmuted into sentimental public, the presence of pain comes to equate to social inequality, pleasure is evidence of freedom, agency signals the capacity for adjustment to lived realities, and the refusal to express hope in the sufferer's movement from trauma to recovery is an attack on the collective. All of this forecloses critique. No hope? No credit.

These dynamics are at play with the socially responsible maquiladora and the child employees, with one amendment: the factory no longer represents the space of harm. The scene of prior trauma is now the environment outside the place of production, with its dysfunctional homes and dangerous streets. The set pieces are inverted, but the child remains the locus of empathetic attachment and affective displacement in a wasteland of racialized economic violence. "Where sentimental solidarity is," Berlant writes, "so there will be a will to separate and compartmentalize fundamental psychically felt social ambivalences, so that a sense of potentiality can be experienced enduringly, motivatingly, and even utopianly."[23] Identification will cut through the source of discomfort. When I'm letting a creditor bully our collective way into a stranger's house or when I am guilty of bystanding the sexual harassment of teenagers or when I am baseline cognizant of what my purchase of out-of-season mangoes means for farmworkers, and when any of these scenarios could and should spark my revolt, I will also take shelter in a story about my empathy with the person being harmed. I will daydream about our mutual disgust toward the system as it is, suppose that I'm sending my ESP solidarity for someone else's refusal, even if I won't instigate the disruption myself.

The capitalist humanitarian psychically invests in the figure of a *somewhat-better-off* child laborer freed to pursue a better life for herself and her family. This attachment—this ability to revalue child labor as gleaning such happy results and this impulse to adjust the labor conditions accordingly—says less about the people stitching the clothes than about the affective lifeworlds of the people issuing the orders. When the investor attaches to the child laborer, he is also attaching to the reproduction of his own social and economic world in its current form, with enough adjustments that, if he squints, he might even convince himself that its trajectory is toward a less-damaging good life for all.[24]

. . . . . .

The rejoinder is still there: Don't I want better options for the global child, given that her world is not destroyed? Would I rather this child be "sniffing glue" on the street or in a well-ventilated factory? Would I rather her family have enough to eat because she works or go hungry because she doesn't? How would I recommend that they manage? What would I have the bankers and investors do instead?

The questions are a trap. They wipe out the dissonance of witnessing the factory. It is better to ask this: How did that scene of young people on an assembly line come to make political, economic, social, and affective sense to the majority of people in that van? The answer is there in the child of the socially responsible maquila, the patron saint of capitalist humanitarianism. She incarnates a hope that life can go on, that for some people life might even get better, in this carved-up landscape. She extends reassurance that the people targeted for "development" are finding a secure place within the global market and the worlds that it ransacks. The promise of capitalist regeneration sticks to the symbolic child, but as a politics it will always exceed her. The issue is not the child herself but the intimate public captivated by her beacon of a durative, maybe-sometimes-slightly-better same.[25] Empowered, future-oriented, yes—but never so much so that her champions would be compelled to stop the machine, never so much that the injunction to imagination would be much else than another postponement.

No Future, No Credit

We'd returned to the hotel for the evening. The local bankers had retreated to wherever they go after hours, and our tour group had again congregated in our reserved conference room. While the majority of us shoveled down beans and rice, the executive director set the stage for her next lesson. She dragged three spare chairs away from the long wooden table and lined them up at the front of the space. She had an exercise for us. Each of the chairs represented a criterion for credit. The first chair was talent. The second was accountability. The third was positive attitude. The director prompted us to recall, one by one, the people we had met that day: the subsistence farmer who hoped his son would go to agronomy school, the woman who used her first-ever loan cycle to purchase chickens and sell their eggs, the shoe factory boss and his teenage workers, the weaver father who hesitated to let us into his house. We, the tourists, who just this morning had been judged remedial in our grasp of microfinance, were now drafted as the evaluative experts. Which of these people were creditworthy?

We proceeded down the list of candidates. As we recalled their various qualities, the executive director paced back and forth among the three chairs. She lingered at the "talent" chair when we conferred over the marketability of their skills. She rested her forearms on the "accountability" chair when we debated the chances that, if someone failed to meet the expectations laid out in their contract, their social network would pressure them into compliance. The director spent the majority of her time at the attitude chair, goading us to discuss this criterion in greater depth. We had achieved quick consensus that, across the board, everyone received full marks on talent and susceptibility to peer pressure. Their hope for the future, or lack thereof, would have to be the deciding factor. Someone had to lose.

The weaver came up short. "He didn't seem happy to see us," someone shrugged. No doubt he possessed the skills, and he had been faithful in his repayment. Unlike the other people we visited, however, he had not expressed enthusiasm about a possible future—manifest in the bank and its representatives—when it was perched on his doorstep. Calling our deliberations to closure, the executive director asked the crucial question: "What do you think? Creditworthy? Not creditworthy?"

No credit.

She was performing the process by which neoliberalism comes to a verdict about who is allowed to continue in its game. The decision commenced in the vague space between the two kinds of commodified labor that we encountered over the course of the day: the labor of producing material goods for eventual sale and the labor pulling off an affected performance for the creditor class. The second kind of labor evades objective quantification. It has more to do with feeling in the atmosphere, the impression that sticks to the encounter once its details dissolve in memory. What were the vibes? Was I comfortable? Was I not comfortable? Was there a resolution to my dissonance? Did I feel a sense of closure, as if I could walk away unburdened?

Part of me wanted to cheer for the weaver, to revel in his failure to pass the audit. The fact that he fell short could be proof of his integrity and backbone, consequences come as they may. As in: Fuck that executive director and her neocolonial ambitions. Forget the creditor with his promises and threats. Run the speculators out of town.

This impulse, too, plunged me deeper into the system that had brought me to his doorstep in the first place. It recruited him, or the idea of him, as palliative for my own affect alienation. None of us could know how the man's failure to express right attitude and correct hope, or how the credit officers' failure to extract such a performance, would play out. The middle managers who screened loan applicants were not here; the US director had higher priorities than meddling in the affairs of an individual borrower of a subsidiary. The credit-scoring exercise had been hypothetical, staged primarily for pedagogical purposes.

Regardless, the situation was untenable. Deem someone creditworthy, and the bank would be in charge. Deny someone credit, and the bank would still be in charge. All movement would take place with some reference to the bank, even if the movement looked like creative refusal or escape. The weaver doesn't have a safe harbor in this scenario. What would a resolution look like, anyway? Where does someone find refuge from the bank? Do they go to the private home? To the factory? The border? The social world of a gang or a church? Some grassroots movement? Off the grid? There are always options. All have advantages and disadvantages. All have been invested by neoliberalism with a story and a moral.

Yes, our boardroom conversation would—most likely—not have significant bearing on the weaver's life. This probability does not deliver relief. It only put a crescendo on what had happened that day. The purpose of the exercise, as with the tour, was not primarily about evaluating the bank's clients. It was to teach our group to experience and to evaluate the world as responsible creditors should: to find redemptive intimacy with the labor that makes possible our good lives, to summon solidarity from the spectacle of their imagined lives, to insinuate reproductive care into scenes of brute expropriation, and to extract hope from the promise that these relations will repeat. These skills aren't hard to master. Once acquired, they mediate the dissonance of living through the gruesome lie that it will be harder to imagine the end of capitalism than to imagine that capitalism, with its compounding crimes and losses, has no end: only a next generation.[26]

May 2017.
I believe that we will win.

I can still feel the asphalt burning my skin and my friends' elbows tugging against mine as police circled to arrest us for gridlocking traffic across the city. Three eight-person pods of women and nonbinary and queer graduate workers had parked ourselves at three intersections in downtown New Haven. We stayed there for two hours in the afternoon heat, throats hoarse from continuous call-and-response chants and our necks blistering under the unforgiving sun.

The graduate teaching union, Local 33, had choreographed the action. At immediate stake was the university's flagrant refusal to institute a transparent, neutral, third-party process for handling graduate employees' allegations of workplace harassment and retaliation. Our need for this recourse, along with the union's more general demands for comprehensive healthcare coverage and equitable compensation for our labor, had risen to the top of the organizing priority list.

It had been a long spring. The euphoria of winning our union vote had faded into the stressed monotony of bureaucratic limbo. We had endured a three-week hearing at the regional National Labor Relations Board (NLRB), where hired lawyers from a firm specializing in "union avoidance" argued that the instructors of Yale seminars in English composition, foreign language, and calculus were an unskilled and interchangeable workforce. Without a trace of embarrassment, Yale had suggested that, for example, a history doctoral candidate with no postsecondary experience in math could be slotted to lead a section of linear algebra, or that a graduate researcher in an astrophysics lab could staff an elementary French section even if he had never studied the language himself.[1] The NLRB had disagreed, and Local 33 secured federal certification—but university officials still stonewalled not just our efforts to bargain but also the court order that compelled it to do so. Their stall tactics had a purpose. The longer the antiunion attorneys drew this out, the greater the likelihood that a new cohort of far-right presidential appointees would overturn the national precedent that allowed graduate workers to unionize at all. We were running out of time. Our appeal to the spectacular—caution tape draped around lamp posts, bumper-to-bumper traffic jams, limp bodies carried to police vans—correlated with our dwindling odds of victory. How could we not try?

. . . . . .

That evening, once everyone was released from detention and back in the church basement that doubled as union headquarters, a senior organizer announced our regrouping and warm-up exercise. We were to go around the table and, one by one, recite the labor movement's favorite cheer—"I believe that we will win"—along with our personal reasons for keeping the faith. My comrades followed on cue. *I believe that we will win because history shows the power of everyday people to challenge power and make their own way. I believe that we will win because we have done the organizing to make it happen. I believe that we will win because Yale is fucking scared.* Was it possible that if we affirmed our optimism with enough conviction, the other factors would recede? Would it matter less that Congress had stacked the deck to favor private, ultrawealthy corporate interests? Would a more fervent faith help feminist organizers ride out the leftist misogyny running rampant *within* Local 33? If we believed harder, could the union's coordinating committee avert an imminent rupture over our own failures of democratic process?[2] My turn came, and I lacked the bandwidth for euphemism: "I actually *don't* believe that we will win." I admitted it, and then I explained that my pessimism didn't alter the strength of my will. I knew there was little to lose.

My off-brand reply alarmed some of the senior organizers. Many of us tended to assume that self-interest motivated activism, and that nobody would jeopardize their career or put their body on the line if they lacked hope that their actions would change something. The prospect was too exhausting. A few of the people in our circle had spent the day in a police station holding cell. All of us had spent the preceding weeks either hunger striking or sleeping outside, on concrete, in defense of our campus occupation. We had managed the adversity with redoubled work and a high dose of compulsory optimism. To doubt these tactics was at best to undermine the collective morale and at worst to signal disloyalty to the entire cause. If I didn't anticipate victory, if I didn't believe that we were righteous underdogs destined to triumph in the end, what was the point of giving so much?³

. . . . . .

But I said what I said. I don't believe that we will win. There is a way I keep reiterating this position, not only in union meetings but also every time I reject the conceit that repair is possible within the frame that capitalism provides. I am constantly tripping over the truism—common to liberal institutions, but not exclusive to them—that critique should be paired with a constructive gesture or an invocation of hope.⁴ These questions have followed this project everywhere: *What is the alternative? What comes after deconstruction? If you have a problem with capitalist humanitarianism, what do you want instead?* Sometimes when I hear these questions, which can sound more like an accusation or like a demand to cough something up, my mind jumps to a memory of my confirmation class. A dozen ten-year-olds gathered in a Sunday school classroom, eyes and ears tuned to my mother, who was also the pastor, while she taught us about one of the core doctrines of reformed Protestant theology. "What is grace? Here's an example. Let's say it's Christmas, and you've been bad that week. You threw a tantrum. You were mean to your brother. But then on Christmas morning you get presents anyway. Grace is like that. Grace is a *gift*. It is a gift from *God*. It is a gift from God that you *do not deserve*." She segued into Original Sin 101 for tweens. The world was broken—depraved, from the Greek word for "warped"—beyond redress. Here is what that meant: My existence is inextricable from the cosmic train wreck, which is so much graver than my petty unkindness to my siblings. Anyone who pretends that there is an out, or that they somehow have earned access to it, is deluding themself about the extent of the damage. Our efforts to live otherwise remain absolutely necessary—both for the small goods they offer and for connecting us to the grace that makes them possible—but have never been and will never be sufficient.

I am tempted to shut down the question of alternatives. I worry that answering it with anything other than refusal will pull this project back into the cul-de-sac of neoliberal slogans, where the arc of bad capitalist conscience moves, in recursive familiarity, toward reformed capitalist futures. *Your coffee is laced with a farmer's blood, but—look—here is some delicious blood-free coffee that actually helps that farmer. I might be working for a billion-dollar corporation with a shady human rights record, but on the other hand, I'm making money that I can donate to social-justice causes.*

Whatever else their material effects, capitalist humanitarian projects siphon negative feelings into acts of capital exchange and form subjects inclined to take comfort in, or at minimum to keep tolerating, these transactions. Dissonance raised by power arrangements can be sublimated into feelings of sentimental solidarity, even as the basic conditions of production remain stable. Any leftover malaise can then be displaced into resentment toward whatever killjoy has interrupted the scene of resolution.[5] Threats of enclosure are most prescient when our collective efforts to refuse and subvert capitalism's itineraries cede the work of self-critique and when grassroots social movements begin to confuse their own institutional preservation and affirmation with the work of collective liberation. It is troubling, then, that a prominent thread of Left cultural discourse has construed critical negativity as tantamount to political nihilism. Prominent intellectuals have alleged that frameworks of philosophical pessimism should be rejected for treating power as uniform, stable, and timeless, thus denying the presence of social difference and the possibility of historical change.[6] These are not serious criticisms. Among many other problems, they often lean on a baseless straw antagonism between radical critique and radical organizing. If a study of capitalist humanitarianism shows anything at all, it is that the power of empire lies in its drive to convert each instance of dissonance and all traces of refusal into an occasion for further expansion. This does not mean that critique is a bankrupt endeavor; it means that critique is a practice of resisting processes of reification and logics of propitiation in every instance, at every turn.[7]

One need not slog through reformist theologies of total depravity to develop this understanding; you can look to the history of philosophy and cultural studies for resonant interventions.[8] Theodor Adorno, writing in exile from Third Reich Germany, wrote against the fantasy of finding an exit from the boundless prison, camp, and sweatshop that he saw surrounding him. "There is no way out of entanglement," he writes. "The only responsible course is to deny oneself the ideological misuse of one's own existence, and for the rest to conduct oneself in private as modestly, unobtrusively, and unpretentiously as required, no longer by good upbringing, but by the shame of still having air to breathe, in hell."[9] If apocalypse has already happened, the question is not about becoming good or doing good. The question that follows critiques of pervasive violence should not be "what is the alternative?" The question is what it would look like to *not misuse existence* in what is already a ruined landscape. If Adorno does not go so far, it should be underlined that, for many intellectuals shaped by philosophical pessimisms, to *not misuse* is to be constantly fighting and critiquing. There is no way out.

This is not a bad lens for Left organizing. The fight for collective bargaining rights or the decision to take arrest when a confrontation escalated—none of this was moral heroism. It was, on my assessment, in light of the contingencies and affordances of the time, the least-unethical way to relate to the gruesome institutions with which my life was entangled. This is where I find a second, more direct, answer to the question about what I want instead of capitalist humanitarianism: I want everything.[10] I want my university to divest from carbon and I want an immediate cessation of all oil drilling. I want you to stop buying things from the ten-headed monster disguised as an online megastore, and then I want to liquidate the assets of billionaires and reinvest them in public housing and public parks. I want us to go to the next zoning board meeting and block whatever property developer is gentrifying our city. I want to read more books and, when we do, to get them from our local library. I want us all to have infinite time for pickup basketball, for going out dancing, for naps, and for whatever other pleasures we have been missing. I want free and universal comprehensive healthcare for all people. I want everyone I know to turn down all promotions into management, even if there is a cost to that refusal. I want you to give all your cash to the next street musician you see. I want to be clear that none of this is adequate.

A politics anchored in pessimism makes impossible and mundane demands, and then it demands more. It is relentless in its critique not only of power but also of its own desires, methods, and expectations. It is in constant motion: each flight triggers another pursuit. In mapping the violence of our surrounds and dreaming ways to break its operations, fleeting solidarities and delicate sanctuaries can emerge. We find space to gasp for air. Don't stop moving. Precisely because power resists uniformity—because it is incomplete and dispersed and suffused in our most intimate attachments—the moment that critique settles on resolution is the moment of its arrest. It has no "after" or "beyond." Every act of deconstruction creates something new—something that will eventually need to be torn down.

. . . . . .

On the first morning of the Local 33 month of action, while twenty of us barricaded the doors to an event for parents of admitted undergraduates, a second team of organizers drove an eighteen-wheeler flatbed truck onto the quad in front of the university's main administrative building. The truck carried furniture, decorations, and materials for a boatshed-shaped structure that our amateur moving crew somehow assembled in minutes. For the next six weeks, the structure was union headquarters. Illuminated by a generator, strung with fairy lights, decked with plants, and encircled by picnic tables perched on temporary grass, it became our home base. In a city that lacks good public space, at a university that makes its campus a fortress against the black and brown neighborhoods that it ransacked, the place that we came to call "33 Wall Street" held a possibility of difference. People from across New Haven—not just graduate students—slept, convened reading groups, plotted our next actions, and met celebrities, politicians, and kids on field trips to learn about collective action.

Time there was a fever dream, shot through with an intensity derived from the absolute fact that this couldn't last. We hadn't even expected it to survive past the first night. The structure remained intact only because, when patrol cars rolled up around midnight, one hundred people formed a human barricade around its perimeter, until Yale finally opted to postpone the standoff. By the time the sun rose, armed police had stationed themselves all around the encampment—which is where they stayed, circling us around the clock for the next three, five, twelve, thirty days. Each new dawn announced the wonder of borrowed time. We drifted awake in the crisp air of spring and peeked out of our sleeping bags to sunbeams glittering through the arched wood—all these little mercies before the sirens, searchlights, and noise weapons that were a foregone conclusion. The place became an oasis not because it would last but because it was destined for splinters. With long-term survival off the table, we made a fragile freedom.[11]

The university unleashed a subcontracted wrecking crew on the structure in the wee hours of May 25, 2017. Yale had tolerated our antics during commencement; under no circumstances would the administration allow the occupation to interrupt the alumni reunion festivities planned for the subsequent weeks. When the workers showed up, they discovered that our lead architect had stripped the screws. The structure could not be dismantled without a bulldozer, which meant that the university had little choice but to play out its violence in a public way rather than quietly deconstruct our creation in the dark. The organizers had known the strategy all along; we had reveled in it. We were looking not toward the win but toward how we would play the loss toward life.

. . . . . .

A week after the tear-down, I pulled my duffel through the automatic airport doors and into the Milwaukee night. It was 2:07 a.m. A trio of Mark's friends—Annica, Max, Miles—met me at the gate. Adamant that I not rely on a ride share, they'd waited out a three-hour flight delay. Max drove his beat-up Subaru back to the Riverwest apartment that had become home base even for the bandmates who didn't live there but who could not be alone in their grief. Paint your mental picture of a crash pad for twenty-five-year-old Type B artists working shitty call-center jobs to make rent, and you've probably approximated the space: the grimy sinks, the watermarked ceilings, the bikes and instruments and clothes strewn across the floor, a mildewed sofa salvaged from a sidewalk, and, pushed to the side of the cluttered living room, a card table stacked with highest-grade, pristinely maintained recording equipment. A feral-looking cat leered at us from under a chair. "That's Lucy," nodded Miles. "Short for Lucifer." Measured by domestic disorder, the two years separating us in age felt like three decades.

They'd reserved a place for me on couch, even dragged the window air-conditioning unit out of a bedroom so that I could sleep in relative cool. Max passed me a grapefruit LaCroix, Mark's single indulgence. Otherwise, they'd stuffed the refrigerator with Soylent. No solid foods; they preferred not to expend their music-making energies on meal prep.

"Here," Annica's voice cracked, "we changed the pillowcase for you." Annica moved to the couch in slow motion, placing the single pillow down as if it were blown from glass. One of the guys had donated it to me and adopted the couch cushions for their own bed. The tenderness, the care: they were trying so hard. I swallowed, squeezed my eyes closed, opened them again. I couldn't give them what they wanted. But I would have stayed forever willing myself to be him, to become the person we all wished were resting here, in all his madness, where I breathed. I said goodnight.

. . . . . .

The next summer, Miles and a couple of others from the music collective routed their do-it-yourself tour through New Haven. Only then did I grasp what happened in that Milwaukee apartment: for me, it was an absurd desperation to magic-wand my two-hundred-square-foot attic hatch into the mansion they deserved, that Mark deserved. But this was impossible, so instead I transferred every pillow from my bed to the futon they shared, borrowed the softest blankets from my local friends, stayed up until their 2 a.m. return from the venue, and woke a few hours later to make pancakes, eggs, yogurt, fruit salad, cold brew, and enough leftovers to last them several more meals on the road. They had mentioned penny-pinched subsistence diet of Wonder bread and gas station coffee. I pressed supplies on them. None of it brought Mark back. Turning toward the wound that could not heal—all the ways we came up short, all the ways we might have kept him alive one more day, all the parts of us that we would not get back—we found each other.

． ． ． ． ． ．

What does it mean to not misuse existence? The question is too abstract. I ask myself, instead: if I woke up trapped in a call center, or a city ruled by finance bankers, or a firm's corporate responsibility office, or a university run on casual labor, and I knew there was no way out of complicity, what would I be doing with my existence? Would I break the windows and computers and other machines? Would I organize a union? Would I be the middle manager who urges moderation while internally deliberating when to break rank? Would I rat out troublemakers to the boss? Would I be the guard, and if I were, would I throw down my badge, or would I mace the uprising? Would I jump out the window, end it now? Would I urge that desperate person to hold on a bit longer because it will get better or maybe because there is something sustaining about the struggle itself? Would I barricade myself in an office with the boss? Would I feed my colleagues on the front lines, do chores behind the scenes to keep us all going? Would I go back to sleep? Would I go ahead and buy the products, attempt to unsee whatever is happening down the supply chain? Would I document how all of these conflicts went down and write what happened next?

To know that I am always and already on compromised ground is to change my relationship to freedom. I am released from the calculating anticipation of what "might" happen in the future. Instead, I am attuned to the forms of life that emerge in these ruins, where the only question is about how we live together and what worlds our practices will create now. Here is what I want for today: to hold the one crossing over. Ask him what horizon he sees. Tell her it's not over. We can make life almost anywhere. We can write a history of the impossible, and survival is not the end.

acknowledgments

I am grateful to all who have accompanied this book as it became the book it wanted to be.

The first draft coalesced at Yale University, where a triple-threat committee of Michael Denning, Noreen Khawaja, and Kathryn Lofton helped me refine the analysis, composition, and rationale. A colloquium with another dream trifecta—Roderick Ferguson, Karen Ho, and Kathi Weeks—catalyzed the second stage of revisions. Two readers, eventually revealed as Kevin O'Neill and Vincent Lloyd, surpassed my highest hopes for generous and energizing peer review. Hannah Beresford coaxed out the book's narrative voice when I could just barely hear it. Nancy Levene, Jodi Melamed, Linn Tonstad, and Tisa Wenger offered readings and insights that led to breakthroughs.

The Yale Working Group on Globalization and Culture has been an oasis. The Political Theology Network, especially the mentoring initiative, has given continual sustenance. Skidmore College welcomed me into its faculty ranks and offered the resources I needed to complete the manuscript. I especially appreciate the support of my Religious Studies colleagues Eliza Kent, Jennifer Lewis, Bradley Onishi, Ryan Overbey, Xander Prince, and Gregory Spinner. For community and encouragement, infinite thanks are due to Lindsay Buchman, Rachel Cantave, Mary Kate Donovan, Winston Grady-Willis, Maggie Greaves, Susanne Kerekes, and Dominique Vuvan.

My students keep me honest and remind me that revision never stops. At Yale, learning with Lauren Chan, David Diaz, CJ Fowler, and Sheau Yun Lim propelled my experiments with written form. At Skidmore, Carla Crawford, Grace Waibel, and Ian Chorlian have been heroic research assistants.

People who know me know it is impossible to overstate the influence of Tina Pippin on my approach to scholarship, organizing, and pedagogy. When I reflect on how Tina along with Marie Marquardt and the entire Agnes Scott College crew of that generation were my first direct models of the kind of work I do now, I cannot believe my luck.

It has been an honor to work with the brilliant (unionized!) team at and around Duke University Press. Thanks to Aimee Harrison for a stunning design, Annie Lubinsky for coordinating the production process, Donald Pharr for superb copyediting, and Paula Durbin-Westby for an expertly engineered index. Finally, special gratitude is due to Sandra Korn, who raised the bar for editorial excellence and solidarity at every juncture.

There are the words on page, and there is the background that sets the text into relief. I imagine that space as a mural to the many colleagues and friends who made this work, and the life around it, possible and sometimes wonderful. Lots of these people are named above. I am also grateful to Eddy Abraham, Bench Ansfield, Rebecca Bartel, Lauren Berlant, Desiree Bernard, Janelle Browning, Rachel Buff, Gavriel Cupita-Zorn, Tiffany Curtis, Lena Eckert-Erdheim, Marko Geslani, Aaron Greenberg, Adrian Hernandez-Acosta, Sophia House, Danube Johnson, Breana Jones, Sarah Koenig, Wendy Mallette, Christopher McGowan, Ben McNair, Erik Nordbye, Emily Owens, Joshua Phillips, Shari Rabin, Peter Raccuglia, Kate Redburn, Michelle Sanchez, Jason Smith, Lewis West, Kenny Wiley, and Sarah Zager. I want to extend special thanks to Amaryah Armstrong, Salonee Bahman, Timothy Byram, Pratima Gopalakrishnan, Mie Inouye, Cody Musselman, and Justin Randolph for the depth with which they read and critiqued, if not every page of this manuscript, then near it. All my love to each of you.

Thank you to the many extended family and many friends who gave me a safe harbor during the research and writing process. Thank you, too, to the people—named and unnamed—who shared their lives and thoughts about capitalist humanitarian existence. Thank you to all of the archivists who helped me. Deepest gratitude to the good people at St. Luke Presbyterian Church for the welcome and the perfect cap to the research.

Annica, Max, Miles: thank you for the worlds you share and create. Thank you to all those who cared for (care for) my brother Mark and who have nurtured his life in theirs.

My parents and my brothers are the condition of possibility for all I do. I hope they will feel my absolute love in these pages, not only in the parts where our stories converge but, more than that, in the differences and departures. I dedicate this book to them.

notes

PREFACE

1. Brown, "Resisting Left Melancholy."
2. Li, *Dear Friend, from My Life I Write to You in Your Life*, 20.

INTRODUCTION

1. Reich, *Saving Capitalism*, 167.
2. Giridharadas, *Winners Take All*.
3. Brown, *Undoing the Demos*, 17.
4. See chapters 1 and 3.
5. Emerson, *The Purpose of Capital*, 202. See also chapter 2.
6. See chapters 4 and 6.
7. By far the best treatment of this general theme is Davis, *Planet of Slums*, 672–88.
8. Bhattacharya and Vogel, *Social Reproduction Theory*; Briggs, *How All Politics Became Reproductive Politics*; Federici, *Caliban and the Witch*; Federici, *Revolution at Point Zero*;; Weeks, *Problem with Work*; Morgan, *Laboring Women*.
9. Of the vast body of scholarship on the expulsions that are the substrate to liberal inclusion, the works that have most influenced my thinking include Byrd, *Transit of Empire*; Cacho, *Social Death*; Silva, *Toward a Global Idea of Race*; Melamed, *Represent and Destroy*; Puar, *Terrorist Assemblages*; Reddy, *Freedom with Violence*; Sharpe, *In the Wake*; and Spillers, "Mama's Baby, Papa's Maybe."
10. Hartman, *Lose Your Mother*, 6.
11. Berlant, *Cruel Optimism*.
12. Melamed, "Proceduralism, Predisposing, Poesis."

13. Moreton, *To Serve God and Wal-Mart*; Phillips-Fein, *Invisible Hands*. Other key works include Dochuk, *From Bible Belt to Sunbelt*; Gloege, *Guaranteed Pure*; Grem, *The Blessings of Business*; and Kruse, *One Nation under God*.

14. On finance discipline and evangelical Christianity in Latin America, see Bartel, *Card-Carrying Christians*, and O'Neill, *Secure the Soul*.

15. On the circulation of liberation theology as a fetish product for white Western audiences, see Althaus-Reid, "Gustavo Gutierrez Goes to Disneyland."

16. Hall, *Cultural Studies: 1983*, 127–54. See also Hall, "Problem of Ideology—Marxism without Guarantees," 24–45.

17. Hall, *Cultural Studies: 1983*, 43, 143, 143–44.

18. Many scholars have attempted to excavate Christianity as the germ that hides inside concepts of political sovereignty, the nation-state, history, and the secular. These analyses trace these terms to the Enlightenment, which they portray as the movement that finally transposed Christianity into the idiom of secular modernity and historical progress. The most vivid example of this is Andijar, *Blood*, viii. Andijar necromances the political philosophy of Carl Schmitt, who wrote nearly a century ago that "all the significant concepts of the modern doctrine of the state are secularized theological concepts." See Schmitt, *Concept of the Political*. For a lucid critique of the search for Protestantism in the secular, see Khawaja, *Religion of Existence*, 235–42. For generative analysis of the implicit disciplinary secularism of modern capitalism, see Jakobsen and Pellegrini, *Secularisms*; Masuzawa, *Invention of World Religions*; and Asad, *Formations of the Secular*.

19. Benjamin, "Theses on the Philosophy of History," 198.

20. Using the figure of "spirit" and "sacred" as a name for what is fugitive to racial capitalism and its anomie has become an increasingly common turn within queer theory and critical-race and ethnic studies. Three examples are Alexander, *Pedagogies of Crossing*; Crawley, *Blackpentecostal Breath*; and Cvetkovich, *Depression*, 154–202.

21. Hall, *Cultural Studies: 1983*, 143.

22. Robinson, *Black Marxism*.

23. Federici, *Caliban and the Witch*.

24. Gramsci, *Selections from the Prison Notebooks*, 405–26, 501–6.

25. Marx, *Capital*, 1:163–77; Marx, "On the Jewish Question," 26–52; Marx, "The German Ideology"; Marx, *Economic and Philosophic Manuscripts*.

26. For an extended engagement with this argument in relation to the academic study of religion, see Bartel and Hulsether, "Introduction: Classifying Capital," 4–7.

27. On the categories of religion, coloniality, and their study, see Chidester, *Savage Systems*; Keane, *Christian Moderns*; Wenger, *We Have a Religion*; and Masuzawa, *Invention of World Religions*.

28. Lofton, *Consuming Religion*, 3, 9.

29. More work should be done on the merits of a relatively Durkheimian framing (oriented toward social solidarity and even uneasy social consensus) versus a more Marxian and conflict-laden framing (attentive to fissures, contestations, and outright violence internal to any society). For example, this conversation can be easily extrapolated to a prior debate about consensus versus conflict in American studies and US

historiography. On this historiography and the problems with consensus, see Denning, "Special American Conditions"; and Pease and Weigman, "Futures."

30. Durkheim, *The Division of Labor in Society*.

31. Lofton, *Consuming Religion*, 282.

32. On political consequences of this epistemology, see Bernstein, "I'm Very Happy to Be in the Reality-Based Community."

33. The language of reparative reading was developed in a now-canonical essay by Eve Sedgwick, who elaborated a distinction between paranoid and reparative critical practices within queer studies scholarship. A more recent cohort of queer and feminist studies scholars has called for a new "turn" to the reparative. For the early essay, see Sedgwick, *Touching Feeling*. For calls for a new reparative turn, see Love, "Truth and Consequences"; and Felski, *Limits of Critique*.

34. Robyn Wiegman identifies in the reparative "turn" a compensatory impulse on the part of the scholar determined to reproduce her own act, even if that means ceding the ground on which a critique or judgment of the conditions of her work rests: "Here, in a present in which the value of critical thinking has undergone attrition in contemporary cultures that prioritise accounting without accountability, discourse without truth, and meaning without interpretation, the reparative turn quite significantly rewrites the critic's value as the consequence of the object's need. . . . [The reparative turn is] a compensatory tactic aimed at redeeming the critic's self perception in the twilight of the hermeneutics of suspicion, where one of the most potent remnants of its critical habits can be found in the repeated accusation that the declining significance of the humanities is the critic's own fault." Wiegman, "Times We're In," 16–18. See also Tonstad, "Ambivalent Loves"; Berlant, *Cruel Optimism*, 120–25; and Shahani, "Future Is Queer Stuff."

35. Stuelke, *Ruse of Repair*, 17.

36. On how the subject who identifies a problem with normative power is identified as the one who is actually causing damage, and on how freedom entails becoming affectively alienated from and tearing down normative institutions that have been a source of belonging and good feeling, see Ahmed, *Promise of Happiness*.

37. Grandin, *The Blood of Guatemala*; McAllister and Nelson, "Aftermath: Harvests of Violence and Histories of the Future"; Smith, "The Militarization of Civil Society in Guatemala."

38. Tsing, *Friction*.

39. Especially helpful have been the following works: Abdurraqib, *They Can't Kill Us until They Kill Us*; Boyer, *Handbook of Disappointed Fate*; Cacho, *Social Death*; Clare, *Brilliant Imperfection*; Cottrell, *Sorry to Disrupt the Peace*; Crosby, *Body, Undone*; Hartman, *Lose Your Mother*; Puar, *Terrorist Assemblages*; Nelson, *Tough Enough*; and Sharpe, *In the Wake*.

40. On post–World War II liberalism and racial capitalism, see Geismer, *Don't Blame Us*; Connolly, *World More Concrete*; and Mittelstadt, *From Welfare to Workfare*.

41. See Taylor, *Race for Profit*; Chakravartty and Silva, "Accumulation, Dispossession, and Debt," 368–85; Roy, *Poverty Capital*; Karim, *Microfinance and Its Discontents*; and Elyachar, *Markets of Dispossession*.

42. On archives and the history of capitalism, see Morgan, "Archives and Histories."

43. Brown, *Undoing the Demos*; Murphy, *Economization of Life*; Lazzarato, *Making of the Indebted Man*.

44. Cooper, *Family Values*.

INTERLUDE ONE

1. Aviv, "The Philosopher of Feelings."

2. Jaycox, "Nussbaum, Anger, and Racial Justice"; Srinivasan, "Would Politics Be Better Off without Anger?"

3. Cohen, *A Consumer's Republic*, 18–61.

4. Davis, "Culture and Struggle," 11–14; Roy, *Reds, Whites, and Blues*, 28–49, 210–15.

5. The workshop description read, "For decades, consumers around the world were encouraged to look for the fair trade seal on commodities such as coffee, a guarantee that the product was purchased from an organization of small farmers and at a 'fair' price, among other things. However, even from the earliest years, products such as tea were permitted into the system under conditions no different than they had been for a century. And then led by certifiers seeking market share, and perhaps permitted by authentic fair traders, the system was manipulated to the benefit of large players, both in the North and the South such that the original set-up was no longer recognizable. What does this mean for our work moving forward?" Notice how the story of declension hinges on an appeal to an original authenticity and sets up, rhetorically, a charge to reclaim it. Equal Exchange, "Summit Schedule: June 8–9," acquired at Citizen Consumer Action Summit, copy in author's possession.

CHAPTER ONE. MAY ANALYZE LIKE A CAPITALIST

1. I am grateful to Pratima Gopalakrishnan for sharpening my thinking on this point. For a smart intervention into public histories of race in classical studies in particular, see Kotrosits, *Lives of Objects*, 145–64. For an outstanding analysis of the presuppositions at play in debates over United States national origin stories, see Jackson, "The 1619 Project and the Demands of Public History," https://www.newyorker.com/books/under-review, accessed December 10, 2021.

2. Trouillot, *Silencing the Past*, 1–30.

3. Tuck and Yang, "Decolonization Is Not a Metaphor," 9–10.

4. Stephen Nolt discusses the relationship between traditional Mennonite commitments to simplicity and separation and economic globalization in the twentieth century: "During the mid-twentieth century Mennonite efforts to distinguish themselves from prevailing Cold War sentiments resulted in new and more frequent encounters with Christians in various contexts around the globe.... Separatism had simultaneously encouraged Mennonites into seeing themselves in a global context, while giving North American Mennonite globalism a distinct cast." Nolt, "Globalizing a Separate People," 488.

5. De Grazia, *Irresistible Empire*; McAlister, *Epic Encounters*.
6. Borgwardt, *New Deal for the World*.
7. On Anabaptists and Heifer, see Kreider, *A Cup of Cold Water*; and Yoder, *Passing on the Gift*. On Oxfam, see Roper, *Change Not Charity*.
8. Ingrid Hess, "Self Help: Crafts of the World: The First 50 Years," thesis written and held by the Mennonite Central Committee, 1994 (copy in author's possession), 11.
9. The historiography on twentieth-century consumer citizenship chronicles consumer-based political action for labor protection, minimum wages, consumer-protection bureaus, and a general public commitment to a strong state. See Cohen, *Consumers' Republic*; Enstad, *Ladies of Labor, Girls of Adventure*; Frank, *Purchasing Power*; Glickman, *Buying Power*; and Jacobs, *Pocketbook Politics*.
10. Hess, "Self Help: Crafts of the World," 11. On postwar consumer cultures, see Cohen, *Consumers' Republic*; and May, *Homeward Bound*.
11. Kevin Rose has studied the early years of Needlework in greater depth and analyzed them, as well as Protestant fair trade movements broadly, as forerunners of a capitalist environmentalism premised on individual consumer lifestyle choice and a romantic orientation toward global poverty. See Rose, "Living Green," 225–60.
12. For a summary of Needlework's first two decades, see Nolt, "Self Help Philosophy and Organizational Change."
13. During World War II the US government conscripted Puerto Rico as a strategic base in the Atlantic Ocean and used the population as a pool of military draftees. Puerto Rico's decolonial and independence movement raged through the 1940s and faced consistent military repression. See Ayala and Bernabe, *Puerto Rico in the American Century*; and Burnett and Marshall, *Foreign in a Domestic Sense*. On the colonial status of Puerto Rico during and immediately after World War II, see Cabán, "Redefining Puerto Rico's Political Status"; and Genova and Ramos-Zayas, "Latino Crossings."
14. Helen King, "Arab Needlework Project Jerusalem: Progress Report January, 1968–August, 1970," Needlework and Crafts Project, Box 12 no. 6, Mennonite Central Committee Archives, Akron, PA.
15. Paul and Loretta Leatherman, "Haiti Trip Report," October 18, 1976, MCC Archives.
16. Mennonite Central Committee News Service, "MCC's Needlework Lady Retires," Akron, PA, January 29, 1971. All News Service press releases were obtained through email correspondence with the MCC Archives in Akron, PA.
17. Mennonite Central Committee News Service, "Self-Help Sales Top 200,000," Akron, PA, December 20, 1974.
18. "Common Visual Identity Project Goals," November 27, 1995, MCC Archives.
19. Charmayne Brubaker to Melodie Wenger, Sue Shultz, Paul Myers, and Tom Wenger, "Re: Feedback about 10 Options for Name," March 26, 1996, MCC Archives.
20. Nolt, "Globalizing a Separate People."
21. Goossen, "Mennonites in Latin America"; Sawatsky, *They Sought a Country*; Bottes, *Old Colony Mennonites in Argentina and Bolivia*, 203–24; Peters, "Mennonites in Mexico and Paraguay."

22. "Middle East Trip Recommendations and Administrative Understandings with Ivan Friesen," report from Executive Office (Snyder) to Overseas Services (Preheim), April 23, 1969, MCC Archives; Ivan Freison to Vern Preheim, Needlework Goals: Preliminary Report, letter August 16, 1969, MCC Archives; Vern Preheim (Director for Africa and Middle East) to Ivan Frieson and Helen King, September 12, 1969, MCC Archives; Griselda Shelly to Reg Toews, "Response to MCC Self-Help Program Review," April 26, 1977, MCC Archives; Jean W. Frieson (Self Help Director B.C.) to Mr. Arthur Driedger, Re: Self-Help Program Review, May 4, 1977, MCC Archives; Neil Janzen to Dorothy Friesen and Gene Stolzfus, Social Justice and Self Help, July 6, 1977, MCC Archives; MCC Self-Help Review, 1978, MCC Archives.

23. Hess, "Self Help," 16.

24. Hess, 16.

25. King, "Arab Needlework Project Jerusalem."

26. The full workshop description read, "You buy our coffee and chocolate. You know we have been around a while. Maybe you know there is something kind of special, different about Equal Exchange. And so you wonder, how did this thing begin? Do they call it a company? A co-op? Some mysterious blend of for profit and non-profit? In this workshop you will meet the founders, get some answers, and hopefully walk away with even more questions." Equal Exchange, "Summit Schedule: June 8–9," Citizen Consumer Action Summit, copy in author's possession.

27. The "story of now" follows two other kinds of stories—"the story of self" and "the story of us"—that Ganz offers as a tool for social change. At this point in the class, the investor had narrated his own motivations as a leader (the story of self) and gestured toward a collective experience of wanting to heal a fragmented world but not knowing how (story of us). Ganz circulates a popular worksheet on these genres of story. Ganz, "What Is Public Narrative: Self, Us, Now."

28. My analysis of the dynamics of coloniality, sovereignty, and recognition is shaped by Povinelli, *Cunning of Recognition*; and Simpson, *Mohawk Interruptus*.

29. SOCAP, home page, accessed October 1, 2018, https://socialcapitalmarkets.net.

30. Povinelli, *Cunning of Recognition*, 17.

31. On the significance of Israel and Palestine to US imperial cultures and racial formation, see Feldman, *Shadow over Palestine*. On Mennonites in Palestine, see Epp, "Mennonites, Palestine, and the Palestinian Right of Return."

32. King, "Arab Needlework Project Jerusalem." On the renaissance of Palestinian textiles work in this period, including but not limited to the appropriation of traditional patterns by the state of Israel, see Peteet, *Landscapes of Hope and Despair*, 148–51.

33. "To All Representatives of Overseas Needlework and Crafts Project," from David and LouAnn Kanagy Re: Arab Needlework from Jordan, October 9, 1967; Ivan Freison to Vern Preheim, Needlework Goals: Preliminary Report, letter August 16, 1969, MCC Archive.

34. King, "Arab Needlework Project Jerusalem," 4.

35. King, 4.

36. McAlister, *Epic Encounters*.

37. Ivan Freison to Vern Preheim, Needlework Goals: Preliminary Report, August 16, 1969, MCC Archives, Akron, PA.

38. King, "Arab Needlework Project Jerusalem," 26.

39. Maskit, home page, accessed October 1, 2018, https://maskit.com/about.

40. King, "Arab Needlework Project Jerusalem," 14.

41. King, 14.

42. King, 14.

43. For examples of the new historiography of missions, see especially King, "New Internationalists"; McAlister, *Kingdom of God Has No Borders*; Tyrell, *Reforming the World*.

44. Hollinger, *Protestants Abroad*.

45. Povinelli, *Empire of Love*; Hartman, *Scenes of Subjection*; Berlant, *Female Complaint*.

46. Hulsether, "Decolonization, TM."

47. Schuessler, "In History Departments, It's Up with Capitalism," *New York Times*, April 6, 2013.

48. Lipartito, "Reassembling the Economic"; Hudson, "Racist Dawn of Capitalism"; Sklansky, "Elusive Sovereign"; Sklansky, "Labor, Money, and the Financial Turn in the History of Capitalism."

49. "Columbia Studies in the History of U.S. Capitalism," Columbia University Press, accessed October 1, 2019, https://cup.columbia.edu/hoc; "Histories of Capitalism and the Environment," West Virginia University Press, accessed October 1, 2019, https://wvupressonline.com/node/594.

INTERLUDE TWO

1. Chen, *Animacies*, 189–221.

2. Marie Kondo writes, "I know some people find it hard to believe that inanimate objects respond to human emotion.... Still, we often hear about athletes who take loving care of their sports gear, treating it almost as if it were sacred. I think the athletes instinctively sense the power of these objects. If we treated all things we use in our daily life, whether it is our computer, our handbag, or our pens and pencils, with the same care that athletes give to their equipment, we could greatly increase the number of dependable 'supporters' in our lives." Kondo, *The Life-Changing Magic of Tidying Up*, 170.

3. I am especially moved by how the novelist Ruth Ozeki imagines and theorizes these relationships. Ozeki, *The Book of Form and Emptiness*.

CHAPTER TWO. ETHICAL VAMPIRES

1. Equal Exchange, advertisement, reprinted in *Equal Exchange Annual Report 1999*, 8, accessed February 1, 2021, https://equalexchange.coop/sites/default/files/annual_report/AR1999.pdf.

2. Glickman, *Buying Power*; Garcia, *From the Jaws of Victory*; Maira, *Boycott!*

3. Marx, *Capital*, 1:165, 342.

4. Equal Exchange, advertisement, *Equal Exchange Annual Report*, April 16, 1987, 8, accessed October 1, 2020, https://equalexchange.coop/about/annual-reports. Italics in original.

5. Grandin, *Empire's Workshop*; Gobat, *Confronting the American Dream*; Smith, *Resisting Reagan*; Westad, *Global Cold War*.

6. Marx, *Capital*, 1:164–77.

7. My analysis of the fetish and my reading of Marx is shaped in part by William Pietz's pivotal discursive archaeology and contextualization of this concept in the Portuguese colonialism in West Africa. See Pietz, "The Problem of the Fetish, I–III." For a classic study of the collision between pre-capitalist "fetishism" and the "commodity fetish" see Taussig, *The Devil and Commodity Fetishism*.

8. Marx, *Capital*, 1:165.

9. The condemnation of "middlemen" as predators in the supply chain is a rhetorical claim that exists both in fair trade circles and in drivers of the gig and "sharing" economies. On the latter phenomenon, see Nelms, Maurer, and Swartz, "Social Payments."

10. For a scholarly argument that consumer culture might be bent in alternative, life-affirming ways, see Lofton, *Consuming Religion*, 1–13.

11. Equal Exchange, advertisement, Equal Exchange Cooperative Campaign, May 2014, accessed November 1, 2018, https://eecampaign.files.wordpress.com/2014/05/coop-grocer-ad.jpg.

12. Marx, *Capital*, 1:176–77.

13. Moten, *In the Break*, 5, 1.

14. See Interlude 1.

15. Hulsether, "Buying into the Dream," 483–508.

16. Fairtrade International, "What Is Fairtrade?," YouTube, www.youtube.com/watch?v=PLKTGWH398Q.

17. Campbell, *Romantic Ethic*.

18. The gift is a site for theorizing varieties of exchange and network building, often in places constructed as outside of capitalist modernity. The classic work is Mauss, *Gift*. For reinterpretations, see especially Godelier, *Enigma of the Gift*; Derrida, *Gift of Death*; Weiner, *Inalienable Possessions*; Elyachar, *Markets of Dispossession*; and Nguyen, *Gift of Freedom*.

19. The story is narrated at length in the first chapter of Mycoskie's biography and in redacted form on the company website and in both marketing and trade publications. For the long version, see Mycoskie, *Start Something That Matters*. For shorter versions, see "Blake Mycoskie's Bio" and Burstein, "TOMS Out to Sell a Lifestyle."

20. This quotation is taken from the Stanford Social Innovation Review, but variations of it can be found in all of the company testimonies above. See Mycoskie, "A New Model of Philanthropy."

21. Hulsether, "TOMS Shoes."

22. Other companies with a "buy one, give one" model include Warby Parker (glasses), Sir Richard's (condoms), Bixbee (children's backpacks), Bomba (merino wool socks), Smile Squared (toothbrushes), SoapBox (soap), This Bar Saves Lives (granola

bars), and Roma (boots). All adopt slightly different models—some give in-kind products, and some donate money for every product sold—but all pitch themselves with this language of reciprocal giving.

23. The foundational work is Mauss, *Gift*.

24. Godelier, *Enigma of the Gift*, 12.

25. Nietzsche, *On the Genealogy of Morality*.

26. Guru Jagat's public profile swelled in the aftermath of her death in 2021. See Phelan, "The Second Coming of Guru Jagat."

27. Malone, "Sexual-Harassment Claims against a 'She-E.O.'"; Tokumitsu, "What a Start-Up's Scandal Says about Your Workplace."

28. Agrawal, *Disrupt-Her*, 81–98.

29. "Meet Our Give Back Partner: Samagra," TUSHY, accessed February 16, 2021, https://hellotushy.com/pages/give-back-program-with-samagra.

30. Marx, *Economic and Philosophic Manuscripts*, 104–5.

31. Marx, 104.

32. Edgar Villanueva, *Decolonizing Wealth*. Villanueva continues: "Money is like water. Water can be a precious live-giving resource. But what happens when water is dammed, or when a water cannon is fired on protestors in subzero temperatures? Money should be a tool of love, used to facilitate relationships.... If it's used for sacred, life-giving, restorative purposes, it can be medicine. Money, used as medicine, can help us decolonize." Villanueva, *Decolonizing Wealth*, 1–4, 9. For an analysis of this text, see Hulsether, "Decolonization, TM."

33. Emerson, *Purpose of Capital*, 202.

34. Emerson, *Purpose of Capital*, 150–51, 184–94. Emerson is most taken by theologian Joerg Rieger's argument that modern capitalism is insinuated with "a kind of hidden religiosity that promotes the worship of gods of the free market." See Rieger, *No Rising Tide*, 33–34.

35. Emerson, *Purpose of Capital*, 194.

INTERLUDE THREE

1. For synthetic analysis of the status of the US religious Left in recent historiography, see especially Danielson, Molin, and Rossinow, "Introduction," 1–17. Historical works that follow the mainline Protestant Left into the 1970s and 1980s without overstating a decline include Hulsether, *Building a Protestant Left*; Rossinow, *Politics of Authenticity*, 335–46; Smith, *Resisting Reagan*.

CHAPTER THREE. MARXISTS IN THE MICROBANK

1. For a longer study of microfinance and development in this period, see Meyerowitz, *A War on Global Poverty*.

2. "Final Script," 35th Anniversary Celebration, November 11, 1996, Box 001, Folder "35th Anniversary Records," ACCION International Records, Tisch Library Special Collections at Tufts University (hereafter AI).

3. Jamie Curran, "Ex-Bruin on Good Will Net Tour," *Los Angeles Times*, March 17, 1959, C5, ProQuest Historical Newspapers (hereafter PHN). On the US federal program, see Von Eschen, *Satchmo Blows Up the World*.

4. ACCION History and Summary of Projects, MS1961001, folder 001:00001, AI.

5. Neil Ulman, "U.S., Venezuela Firms Help Support Yankee 'Private Peace Corps,'" *Wall Street Journal*, July 1, 1963, 1, PHN.

6. Wright, *Latin America in the Era of the Cuban Revolution*.

7. Adelman, "Andean Impasses."

8. Henry Sutherland, "Student's Idea Grew to Junior Peace Corps," *Los Angeles Times*, February 3, 1963, G2, PHN.

9. Henry Sutherland, "ACCION Tells Hopes for Expanding Results," *Los Angeles Times*, February 6, 1963, C14, PHN.

10. Ernest A. Lotito, "Private Peace Corps Aiding Latin America," *Washington Post*, December 4, 1963, PHN. Even ACCION workers reported having received a positive education in the potential of capitalism. One Mt. Holyoke graduate volunteering in Caracas reported back to the board that the work "is giving me a fine lesson in private enterprise, both the development of a capitalistic spirit of competition and the great role that private companies can and should play in the economic and political stability of a nation." Christina Downey to G. Forrest Murden, February 18, 1965, 5, ACCION International Collection, Tufts Digital Collections and Archives (hereafter TDCA).

11. Jack Smith, "Private 'Peace Corps' Extending Its Horizons," *Los Angeles Times*, October 31, 1965, C2, PHN.

12. "'Little Peace Corps' Picks Venezuela," *Christian Science Monitor*, December 4, 1962, 22, PHN; "Private Peace Corps Working in Venezuela," *Los Angeles Times*, December 5, 1962, C4, PHN.

13. Sutherland, "ACCION Tells Hopes," C4. This principle was reiterated throughout the first decade. See also Terry Holcombe, "Minutes of Executive Committee of the Board of Directors of ACCION," New York, October 12, 1971, 5, TDCA.

14. ACCION International, "Proposal to Support the Launching of Action International as a New York Based International Development Agency," October 4, 1965, 2, TDCA.

15. Although ACCION's public documents suggest that the small-lending idea arose only in 1973 in its Recife, Brazil, research, minutes from board meetings suggest that the idea of setting up "small enterprise development" projects that involved banks had been on their minds earlier. See Hans Neumann, "Remarks to the Board of Directors," December 12, 1967, TDCA; ACCION International, "Minutes of the Postponed Annual Meeting of the Board of Directors," June 25, 1968, TDCA. Michael Chu, director of ACCION in the 1990s, would refer to this transformation as the organization's move from "a project of the redistribution of wealth" to "a project of the creation of wealth." The former involved volunteers doing manual labor alongside locals while "consciousness-raising" with them about their collective needs. The latter involved withdrawing this facilitation and empowering poor people to direct their own futures. See "Brief History and Evolution," Box 001, Folder "ACCION Int'l History," AI.

16. On the Peace Corps, see Hoffman, *All You Need Is Love*.

17. "Brief History and Evolution."

18. Cecy Faster, interview by author, Minnetonka, MN, October 27, 2019.

19. St. Luke Presbyterian Church, "Our History," accessed October 15, 2019, www.stluke.mn/our-history.

20. Kay Miller, "Church Shelters Salvadoran Refugee," *Minneapolis Star Tribune*, December 13, 1982, 1, PHN.

21. Ashe et al., *Pisces Studies*, ix.

22. Ashe et al., x.

23. "Brief History and Evolution."

24. Chu and Cuellar, "Banco Compartamos."

25. Roediger, "Making Solidarity Uneasy." For an excellent discussion of the potential of solidarity and coalitions, see Jakobsen, *Working Alliances and the Politics of Difference*.

26. Durkheim, *Division of Labor in Society*. From one angle, Durkheim's account sounds like a typical narrative of religious declension into secular disarray. His later work in *Elementary Forms* clarifies that it is not: this is a story not of declining religion but of a "transformation" in the substance of religion. Durkheim is speaking about a moment of perceived crisis wherein there is no clear source of social order, and he is urging the discovery of a possible source in the corporate form.

27. Durkheim, *Suicide*, 252. As Durkheim writes, "Man's characteristic privilege is that the bond he accepts is not physical but moral; that is, social. He is governed not by a material environment brutally imposed on him, but by a conscience superior to his own."

28. Durkheim, 252, 253.

29. Durkheim, 26–29, 14, 28.

30. Durkheim, *Suicide*, 14–18. Durkheim makes these claims in the context of rehearsing a multi-century history of the worker corporation. He focuses on its social role in both ancient Rome and the European Middle Ages, concluding that it is both "above all . . . a religious organization" in terms of its provision of a "common cult" to members and an "heir to the family" in terms of its regulation of "occupational ethics and law." Durkheim interprets these previous functions as evidence that the modern worker corporation might assume a related role—not as a return to some previous order, but as a reform of the current one. Further work should be done to compare Durkheim's history of the corporation to his history of religion.

31. Durkheim, *Suicide*, 27–31.

32. Even if people were born into a state of equal wealth and power, Durkheim writes, "Life will be just as complex as ever. Because riches will not be transmitted any longer as they are today will not mean that the state of anarchy has disappeared, for it is not a question as to the ownership of riches, but as to the regulation of the activity to which these riches give rise." Durkheim, 30. Appropriating Durkheim for an analysis of religion capitalism, Kathryn Lofton expresses this point in a passage on overlapping discourses of abstention in radical religious movements and mainstream addiction literature: "You know you're in trouble if [addiction] is affecting your relationships with other people. You're using too much porn if you can't have a real sexual interaction without it; you're drinking too much if your loved one can't trust your voice or

person to be a sober one. *You know you're an addict if your idea of society has become one driven by your hungers rather than by your society.*" This final line inherits Durkheim's concern: pathology is desire out of alignment with social discipline. Lofton, *Consuming Religion*, 33 (italics mine).

33. Ashe et al., *Pisces Studies*, 175.
34. Berenbach and Guzmán, "Solidarity Group Experience Worldwide," 12.
35. Elyachar, *Markets of Dispossession*, 1–30.
36. Yunus, *Banker to the Poor*, 105.
37. Nietzsche, *On the Genealogy of Morality*, book 2.
38. For this reason I am suspicious of how Durkheim's reformist social theories have been revived within the academic study of religion, consumer culture, and capitalism. Influentially for many scholars in this field, Kathryn Lofton has used Durkheim to undergird a call to rethink the contours of the academic study of religion, beyond the positivist "world religions" rubric that reigned supreme for the last several decades. For Lofton, Durkheim founds the study of religion as the study of social organization, including the study of how social groups have delineated what does and does not count as "religious" in the first place. "Many of us have never seen the inside of a cathedral, a temple, or a seminary offering theological education, but don't worry," Lofton writes. This nineteenth-century father of sociological theory makes clear that "no matter what you think you are relative to some abstract notion of religion, you are, as a social actor, being determined by it. That is, if you're socialized." See Lofton, *Consuming Religion*, 1–13. For Lofton and for Durkheim, one of the primary referents for establishing such distinctions, and a singularly potent source of social discipline, is corporate culture and commodity capitalism. To shop, to go to work, to use a credit card, and to exist in reference to an economy that monetizes value is to participate in and be organized by a religious system. Likewise, to imagine one set of persons or actions as "religious" while imagining another set as outside of religion is to engage in the very rituals of sacred/profane distinction that define social (religious) life. These distinctions are also shaped by the social worlds that a study of religion diagnoses. Lofton's recuperation of Durkheim has opened up space for new questions and more inclusive scholarship within the field of religious studies. The questions that now have to be asked are those that should be asked about any moment of apparent institutional progress toward equality: What is the relationship of power to difference in this framework? What forms of difference does it oblige and accommodate, and what registers of critique remain illegible to or expelled from it? What techniques of management do we take on board when we adopt one intellectual tradition, and not another, to theorize modern capitalism? Durkheim's excavation of the religious practices of Aboriginal Australians is no mere descriptive project, just as Lofton's analysis of consumer religion is more than a detached narrative of contemporary consumer life. For Lofton, religion—consumer culture—names less alienation than the possibility of "the beginning of a new self-consciousness to liberate us from the very obsessions that it compels." Durkheim writes out of a hope that is visible when we understand his final study through the point that showed up again and again in his earlier studies: the religious function of the social organism had gone haywire in industrial capitalism; religion was also the thing that would make

industrial capitalism better. It was here that Durkheim wrote in earnest disavowal of a Marxian tradition that had gained momentum both on the page and in the transnational labor movement. This is the legacy that we bring into the room when postures of functionalist social reform ground our primary theories of capitalism.

39. The front-page press coverage of Hurtado is vast and spans more than twenty-five years. See "Haven for Refugees," *Los Angeles Times*, December 13, 1982, A2; "Church-Protected Refugee Says He Raped, Tortured," *Minneapolis Star-Tribune*, July 8, 1984, 1A; Josephine Marcetty and Jim Parsons, "Hurtado Begins Long Fight to Stay in U.S.," *Minneapolis Star-Tribune*, February 6, 1985, 1B.

40. Dick Youngblood, "His Notion of Foreign Aid Goes Directly to Those Who Need It," *Minneapolis Star-Tribune*, June 2, 1985, 1D and 8D, PHN.

41. Nelson et al., *Village Banking*, 10–11.

42. Don Davies, interview by author, Minnetonka, MN, October 27, 2019.

43. Richard Lundy, interview by author, Minnetonka, MN, October 27, 2019.

44. Cecy Faster, interview by author, Minnetonka, MN, October 27, 2019.

45. Jean Clarke, interview by author, Minnetonka, MN, October 28, 2019.

46. Daley-Harris, *Reclaiming Our Democracy*.

47. Daley-Harris, chapter 15.

48. Kristen Helmore, "Debate over Capability of World's Poorest People Ruffles US Aid Issue," *Christian Science Monitor*, October 28, 1987, 7, PHN.

49. Cusicanqui, *Bircholas*.

50. Quoted in Robin Ratcliffe, "World's First Commercial Microlending Bank Pays Dividends," ACCION International, Box 5.1, Folder "BancoSol Dividends Release," A1.

51. The apparent entanglements between Compartamos and Regnum Christi merit further scholarly study. See Olmos, "La mafia financiera de los Legionarios de Cristo."

52. Armendariz and Morduch, *Economics of Microfinance*, 17.

53. Chu and Cuellar, "Banco Compartamos."

54. Chu and Cuellar. See also Hillion, Wee, and Rousset, "Microfinance at Credit Suisse," 8–9, https://hbr.org/product/microfinance-at-credit-suisse-linking-the-top-with-the-bop/INS125-PDF-ENG.

55. On these dynamics, see Cull, Demirgüç-Kunt, and Morduch, "Microfinance Meets the Market."

56. Chu and Cuellar, "Banco Compartamos."

57. Richard Lundy, interview by author, Minnetonka, MN, October 27, 2019.

58. Richard Lundy, Cecy Faster, Don Davies, Connie Bell, Lucille Goodwyne, Larry Stickler, Sandy Zeiss, and Frank Kampel, interview by author, Minnetonka, MN, October 27, 2019.

CHAPTER FOUR. REPRESENTING INCLUSION

1. Melamed, *Represent and Destroy*, 42.

2. See Bank of America, "Bank of America Employees around the Country Celebrate Pride," December 15, 2016, https://about.bankofamerica.com/en-us/global-impact/lhnl-pride-events-2016.html#fbid=mvCoK4cd0e0; Coca-Cola Company

Journey Staff, "America Is Beautiful and Coca-Cola Is for Everyone," February 7, 2014, www.coca-colacompany.com/stories/america-is-beautiful-and-coca-cola-is-for-everyone; Walmart, Workplace Diversity 2012, accessed August 29, 2017, http://cdn.corporate.walmart.com/d5/34/df2a49394a7797f5399beeb67f9d/2012-workforce-diversity-report.pdf.

3. Postel, *Populist Vision*, 139–66.

4. Huntington, *Usurer's Grip*, silent film, produced by Thomas A. Edison Inc. and sponsored by the Russell Sage Foundation, rereleased by the National Film Preservation Foundation (Chatsworth, CA: Image Entertainment, [1912] 2007).

5. Gallert, *Small Loan Legislation*, 90–94. This history is also summarized in Calder, *Financing the American Dream*, 22–25.

6. Monograph-length histories of the Russell Sage Foundation include Glenn, Brandt, and Andrews, *Russell Sage Foundation, 1907–1946*; and O'Connor, *Social Science for What?*

7. The motto is taken from the New Testament, Matthew 25:41, from a story in which Jesus informs his disciples that they will be judged by the extent to which they fed the hungry, clothed the naked, and visited the prisoner. Glenn, Brandt, and Andrews, *Russell Sage Foundation, 1907–1946*, 17.

8. Glenn, Brandt, and Andrews, 57–69, 136–51.

9. Wassam, *Salary Loan Business in New York City*; Ham, *Chattel Loan Business*.

10. Wassam, *Salary Loan Business in New York City*; Ham, *Chattel Loan Business*; Robinson, *Ten Thousand Small Loans*.

11. Jackson, *The World and Its Witness*, 276, 236.

12. Gallert, *Small Loan Legislation*, 90–94. This history is also summarized in Calder, *Financing the American Dream*, 111–55; and Hyman, *Debtor Nation*, 22–25.

13. Robinson and Nugent, *Regulation of the Small Loan Business*, 206, 207.

14. The Russell Sage Foundation harbored suspicions about unmarried borrowers and, in an early draft of the Uniform Small Loans model law, required borrowers to obtain consent of their wives in loan applications. See Arthur H. Ham, "Running the Usurer Out of Business," Louisville *Courier-Journal*, November 14, 1909, B2. On racialized sexuality and gender in progressive reform, see Gordon, *Pitied but Not Entitled*; Mink, *Wages of Motherhood*; and Ferguson, "Race-ing Homonormativity." For accounts that focus more on race and deemphasize gender and sexuality, see Muhammad, *Condemnation of Blackness*; and Jacobson, *Whiteness of a Different Color*.

15. O'Neill, "Caught on Camera."

16. Robinson and Nugent, *Regulation of the Small Loan Business*, 13.

17. Robinson and Nugent, 14, 15–16, 17–19, 19–23, 23–25, 25–26, 26–28, 28–30.

18. On anti-Semitic associations between Jews and usury, see Penslar, *Shylock's Children*. On the visual cultures of Christian supersessionism, see Biddick, *Typological Imaginary*.

19. On the role of financial institutions in turn-of-the-century empire in the Americas, see Hudson, *Bankers and Empire*.

20. Wenger, *Religious Freedom*; Jacobson, *Barbarian Virtues*; Kramer, *Blood of Government*.

21. Hartman, *Scenes of Subjection*; Sexton, *Amalgamation Schemes*; Wilderson, *Red, White, and Black*; Sharpe, *Monstrous Intimacies*.

22. Muhammad, *Condemnation of Blackness*.

23. Robinson and Nugent, *Regulation of the Small Loan Business*, 139–41.

24. "Moneylenders See Problem in Strikes," *New York Times*, September 21, 1922, 35.

25. Franklin W. Ryan, "Why Usury Laws Have Failed," *New York Times*, April 9, 1922, 95.

26. Historical treatments of the social gospel have tended to underscore the well-intentioned critiques of its members over and against the profit motives that surrounded them. The primary critiques of the social gospel are that despite good intentions, its middle-class and elite spokespeople did not connect well enough with the protests of workers themselves; the constructive response to this problem has been to recuperate depictions of working-class Christianity among the poor. Switching between the two poles of elite good intention and worker innovation, this pattern of interpretation takes place alongside rich literature on the multifaceted progressive movement of which the social gospel, also internally contested and diverse, is a part. Many historians who dismiss the role of Christianity in progressive movements have argued convincingly that the era of turn-of-the-century industrialization and progressive reform was one of expanded forms of institution building and consolidation of state power in the service of industrial markets. I am building on this literature to suggest that moral and theological critiques of tycoon capitalism were not mutually exclusive to collaboration with tycoon capitalism as it moved into its next phase; the former critique was the motor for the latter change. On the social gospel, see, for example, Cantwell, Carter, and Drake, "Introduction: Between the Pew and the Picket Line"; Carter, *Union Made*; Dorrien, *Social Ethics in the Making*; Fox, "Culture of Liberal Protestant Progressivism, 1875–1925"; Fones-Wolf, *Trade Union Gospel*; and May, *Protestant Churches and Industrial America*. For synthetic work on progressives, see McGerr, *Fierce Discontent*; Gilmore, "Responding to the Challenges of the Progressive Era"; Rodgers, *Atlantic Crossings*; and Diner, *Very Different Age*. To date, the most balanced treatment on the role of liberal and Left interiority in shaping political activism—with mixed consequences—is Rossinow, *Politics of Authenticity*.

27. For broad outlines, see Hyman, *Debtor Nation*; and Calder, *Financing the American Dream*.

28. Muhammad Yunus, "Opening Plenary," February 2, 1997, www.grameen.com/category/microcredit-summit-1997.

29. "Key Points: Microenterprise Award Winners," January 23, 1997, Folder "Presidential Award 1997," ACCION International Records, Tisch Library Special Collections at Tufts University (hereafter AI).

30. "ACCION International's United States Network," n.d., Box 001, Folder "ACCION US Project," AI.

31. "Additional Background Prep for ACCION Staff," n.d., Box 001, Folder "More Staff Resources," AI.

32. "ACCION International's United States Network."

33. Gabriela Roman to Program Directors of the AWARD WINNING US Network, January 23, 1997, Box 196 006.002, Folder "Presidential Award 1997," AI.

34. Draft Press Release for Presidential Award, January 24, 1997, Box 006.002, Folder "Presidential Awards," AI.

35. Logemann, "From Cradle to Bankruptcy."

36. C. K. Prahalad and his colleague Stuart L. Hart introduced the concept of a "world economic pyramid" in a 2002 coauthored article published under the same title as Prahalad's eventual book. Both this article and Prahalad's book list the pyramid's source as "U.N. World Development Reports" but do not name any specific report or release date. It is so far unclear to me whether they are discussing a report from the World Bank (the UN does not appear to publish "world development reports," but the World Bank does) and whether they are diagramming numbers in a report or reproducing an actual chart. Ambiguous provenance notwithstanding, this diagram has been widely reproduced in NGO reports and articles on economic development, generally with the sourcing provided by Prahalad and Hart. That this has been the citation practice speaks to the influence of Prahalad's exposition of the economic pyramid; I have so far been unable to find any citation of this diagram that cites the original UN report. See Prahalad and Hart, "Fortune at the Bottom of the Pyramid"; and Prahalad, *Fortune at the Bottom of the Pyramid*.

37. Prahalad, *Fortune at the Bottom of the Pyramid*, 1, 60–61.

38. The pyramid also works within development theories that distinguish themselves from Prahalad's. The most well-known direct critique of Prahalad is from Aneel Karani, who charges Prahalad with investing in a "mirage at the bottom of the pyramid." He argues that Prahalad errs in recognizing the poor as "consumers" rather than "producers" and that Prahalad romanticizes the private sector in a way that downplays the role of government in providing "public safety, basic education, public health, and infrastructure, all of which increase the productivity and employability of the poor, and thus their income and well being." Karani and Prahalad disagree on whether it is better to include the poor as producers (Karani) or consumers (Prahalad) and whether the state should aid their participation through providing public infrastructure (Karani) or deregulating business (Prahalad). But their common ground is greater than their difference. The shared basic message is that the state should support market participation of the poor and that business should recognize the poor as candidates for global economic citizenship. Karnani, "Mirage at the Bottom of the Pyramid."

39. On crisis ordinary, see Berlant, *Cruel Optimism*. On disaster capitalism, see Harvey, *A Brief History of Neoliberalism*.

40. Hillion, Wee, and Rousset, "Microfinance at Credit Suisse," 8–9; Chu and Cuellar, "Banco Compartamos."

41. For a quantitative overview of the mortgage securities collapse, see Joint Center for Housing Studies of Harvard University, "State of the Nation's Housing 2008."

42. Edward Gramlich, "Subprime Mortgage Lending: Benefits, Costs, and Challenges," Remarks at the Financial Services Roundtable Annual Housing Policy Meeting, May 21, 2004, www.federalreserve.gov/boarddocs/speeches/2004/20040521.

43. Micheline Maynard, "Edward Gramlich, a Former Governor of the U.S. Federal Reserve, Dies at 68," *New York Times*, September 7, 2007. https://www.nytimes.com/2007/09/07/business/worldbusiness/07iht-obits.1.7417292.html.

44. Ben S. Bernanke, "The Subprime Mortgage Market," Remarks at the Federal Reserve Bank of Chicago's 43rd Annual Conference on Bank Structure and Competition, May 17, 2007, www.federalreserve.gov/newsevents/speech/bernanke20070517a.htm.

45. For a fuller analysis on this "predatory inclusion," see Taylor, *Race for Profit*.

46. Chakravartty and Silva, "Accumulation, Dispossession, and Debt," 367.

47. Harney and Moten, *Undercommons*, 61–70.

48. Prahalad and Lieberthal, "End of Corporate Imperialism."

49. Center for Financial Inclusion, "About Us," accessed December 19, 2016, www.centerforfinancialinclusion.org. The CFI website was revamped in 2018, so the video has moved. It is now available at Center for Financial Inclusion, "Constance Considers Financial Inclusion," www.centerforfinancialinclusion.org/constance-considers-financial-inclusion-video.

INTERLUDE FIVE

1. The video of the lecture has been taken down. The scholar who it depicted is Stefano Harney. There is a statement almost like the one that Mark transcribed in Harney, "Governance and the Undercommons." This argument is developed in Harney and Moten, *Undercommons*, 55–57.

CHAPTER FIVE. THE HUNT FOR YES

1. During my fieldwork I interacted with a total of ten MFIs for some period of time (ranging from three months of residency to day visits). This is only a very small fraction of the minimum of two thousand MFIs estimated to operate in Guatemala. These MFIs include commercial banks, small nonprofits, church and parachurch bodies, employer-based lending programs, and cooperatives. Observers within the microfinance industry have made efforts to differentiate MFIs by their nonprofit or for-profit affiliation, by their gender demographics, by the interest rates they charge, by presence and style of educational programming, by longevity in the country, and more. This study is less interested in parsing these comparisons than it is in understanding the installation of the common sense that capitalism provides a solution to ravages caused by capitalism. The conviction is not limited to agents of finance capitalism, although the particular intensity of finance's investment in abstraction—everything and anything can be fashioned into a source of capital, even poverty itself—makes it a particularly fruitful site of inquiry. For an overview of the sorts of NGOs operating in Guatemala, see Beck, *How Development Projects Persist*, 45–57; and McIntosh and Wydick, "Competition and Microfinance." On poverty as a form of capital, see Roy, *Poverty Capital*; and Elyachar, *Markets of Dispossession*.

2. Social Performance Management Center at the Grameen Foundation, *Piloting the PPI*.

3. Innovations for Poverty Action, "PPI Users."

4. Social Performance Management Center at the Grameen Foundation, *Piloting the PPI*.

5. On anger, feminism, and what counts as reasonable, see Ahmed, *Cultural Politics of Emotion*, 172–78. Ahmed focuses particularly on the attribution of anger to feminists when they protest injustice and, more importantly for Ahmed, the fundamental rightness of anger as a feminist response to pains inflicted by misogyny. Ahmed's observations sit uncomfortably with the anger of the financier toward the weaver, given the skewed dynamic of racial, economic, and gendered power in the situation. If anger is a response to a feeling of pain—and if "reasonability" is also affectively produced—we could inquire why the financier felt the "no" as painful. What idea of relation did it pain? What part of his desire, and the desire of capitalist humanitarian data-contract culture more generally, did it interrupt? These are the questions that this chapter explores.

6. Stanley, *From Bondage to Contract*, x. For a concise overview of key debates within contract theory as they pertain to perennial concerns in American studies scholarship, see Stanley, "Contract," in *Keywords for American Cultural Studies*, 61.

7. The most prominent early modern-contract theorists are Thomas Hobbes, John Locke, John-Jacques Rousseau, and Immanuel Kant. The contemporary heir to these thinkers is John Rawls. Rawls speaks less of "consent" to be governed than in terms of "agreement" to common principles of governance. The exercise of coercive power is legitimate when it is premised on terms that free and equal citizens "may reasonably be expected to endorse in the light of principles and ideals acceptable to their common human reason." His notion of the human is optimistic (she is rational; she is capable of toleration; she seeks life in common). Rawls, *Political Liberalism*, 137.

8. The temporality of indenture and contract labor (which at least in theory ends when one has paid off one's debt) comes into direct contrast with the temporality of slavery (which remains in perpetuity). The contract as a document that both commits its signatory to a set of terms and recognizes this signatory as an agentive self would seem to perform a racial politics that understands the self as owner: if you have debt, it is temporary. But maybe there is something else here. The surrounds of the contract scene—which first is one of data accumulation and exchange—suggest that the equal trade of wills is not the only thing being aided by the contract. As is elaborated below, the contract is also becoming a vehicle through which to articulate a *desire* for an equal agency that may always be deferred. The historical literature on indenture is vast. On temporality and indenture, see Stanley, *From Bondage to Contract*, 60–97; Valenze, *Social Life of Money in the English Past*; and Steinfield, *Coercion, Contract, and Free Labor in the Nineteenth Century*, 253–89. On indenture in relation to other forms of labor in the early United States, see Montgomery, *Citizen Worker*, 1–40; Rockman, *Scraping By*; and Salinger, *"To Serve Well and Faithfully."* For a critical-race analysis of indenture and slavery, see Fields, "Slavery, Race, and Ideology in the United States of America."

9. Critiques of contract overlap significantly with critiques of liberalism. They crosscut fields of labor and economic studies (critiques of the wage, contract between

free and unfree labor), feminist theory and gender/sexuality studies (the marriage contract), critical-race and ethnic studies (the relationship between self-ownership and whiteness), and postcolonial and decolonial theory (contract as an instrument of dispossession and genocide). Key works include Pateman, *Sexual Contract*; Mills, *Racial Contract*; and Mills and Pateman, *Contract and Domination*.

10. Conrad, *Against Equality*; Weiss, "Reinvigorating the Queer Political Imagination," 845–49.

11. The turn to new materialisms might be read as a flight from the liberal, secular subject and her human exceptionalism. This is happening across subdisciplines. See, for example, Barad, "Posthumanist Performativity"; Chen, *Animacies*; Haraway, *When Species Meet*; and Muñoz, "The Sense of Brownness."

12. The death drive is taken up by what is loosely known as the antisocial or antirelational school of queer theory, whose standard bearers build primarily on Lacanian psychoanalysis. See Bersani, *Homos*; Edelman, *No Future*; Scott, *Extravagant Abjection*; and Viego, *Dead Subjects*.

13. To use the figure of "spirit" and "sacred" as a name for what is fugitive to racial capitalism and its anomie has become an increasingly common turn within queer theory and critical-race and ethnic studies. Three examples are Alexander, *Pedagogies of Crossing*; Crawley, *Blackpentecostal Breath*; and Cvetkovich, *Depression*, 154–202.

14. Gumbs, *Undrowned*.

15. Boyer, *Handbook of Disappointed Fate*.

16. Mivera, "Move Slow and Break Things."

17. McAlevy, *No Shortcuts*.

18. Some of the richest parts of this conversation have been anchored in performance studies. The concept of fugitivity is theorized at length in Harney and Moten, *Undercommons*. See also Moten, *In the Break*; Muñoz, *Cruising Utopia*; Brooks, *Bodies in Dissent*; Brown, *Babylon Girls*;.

19. My thinking is influenced by Silva, *Toward a Global Idea of Race*; and Moreiras, *Exhaustion of Difference*. I am grateful to Adrian Hernandez-Acosta for conversation on this point.

20. Murphy, *Economization of Life*.

21. Cheah, "Biopower and the New Division of Reproductive Labor."

22. I have cited in this chapter the questions from the 2009 version of the Progress Out of Poverty Index, which were developed in advance of the institutional name change. The copy of this survey is in the author's possession; the questions asked for Guatemala have since changed to focus even more intensely on personal possessions. Questions about employment have been replaced with questions about whether or not the family has cable-television and cell-phone service. For the 2014 Guatemala scorecard and its conversion chart, see Schreiner, "PPI for Guatemala 2014." For current versions of PPI scorecards for different countries, see Innovations for Poverty Action, "PPI by Country."

23. Jacques Derrida's canonical footnoted line resonates here: "There is no political power without control of the archive, if not memory. Effective democratization can always be measured by this essential criterion: the participation in and access to the

archive, its constitution, and its interpretation." Derrida, *Archive Fever*, 4. Derrida and many of his readers have suggested that the reproduction of state power depends upon the archive as legitimator of collective memory and forger of collective consciousness. The claim can spark a complementary rush to identify exactly *when* and *how* historical archives become tools of a gendered domination, and when and how they can preserve insurgent knowledges or shore up resistance. See Hamilton et al., *Refiguring the Archive*; and Blouin and Rosenberg, *Archives, Documentation, and Institutions of Social Memory*. The flight to resistance amid domination recapitulates the drive to legibility and classification within normative regimes. The critique of archival power can get displaced into a conversation about which specific archives serve what ends. So: here is an archive of an empire that controlled its subjects with tight taxonomic knowledge, but there is an archive that bespeaks the contingency and anxiety of that same empire. There is an archive of a tyrannical state, recording its every victim by name, address, family, and photo. And, still, here are human-rights defenders, some of them professional historians, recovering these same documents to create a counterhistory. There is an archive that interpolates its user into the racializing violence it both represents and reinstates; here is how nevertheless it reveals better alternatives. As our archival judgments swing between its poles, they index less a final clarity on truths that scholars have revealed than anxieties about and strategies relative to the afterlives of colonialism and slavery. Recent work among scholars who work in the black Atlantic and the history of slavery have engaged the paradox of the archive as, in Jennifer Morgan's words, "both the home of those who commanded and the tantalizing place from which that command might be subverted" such that "engagement with the archive is an opportunity to confront the exclusionary powers that position racialized subjects as outside the national project." For essays that introduce the question of slavery's archive and its command-subversion paradox, see Helton et al., "Question of Recovery"; Connolly and Fuentes, "Introduction"; Hartman, "Venus in Two Acts"; and Morgan, "Archives and Histories of Racial Capitalism." For works that straddle both the "state control" and the "vulnerable state" lines in order to underscore the contingency of state narrative, see, for example, Weld, *Paper Cadavers*; and Azoulay, "Imperial Condition of Photography in Palestine." My thinking is especially influenced by Roderick Ferguson's analysis of universities through Derrida. See Ferguson, *Reorder of Things*, 1–20.

24. That women supposedly are more likely to invest loans in the businesses and in their children—whereas men are more likely to spend loan payments on gambling, tobacco, and alcohol—is a perennial justification for women-only loan programs. This idea is ingrained enough as a truism that economists of microfinance now debate the extent of its veracity. I am interested in this debate less for what it reveals about actual household spending than for how it reveals the characteristics of general "women" as a question for debate, quantification, and economic optimization. See Armendariz and Morduch, *Economics of Microfinance*, 2nd ed., 211–37; and Kevane and Wydick, "Microenterprise Lending to Female Entrepreneurs."

25. On neoliberal intervention and women's empowerment, see Dolhinow, *Jumble of Needs*, 141–77; and Karim, *Microfinance and Its Discontents*, xiii–xxxiii.

26. For diagnoses mainly focused on the subject of humanitarian development, see especially Bernal and Grewal, *Theorizing NGOs*; Bornstein, *Spirit of Development*; and Ferguson, *Anti-Politics Machine*. For diagnoses mainly focused on debt subjectivity within late capitalism and especially post-2008, see Berlant, *Cruel Optimism*; Chakravartty and Silva, "Accumulation, Dispossession, and Debt," 368–85; Kish and Leroy, "Bonded Life"; and Lazzarato, *Making of the Indebted Man*.

27. See Meta and Sanford, "My Turn to Speak."

28. Schacher and Schmidtke, "Harmful Returns," 1.

29. BPO Guatemala, "Finishing School."

30. For a much closer account of call-center policy and practice in Guatemala, see O'Neill, *Secure the Soul*, 96–119.

31. Mankekar and Gupta, "Intimate Encounters"; O'Neill, *Secure the Soul*, 96–98; Rodkey, "Disposable Labor, Repurposed."

INTERLUDE SIX

1. Ryan, "The Job," 193.

CHAPTER SIX. HOPE FOR THE FUTURE

1. Narciso et al., "Totonicapán 2013."

2. This discourse shows up in a lot of places, but it is especially easy to witness on the microlending website www.kiva.org. The site invites users to browse the individual profiles of mostly international small-scale entrepreneurs in need of financing and to choose whom they want to support. Something like a cross between switchboard for crowd-funding and an online dating service, the site has tended to deemphasize the fact that lenders' money does not (necessarily) go to the individual subject of the profile they selected. The money goes into a general financing pool administered by the local microfinance institution from which that borrower received financing. On Kiva, see Shuster, *Social Collateral*, 103–37.

3. Murphy, *Economization of Life*; Brown, *Undoing the Demos*, 35.

4. For documentation of this trend within scholarship on development, see Leatherman et al., "Integrating Microfinance and Health Strategies."

5. The public-facing materials from Grameen are intentionally vague about this. In addition to promoting the higher rate of contraceptive use among its clients, Grameen requires its borrowers to take a pledge called the "Sixteen Decisions." Among them is this commitment: "We shall keep our families small. We shall minimize our expenditures. We shall look after our health." That these all are one pledge constructs family size and sees it as valuable for reasons of public health and financial expediency. See Yunus with Jolis, *Banker to the Poor*, 135–37. Sam Daley-Harris, an associate of Yunus whose antihunger advocacy introduced Grameen to US audiences in the 1990s, lauded Grameen as "the only bank in the world with its own birth control policy." Daley-Harris, *Reclaiming Our Democracy*, 111.

6. I have kept the details of this lending program intentionally vague to protect the anonymity of the employees who disclosed the details of this program. This bank is not the only one employing such a program, however. For a policy example of how managed reproductivity is articulated as a rationale for microlending, see Kuchler, "Do Microfinance Programs Change Fertility?" For an example of popular coverage of these programs, see Nadia Sussman, "In the Most Isolated Areas of Latin America, Microcredits Are Saving the Lives of Indigenous Women," *Univision News*, March 26, 2018, www.univision.com/univision-news/health/in-the-most-isolated-areas-of-latin-america-microloans-are-saving-the-lives-of-indigenous-women?platform=hootsuite.

7. Scholars have shown how the convergence of private profit motives and welfare provisions can decimate public infrastructures that struggle to compete with investment capital. For an overview, see Harvey, *Brief History of Neoliberalism*. For studies related to health care, see Turshen, *Privatizing Health Services in Africa*; Homedes and Ugalde, "Why Neoliberal Health Reforms Have Failed in Latin America"; Boris and Klein, *Caring for America*; and Winant, *Next Shift*.

8. Murphy, *Economization of Life*, 144.

9. During fieldwork I was struck by the example of "Starfish," formerly known as "Maia Impact," a US-based NGO whose CEO also founded a large microfinance institution in Guatemala that selects indigenous "Girl Pioneers" for private schooling focused on leadership and entrepreneurship. These goals tie reproduction—"delay marriage and pregnancy to the age of 25"—to the generation of wealth, defined as working for an NGO or as an elected leader in a position of institutional hierarchy over other women (success in this world means becoming a manager of others). Simultaneously, it extends the period of protected girlhood to age twenty-five. Individual profiles of program graduates mention not only their job or degree program but also that they are "unmarried and without children." See Maia: Her Infinite Impact, accessed January 1, 2021, www.maiaimpact.org.

10. For an overview of social reproduction theory, see Bhattacharya and Vogel, *Social Reproduction Theory*. On the valuation of the family within both neoliberalism and neoconservatism, see Cooper, *Family Values*. Cooper introduces the phrase "theology of the social" to describe transfer of welfare provisions to private religious—usually right-wing Christian—providers. I diverge from this analysis in that I analyze the religious beyond what the state designates by this term. Building on but departing from Cooper, I want to suggest that a singular focus on the activities of explicitly religious institutions—and especially an overwrought concern about the mobilization of the Right—hampers our capacity to demonstrate the full scope of an alliance between Christianity and the constitution of the social.

11. There is awkward synergy between this financial rhetoric on banks as a check on machismo and scholarly diagnoses of conversion to Pentecostal Christianity as a check on machismo—including and especially Elizabeth Brusco's consequential construal of Pentecostal conversion as a "strategic women's movement" insofar as involvement in these church communities inspires men to provide for their families rather than congregate with their rowdy guy friends. As Rebecca Bartel makes clear in her recent work, this analysis rests on deeply flawed premises. The first of these is a presumption

of a racialized gender binary wherein "women" are communal and "men" are individualistic, and where Latin American men in particular have expressed this individualism through drinking, gambling, and prostitution. This second is a baseless disaggregation of men's economic productivity—the choice to work and invest in the family rather than blow money on alcohol, gambling, and sex workers—from patriarchy. To Bartel's salient points, I would add that that men's productivity is delinked from patriarchy *through* the assignation of women's productivity as "feminist" and the designation of the home as a site of capital production. When men's "individualism" is ostensibly reincorporated into the (economic-value–bearing) family, it becomes possible to imagine a woman's successful economic production triggering her husband's putative impulse toward recovered dominance in family and market, even as the two domains blur. The implication of these arguments about women inspiring men to invest in family—whether anchored in scholarly analyses of Pentecostal conversion or financial-sector analyses of microfinance outcomes—rests on a logic where women's agency is valuable insofar as it helps to recover heteropatriarchal inclinations to paternalist productivity. See Bartel, *Card-Carrying Christians*, 237–38; and Brusco, *Reformation of Machismo*.

12. DeTemple, *Making Market Women*, 41–64; Lughod, *Do Muslim Women Need Saving?*, 121–36; Sharma, *Logics of Empowerment*.

13. For an outstanding study of how microfinance programs that target women reinforce patriarchy while extracting maximum capital value from their participants, see Radhakrishnan, *Making Women Pay*.

14. This discourse, in Christian contexts, will point to the Apostle Paul's announcement that "there is no longer Jew or Greek, there is no longer slave or free, there is no longer male and female; for all of you are one in Christ Jesus. And if you belong to Christ, then you are Abraham's offspring, heirs according to the promise" (Galatians 3: 28–29, New Revised Standard Version). This passage and ones related to it have been subject to a great deal of criticism within the field of New Testament studies. Works that focus on its race and reproductive politics include Boyarin, *Radical Jew*; Buell, *Why This New Race?*; and Hodge, *If Sons, then Heirs*. Significant scholarship on this text reads it in relation to Paul as a political subject within the Roman Empire and uses it to reflect on issues of subjectivity, difference, and universality within contexts of domination. Feminist and postcolonial critics have pointed out how the field's focus on Paul as a singular voice—whether that voice is imagined as liberatory or oppressive, supportive of empire or against it—obscures differences among many actors who, within early Christianity and beyond, struggled with these issues. For an overview of some of the literature on Paul the subject and an argument for attending to the dialogical context of his writings, see Nasrallah and Johnson-DeBaufre, "Beyond the Heroic Paul." This critique notwithstanding, the fact that there is a context for such a correction reflects the dominance of Paul as a resource for theories of difference and universalism within and beyond Christian communities. See, for example, philosophers who draw on Paul's universalist pronouncements as resources for political reflection, such as Badiou, *St. Paul*; and Zizek, *The Fragile Absolute*.

15. Armstrong, "Of Flesh and Spirit"; Jay, *Throughout Your Generations Forever*.

16. Theologians have seized upon these metaphors to mount their own anticapitalist critiques. They explain that the family of Christ has been recast as the family of global capitalism, in which one becomes a subject of capitalism through inheritance of the Christian promise of salvation. These analogies then support a historical argument in which the family of Christ has become secularized as the family of the global free market. I sketch quickly here the kinds of historical gestures made by those theologians who critique capitalism as a forgery of authentic Christian community. Notable too are secular critics who espouse the inverse argument, that the seeming secularity of capitalism is but veneer over the Christian truth that underlies it. I do not wish to take a position in theological debates about who speaks for Christianity. Rather, I am arguing that we can better grasp the work of capitalist humanitarian discourse if we understand something about the ingrained tropes that it samples and reworks. See, for example, Goodchild, *Theology of Money*.

17. Levy, *Freaks of Fortune*.

18. Moreton, *To Serve God and Wal-Mart*.

19. Peretti, "My Nike Media Adventure."

20. Berlant, "Subject of True Feeling," 56. See also Berlant, *Queen of America*.

21. For an ethnographic study of these affects, see Kaell, *Christian Globalism at Home*.

22. Berlant, "Subject of True Feeling," 57.

23. Berlant, 21.

24. In conversation with Berlant, Lee Edelman has analyzed how the figural "Child" cinches a politics that has become a name for "the temporalization of desire, for its translation into a narrative, for its teleological determination." When political promise and political desire are vested in a sentimentalized "next generation," it is easier to remain accommodated to the material, social world in its current form. The symbolic Child is not only an "it-gets-better" promissory note always deferred, but also a license to annihilate whatever critiques would undermine the narrative resolution and affective closure that she ensures. Reading back and forth between Edelman and Berlant, it is possible to find a feminist theory of social reproduction shifted so that the question of the production of *desire* for politics and social life is the central object of critique. The reproductive family underwrites economic production, not only at the level of material output but also at the level of maintaining an attachment to a social world and social future that is premised on a sacrifice of its negative. See Edelman, *No Future*, 1–12.

25. The fact that the idealized child—the child that capitalist humanitarianism is supposed to protect—is the child laborer complicates both Edelman's analysis and José Muñoz's retort that "the future is only the stuff of *some* kids. Racialized kids, queer kids, are not the sovereign princes of futurity." The racialized child factory worker is always the sovereign prince of futurity, and it is the futurity of neoliberal multicultural free markets and the reproduction of their labor force. The child guarantees not only the physical maintenance of this world but also the possibilities of the good—of learning, of relative upward mobility, of diversity—despite everything that the world is. The imagined symbolic child is always available regardless of what is in front of you, regardless of the materiality of actual children who might be right there but who are

constantly being disappeared in the presumptive whiteness of the capitalist humanitarian form. Muñoz, *Cruising Utopia*, 95.

26. Fisher, "Precarious Dystopias," 27–28.

EPILOGUE

1. For records of the case, see National Labor Relations Board, Case 01-RC-183022, https://www.nlrb.gov/case/01-RC-183022 (accessed July 19, 2022).

2. For theory on union democracy and organizing methods, see Inouye, "Antinomies of Organizing"; McAlevey, *Raising Expectations*; Pitkin, *On the Line*.

3. For a lucid reflection on some of these themes, see Battistoni, "Spadework."

4. The language of reparative reading was developed by Eve Sedgwick, who elaborated a distinction between paranoid and reparative critical practices within queer studies scholarship. Sedgwick's language has been taken up by a cohort of queer feminist studies scholars who have called for a new "turn" to the reparative. For an excellent overview and analysis of this conversation, see Wiegman, "The Times We're In." For the early essay, see Sedgwick, *Touching Feeling*, 123–51. For visions of reparative reading, see Love, "Truth and Consequences"; Felski, *Limits of Critique*; and Nash, *Black Feminism Reimagined*.

5. On how the subject who identifies a problem with normative power is identified as the one who is actually causing damage, and on how freedom entails becoming affectively alienated from and tearing down institutions that we imagine as the source of belonging and good feeling, see Ahmed, *Promise of Happiness*.

6. These arguments have been lodged against many traditions of philosophical pessimisms, including queer pessimisms, black pessimisms, and Marxist pessimisms (especially those associated with the Frankfurt school). Jared Sexton has written an especially lucid analysis of these conversations as they have been staged within—and as they have been preoccupied about—the broad discursive field of Black studies. Sexton, "Social Life of Social Death." For helpful interventions into these debates as they have unfolded in queer and feminist studies subfields, see Mallette, "Lesbian Feminist Killjoy," Tonstad, "Ambivalent Loves"; Shahani, "Future Is Queer Stuff."

7. My thinking on reification is shaped by Alberto Moreiras's critique of historicist methods and identitarian epistemologies in Latin American cultural studies, as well as his call for "a nonprogrammable program of thinking that refuses to find satisfaction in appropriation at the same time as it refuses to fall into appropriative drives." See Moreiras, *The Exhaustion of Difference*, 22–24. My thinking on logics of propriation—as the "pivot of appropriation and expropriation"—is indebted to the scholarship of Jodi Byrd, Alyosha Goldstein, Jodi Melamed, and Chandan Reddy. See Byrd et al., "Predatory Value," 3–4.

8. Sexton, "Affirmation in the Dark," 90–98.

9. Adorno, *Minima Moralia*, 122.

10. Balestrini, *We Want Everything*.

11. For additional description, see Barker et al., "Just the Beginning, Yale."

bibliography

Abdurraquib, Hanif. *The Can't Kill Us until They Kill Us: Essays*. Columbus, OH: Two Dollar Radio, 2017.

Abu-Lughod, Lila. *Do Muslim Women Need Saving?* Cambridge, MA: Harvard University Press, 2013.

Adelman, Jeremy Adelman. "Andean Impasses." *New Left Review* 18 (November–December 2002): 40–72.

Agrawal, Miki. *Disrupt-Her: A Manifesto for the Modern Woman*. Carlsbad, CA: Hay House, 2018.

Ahmed, Sara. *The Cultural Politics of Emotion*. Durham, NC: Duke University Press, 2004.

Ahmed, Sara. *The Promise of Happiness*. Durham, NC: Duke University Press, 2010.

Alexander, Jacqui. *Pedagogies of Crossing: Meditations of Feminism, Sexual Politics, Memory, and the Sacred*. Durham, NC: Duke University Press, 2007.

Althaus-Reid, Marcella María. "Gustavo Gutierrez Goes to Disneyland: *Theme Park Theologies* and the Diaspora of the Discourse of the Popular Theologian in Liberation Theology." In *Interpreting beyond Borders,* edited by Fernando Segovia, 36–58. Sheffield, UK: Sheffield University Press, 2000.

Andijar, Gil. *Blood: A Critique of Christianity*. New York: Columbia University Press, 2015.

Armendariz, Beatriz, and Jonathan Morduch. *The Economics of Microfinance*. Cambridge, MA: MIT Press, 2010.

Armendariz, Beatriz, and Jonathan Morduch. *The Economics of Microfinance*. 2nd ed. Cambridge, MA: MIT Press, 2014.

Armstrong, Amaryah. "Of Flesh and Spirit: Race, Reproduction, and Sexual Difference in the Turn to Paul." *Journal for Cultural and Religious Theory* 16, no. 2 (Spring 2017): 126–41.

Asad, Talal. *Formations of the Secular: Christianity, Islam, Modernity*. Stanford, CA: Stanford University Press, 2003.

Ashe, Jeffrey, et al. *The PISCES Studies: Assisting the Smallest Economic Activities of the Urban Poor*. Washington, DC: Office of Urban Development, Bureau for Science and Technology, Agency for International Development, International Development Cooperation Agency, 1981.

Aviv, Rachel. "The Philosopher of Feelings." *New Yorker*, July 25, 2016. https://www.newyorker.com/magazine/2016/07/25/martha-nussbaums-moral-philosophies.

Ayala, César J., and Rafael Bernabe. *Puerto Rico in the American Century: A History since 1898*. Chapel Hill: University of North Carolina Press, 2007.

Azoulay, Ariella. "The Imperial Condition of Photography in Palestine: Archives, Looting, and the Figure of the Infiltrator." *Visual Anthropology Review* 33, no. 1 (2017): 5–17.

Balestrini, Nanni. *We Want Everything: The Novel of Italy's Hot Autumn*. London, England: Verso, 2016.

Badiou, Alain. *St. Paul: The Foundation of Universalism*. Translated by Ray Brassier. Stanford, CA: Stanford University Press, 2003.

Barad, Karen. "Posthumanist Performativity: Toward an Understanding of How Matter Comes to Matter." *Signs: Journal of Women and Culture in Society* 28, no. 3 (2003): 801–31.

Barker, Tim, Alyssa Battistoni, Tobi Haslett, Michael Paulson, and Gabriel Winant. "Just the Beginning, Yale: On Graduate Labor and the Yale Commencement Protest." *n+1*. May 26, 2017. https://www.nplusonemag.com/online-only/online-only/just-the-beginning-yale/.

Bartel, Rebecca C. *Card-Carrying Christians: Debt and the Making of Free Market Spirituality in Colombia*. Berkeley: University of California Press, 2021.

Bartel, Rebecca C., and Lucia Hulsether. "Introduction: Classifying Capital." *Journal of the American Academy of Religion* 87, no. 3 (September 2019): 1–15.

Battistoni, Alyssa. "Spadework: On Political Organizing." *n+1* 34 (Spring 2019). https://www.nplusonemag.com/issue-34/politics/spadework/.

Beck, Erin. *How Development Projects Persist: Everyday Negotiations with Guatemalan NGOs*. Durham, NC: Duke University Press, 2017.

Benjamin, Walter. "Theses on the Philosophy of History." In *Illuminations: Essays and Reflections*, 253–64. New York: Schocken, (1968) 2007.

Berenbach, Shari, and Diego Guzmán. "The Solidarity Group Experience Worldwide." ACCION International, (1989) 1999. Accessed October 20, 2019. https://centerforfinancialinclusionblog.files.wordpress.com.

Berlant, Lauren. *Cruel Optimism*. Durham, NC: Duke University Press, 2011.

Berlant, Lauren. *The Female Complaint*. Durham, NC: Duke University Press, 2008.

Berlant, Lauren. *The Queen of America Goes to Washington City*. Durham, NC: Duke University Press, 1997.

Berlant, Lauren. "The Subject of True Feeling." In *Cultural Pluralism, Identity Politics, and the Law*, edited by Austin Sarat and Thomas R. Kearns, 49–84. Ann Arbor: University of Michigan Press, 1999.

Bernal, Victoria, and Inderpal Grewal, eds. *Theorizing NGOs: States, Feminism, and Neoliberalism.* Durham, NC: Duke University Press, 2014.

Bernstein, Robin. "'I'm Very Happy to Be in the Reality-Based Community': Alison Bechdel's *Fun Home*, Digital Photography, and George W. Bush." *American Literature* 89, no. 1 (March 2017): 121–55.

Bersani, Leo. *Homos.* Cambridge, MA: Harvard University Press, 1996.

Bhattacharya, Tithi, and Lisa Vogel, eds. *Social Reproduction Theory: Remapping Class, Recentering Oppression.* London: Pluto, 2017.

Biddick, Kathleen. *The Typological Imaginary: Circumcision, Technology, History.* Philadelphia: University of Pennsylvania Press, 2011.

"Blake Mycoskie's Bio." TOMS Shoes. Accessed October 10, 2018. www.toms.com/blakes-bio.

Blouin, Francis X., Jr., and William G. Rosenberg, eds. *Archives, Documentation, and Institutions of Social Memory: Essays from the Sawyer Seminar.* Ann Arbor: University of Michigan Press, (2006) 2010.

Borgwardt, Elizabeth. *A New Deal for the World: America's Vision for Human Rights.* Cambridge, MA: Harvard University Press, 2005.

Boris, Eileen, and Jennifer Klein. *Caring for America: Home Health Workers in the Shadow of the Welfare State.* New York: Oxford University Press, 2012.

Bornstein, Erica. *The Spirit of Development: Protestant NGOs, Morality, and Economics in Zimbabwe.* Stanford, CA: Stanford University Press, 2005.

Bottes, Lorenzo Canas. *Old Colony Mennonites in Argentina and Bolivia: Nation Making, Religious Conflict, and Imagination of the Future.* Leiden: Brill, 2008.

Boyarin, Daniel. *A Radical Jew: Paul and the Politics of Identity.* Berkeley: University of California Press, 1994.

Boyer, Anne. *A Handbook of Disappointed Fate.* New York: Ugly Duckling, 2019.

BPO Guatemala. "Finishing School." http://bpoguatemala.com/finishing-school-page.php.

Briggs, Laura. *How All Politics Became Reproductive Politics.* Berkeley: University of California Press, 2018.

Brooks, Daphne. *Bodies in Dissent: Spectacular Performances of Race and Freedom.* Durham, NC: Duke University Press, 2006.

Brown, Jayna. *Babylon Girls: Black Women Performers and the Shaping of the Modern.* Durham, NC: Duke University Press, 2008.

Brown, Wendy. "Resisting Left Melancholy." *boundary 2* 26, no. 3 (1999): 19–27. muse.jhu.edu/article/3271.

Brown, Wendy. *Undoing the Demos: Neoliberalism's Stealth Revolution.* Cambridge, MA: Zone, 2015.

Brusco, Elizabeth E. *The Reformation of Machismo: Evangelical Conversion and Gender in Colombia.* Austin: University of Texas Press, 1995.

Buell, Denise Kimberly. *Why This New Race? Ethnic Reasoning in Early Christianity.* New York: Columbia University Press, 2005.

Burgett, Bruce, and Glenn Hendler. *Keywords for American Cultural Studies.* 2nd ed. New York: NYU Press, 2014.

Burnett, Christina Duffy, and Burke Marshall, eds. *Foreign in a Domestic Sense: Puerto Rico, American Expansion, and the Constitution*. Durham, NC: Duke University Press, 2001.

Burstein, David. "TOMS Out to Sell a Lifestyle, Not Just Shoes." *Fast Company*, June 17, 2013. https://www.fastcompany.com/3012568/blake-mycoskie-toms.

Byrd, Jodi. *The Transit of Empire: Indigenous Critiques of Colonialism*. Durham, NC: Duke University Press, 2017.

Cabán, Pedro. "Redefining Puerto Rico's Political Status." In *Colonial Dilemma: Critical Perspectives on Contemporary Puerto Rico*, edited by Edwin Meléndez and Edgardo Meléndez, 19–39. Boston: South End, 1993.

Cacho, Lisa Marie. *Social Death: Racialized Rightlessness and the Criminalization of the Unprotected*. New York: New York University Press, 2012.

Calder, Lendol. *Financing the American Dream: A Cultural History of Consumer Credit*. Princeton, NJ: Princeton University Press, 1999.

Campbell, Colin. *The Romantic Ethic and the Spirit of Modern Consumerism*. New York: Blackwell, 1987.

Cantwell, Christopher, Heath W. Carter, and Janine Giordano Drake. "Introduction: Between the Pew and the Picket Line." In *The Pew and the Picket Line: Christianity and the American Working Class*, edited by Cantwell, Carter, and Drake, 1–20. Chicago: University of Illinois Press, 2016.

Carter, Heath. *Union Made: Working People and the Rise of Social Christianity in Chicago*. New York: Oxford University Press, 2015.

Chakravartty, Paula, and Denise Ferreira da Silva. "Accumulation, Dispossession, and Debt: The Racial Logic of Global Capitalism—An Introduction." In "Race, Empire, and the Crisis of the Subprime." Special issue, *American Quarterly* 64, no. 3 (2012): 361–85.

Cheah, Pheng. "Biopower and the New Division of Reproductive Labor." *boundary 2* 34, no. 1 (2008): 90–113.

Chen, Mel. *Animacies: Biopolitics, Racial Mattering, and Queer Life*. Durham, NC: Duke University Press, 2014.

Chidester, David. *Savage Systems: Colonialism and Comparative Religion in Southern Africa*. Charlottesville: University Press of Virginia, 1996.

Chu, Michael, and Regina Garcia Cuellar. "Banco Compartamos: Life after the IPO." Harvard Business School. Cambridge, MA: Harvard Business School Publishing, 2008.

Clare, Eli. *Brilliant Imperfection: Grappling with Cure*. Durham, NC: Duke University Press, 2018.

Cohen, Lizabeth. *A Consumers' Republic: The Politics of Mass Consumption in Postwar America*. New York: Random House, 2003.

Connolly, Brian, and Marisa Fuentes. "Introduction: From Archives of Slavery to Liberated Futures?" *History of the Present* 6, no. 2 (2016): 105–16.

Connolly, N. D. *A World More Concrete: Real Estate and the Remaking of Jim Crow South Florida*. Chicago: University of Chicago Press, 2014.

Conrad, Ryan, ed. *Against Equality: Queer Revolution, Not Mere Inclusion*. Oakland, CA: AK Press, 2014.
Cooper, Melinda. *Family Values: Between Neoliberalism and the New Social Conservatism*. New York: Zone, 2017.
Cottrell, Patrick Yumi. *Sorry to Disrupt the Peace*. New York: McSweeney's, 2017.
Crawley, Ashon. *Blackpentecostal Breath: The Aesthetics of Possibility*. New York: Fordham University Press, 2017.
Crosby, Christina. *A Body, Undone: Living on after Great Pain*. New York: NYU Press, 2016.
Cull, Robert, Asli Demirgüç-Kunt, and Jonathan Morduch. "Microfinance Meets the Market." *Journal of Economic Perspectives* 23, no. 1 (Winter 2009): 167–92.
Cusicanqui, Silvia Rivera. *Bircholas: Trabajo de mujeres, explotación capitalista o opresión colonial entre la migrantes Aymaras de La Paz y El Alto*. 2nd ed. La Paz, Bolivia: Mama Huaco, (1996) 2004.
Cvetkovich, Ann. *Depression: A Public Feeling*. Durham, NC: Duke University Press, 2007.
Daley-Harris, Sam. *Reclaiming Our Democracy: Healing the Break between People and Government*. Philadelphia: Camino, (1992) 2002.
Daley-Harris, Sam. *Reclaiming Our Democracy: Healing the Break between People and Government*. Philadelphia: Camino, 2013.
Danielson, Leilah, Mariam Mollin, and Doug Rossinow, eds. *The Religious Left in America: Doorkeepers of a Radical Faith*. Cham, Switzerland: Springer International Publishing, 2018.
Davis, Lizzy Cooper. "Culture and Struggle: The Organizing History of 'We Shall Overcome.'" *No Depression: The Journal of Roots Music* (Fall 2016): 1–17.
Davis, Mike. *Planet of Slums*. New York: Verso, 2006.
De Grazia, Victoria. *Irresistible Empire: America's Advance through 20th-Century Europe*. Cambridge, MA: Harvard University Press, 2005.
Denning, Michael. "The Special American Conditions: Marxism and American Studies." *American Quarterly* 38, no. 3 (1986): 356–80.
Derrida, Jacques. *Archive Fever: A Freudian Impression*. Translated by Eric Prenowitz. Chicago: University of Chicago Press, 1995.
Derrida, Jacques. *The Gift of Death*. 2nd ed. Translated by David Wills. Chicago: University of Chicago Press, 2007.
DeTemple, Jill. *Making Market Women: Gender, Religion, and Work in Ecuador*. South Bend, IN: University of Notre Dame Press, 2020.
Diner, Steven J. *A Very Different Age: Americans of the Progressive Era*. New York: Hill and Wang, 1998.
Dochuk, Darren. *From Bible Belt to Sunbelt: Plain-Folk Religion, Grassroots Politics, and the Rise of Evangelical Conservatism*. New York: W. W. Norton, 2010.
Dolhinow, Rebecca. *A Jumble of Needs: Women's Activism and Neoliberalism in the Colonias of the Southwest*. Minneapolis: University of Minnesota Press, 2010.
Dorrien, Gary. *Social Ethics in the Making: Interpreting an American Tradition*. New York: Wiley, 2008.

Durkheim, Émile. *The Division of Labor in Society*. Translated by George Simpson. Glencoe, IL: Free Press, 1960.

Durkheim, Émile. *Suicide: A Study in Sociology*. Translated by John A. Spaulding and George Simpson. Glencoe, IL: Free Press, 1951.

Edelman, Lee. *No Future: Queer Theory and the Death Drive*. Durham, NC: Duke University Press, 2004.

Elyachar, Julia. *Markets of Dispossession: NGOs, Economic Development, and the State in Cairo*. Durham, NC: Duke University Press, 2005.

Elyachar, Julia. "Next Practices: Knowledge, Infrastructure, and Public Goods at the Bottom of the Pyramid." *Public Culture* 24, no. 1 (2012): 109–31.

Emerson, Jed. *The Purpose of Capital: Elements of Impact, Financial Flows, and Natural Being*. San Francisco: Blended Value, 2018.

Enstad, Nan. *Ladies of Labor, Girls of Adventure: Working Women, Popular Culture, and Labor Politics at the Turn of the Twentieth Century*. New York: Columbia University Press, 1999.

Federici, Silvia. *Caliban and the Witch*. Brooklyn, NY: Automedia, 2004.

Federici, Silvia. *Revolution at Point Zero: Housework, Reproduction, and Feminist Struggle*. 2nd ed. Oakland, CA: PM, (2007) 2020.

Feldman, Keith. *A Shadow over Palestine: The Imperial Life of Race in America*. Minneapolis: University of Minnesota Press, 2016.

Felski, Rita. *The Limits of Critique*. Chicago: University of Chicago Press, 2015.

Ferguson, James. *The Anti-Politics Machine: Development, Depoliticization, and Bureaucratic Power in Lesotho*. Minneapolis: University of Minnesota Press, 1994.

Ferguson, Roderick. "Race-ing Homonormativity: Citizenship, Sociology, and Gay Identity." In *Black Queer Studies: A Critical Anthology*, edited by E. Patrick Johnson and Mae G. Henderson, 52–67. Durham, NC: Duke University Press, 2004.

Ferguson, Roderick. *The Reorder of Things: The University and Its Pedagogies of Minority Difference*. Durham, NC: Duke University Press.

Fields, Barbara Jeanne. "Slavery, Race, and Ideology in the United States of America." *New Left Review* 1, no. 181 (May–June 1990): 95–118.

Fisher, Mark. "Precarious Dystopias: *The Hunger Games, In Time,* and *Never Let Me Go*." *Film Quarterly* 65, no. 4 (Summer 2012): 27–33.

Fones-Wolf, Ken. *Trade Union Gospel: Christianity and Labor in Industrial Philadelphia, 1865–1915*. Philadelphia: Temple University Press, 1989.

Fox, Richard Wightman. "The Culture of Liberal Protestant Progressivism, 1875–1925." *Journal of Interdisciplinary History* 23 (Winter 1993): 639–60.

Frank, Dana. *Purchasing Power: Consumer Organizing, Gender, and the Seattle Labor Movement, 1919–1929*. Cambridge: Cambridge University Press, 1994.

Gallert, David J. *Small Loan Legislation: A History of the Regulation of the Business of Lending Small Sums*. New York: Russell Sage Foundation, 1932.

Ganz, Marshall. "What Is Public Narrative: Self, Us, Now." Working paper, Harvard Office for Scholarly Communication, 2009.

Garcia, Matt. *From the Jaws of Victory: The Triumph and Tragedy of the Cesar Chavez and the United Farmworkers Movement*. Berkeley: University of California Press, 2012.

Geismer, Lily. *Don't Blame Us: Suburban Liberals and the Transformation of the Democratic Party*. Princeton, NJ: Princeton University Press, 2015.

Genova, Nicholas J., and Ana Ramos-Zayas. "Latino Crossings." In *Latino Crossings: Mexicans, Puerto Ricans, and the Politics of Race and Citizenship*, 1–28. New York: Routledge, 2001.

Gilmore, Glenda Elizabeth. "Responding to the Challenges of the Progressive Era." In *Who Were the Progressives?*, edited by Glenda Elizabeth Gilmore, 1–24. Boston: Bedford, 2002.

Giridharadas, Anand. *Winners Take All: The Elite Charade of Changing the World*. New York: Alfred A. Knopf, 2018.

Glenn, John, Lillian Brandt, and Emerson F. Andrews. *Russell Sage Foundation, 1907–1946*. New York: Russell Sage Foundation, 1947.

Glickman, Lawrence. *Buying Power: A History of Consumer Activism in America*. Chicago: University of Chicago Press, 2009.

Gloege, Timothy E. W. *Guaranteed Pure: The Moody Bible Institute, Business, and the Making of Modern Evangelicalism*. Chapel Hill: University of North Carolina Press, 2015.

Gobat, Michael. *Confronting the American Dream: Nicaragua under US Imperial Rule*. Durham, NC: Duke University Press, 2005.

Godelier, Maurice. *The Enigma of the Gift*. Translated by Nora Scott. Chicago: University of Chicago Press, 1999.

Goodchild, Philip. *Theology of Money*. London: SCM, 2007.

Goossen, Benjamin W. "Mennonites in Latin America: A Review of the Literature." *Conrad Grebel Review* 34, no. 3 (Fall 2016): 236–65.

Gordon, Linda. *Pitied but Not Entitled: Single Mothers and the History of Welfare, 1890–1935*. New York: Free Press, 1994.

Gramsci, Antonio. *Selections from the Prison Notebooks of Antonio Gramsci*. New York: International Publishers, 1971.

Grandin, Greg. *The Blood of Guatemala: A History of Race and Nation*. Durham, NC: Duke University Press, 2000.

Grandin, Greg. *Empire's Workshop: Latin America, the United States, and the Rise of the New Imperialism*. New York: Metropolitan, 2006.

Grem, Darren E. *The Blessings of Business: How Corporations Shaped Conservative Christianity*. New York: Oxford University Press, 2016.

Gumbs, Alexis Pauline. *Undrowned: Black Feminist Lessons from Marine Mammals*. Chico, CA: AK Press, 2020.

Hall, Stuart. *Cultural Studies: 1983*. Durham, NC: Duke University Press, 2016.

Hall, Stuart. "The Problem of Ideology—Marxism without Guarantees." In *Stuart Hall: Critical Dialogues in Cultural Studies*, edited by Kuan-Hsing Chen and David Morley, 28–44. London, UK: Routledge, 1996.

Ham, Arthur. *The Chattel Loan Business*. New York: Charities Publication Committee, 1909.

Hamilton, Carolyn, et al. *Refiguring the Archive*. Dordrecht, Netherlands: Kluwer Academic, 2002.

Haraway, Donna. *When Species Meet*. Minneapolis: University of Minnesota Press, 2008.
Harney, Stefano. "Governance and the Undercommons." April 7, 2008. http://dev.autonomedia.org/node/10926.
Harney, Stefano, and Fred Moten. *The Undercommons: Fugitive Planning and Black Study*. New York: Minor Compositions, 2013.
Hartman, Saidiya. *Lose Your Mother: A Journey along the Atlantic Slave Route*. New York: Farrar, Straus and Giroux, 2007.
Hartman, Saidiya. *Scenes of Subjection: Terror, Slavery, and Self-Making in Nineteenth-Century America*. New York: Oxford University Press, 1997.
Hartman, Saidiya. "Venus in Two Acts." *Small Axe* 26 (2008): 1–14.
Harvey, David. *A Brief History of Neoliberalism*. Oxford: Oxford University Press, 2011.
Helton, Laura, Justin Leroy, Max Mischler, Samantha Seely, and Shauna Sween. "The Question of Recovery." *Social Text* 33, no. 4 (December 2015): 1–18.
Hillion, Pierre, Jean Wee, and Oliver Rousset. "Microfinance at Credit Suisse: Linking the TOP with the BOP." INSTEAD Case Study, 2002. https://hbr.org/product/microfinance-at-credit-suisse-linking-the-top-with-the-bop/INS125-PDF-ENG.
Hodge, Caroline Johnson. *If Sons, then Heirs: A Study of Kinship and Ethnicity in the Letters of Paul*. New York: Oxford University Press, 2007.
Hoffman, Elizabeth Cobbs. *All You Need Is Love: The Peace Corps and the Spirit of the 1960s*. Cambridge, MA: Harvard University Press, 1998.
Hollinger, David. *Protestants Abroad: How Missionaries Tried to Change the World but Changed America*. Princeton, NJ: Princeton University Press, 2017.
Homedes, Nuria, and Antonio Ugalde. "Why Neoliberal Health Reforms Have Failed in Latin America." *Health Policy* 71, no. 1 (2005): 83–96.
Hudson, Peter. *Bankers and Empire*. Cambridge, MA: Harvard University Press, 2017.
Hudson, Peter James. "The Racist Dawn of Capitalism." *Boston Review*, March 16, 2016. https://bostonreview.net/articles/peter-james-hudson-slavery-capitalism.
Hulsether, Lucia. "Buying into the Dream: The Religion of Racial Capitalism in Coca-Cola's World." *Public Culture* 30, no. 3 (September 2018): 483–508.
Hulsether, Lucia. "Decolonization, TM." In *Religion and US Empire*, edited by Tisa Wenger and Sylvester Johnson, 298–319. New York: New York University Press, 2022.
Hulsether, Lucia. "TOMS Shoes and the Spiritual Politics of Neoliberalism." *Religion and Politics* (October 2013). https://religionandpolitics.org/2013/10/01/toms-shoes-and-the-spiritual-politics-of-neoliberalism.
Hulsether, Mark. *Building a Protestant Left: Christianity and Crisis Magazine*. Knoxville: University of Tennessee Press, 1999.
Huntington, Theodora, dir. *The Usurer's Grip*. Image Entertainment, (1912) 2007.
Hyman, Louis. *Debtor Nation: A History of America in Red Ink*. Princeton, NJ: Princeton University Press, 2011.
Innovations for Poverty Action. "PPI by Country." Poverty Probability Index, 2018. www.povertyindex.org/materials-piloting-and-implementing-ppi.
Innovations for Poverty Action. "PPI Users." Poverty Probability Index, 2018. www.povertyindex.org/materials-piloting-and-implementing-ppi.

Inouye, Mie. "Antinomies of Organizing." PhD diss., Yale University, 2022.
Jackson, Gregory S. *The World and Its Witness: The Spiritualization of American Realism*. Chicago: University of Chicago Press, 2009.
Jacobs, Meg. *Pocketbook Politics: Economic Citizenship in 20th-Century America*. Princeton, NJ: Princeton University Press, 2005.
Jacobson, Matthew Frye. *Barbarian Virtues: The United States Encounters Foreign Peoples at Home and Abroad, 1876–1917*. New York: Hill and Wang, 2001.
Jacobson, Matthew Frye. *Whiteness of a Different Color: European Immigrants and the Alchemy of Race*. Cambridge, MA: Harvard University Press, 1998.
Jakobsen, Janet. *Working Alliances and the Politics of Difference: Diversity and Feminist Ethics*. Bloomington: Indiana University Press, 1998.
Jakobsen, Janet, and Ann Pellegrini. *Secularisms*. Durham, NC: Duke University Press, 2008.
Jay, Nancy. *Throughout Your Generations Forever: Sacrifice, Religion, and Paternity*. Chicago: University of Chicago Press, 1992.
Jaycox, Michael P. "Nussbaum, Anger, and Racial Justice: On the Epistemological and Eschatological Limitations of White Liberalism." *Political Theology* 21, no. 5 (2020): 415–33.
Joint Center for Housing Studies of Harvard University. "The State of the Nation's Housing 2008." President and Fellows of Harvard College, 2008.
Kaell, Hilary. *Christian Globalism at Home: Child Sponsorship in the United States*. Princeton, NJ: Princeton University Press, 2020.
Karim, Lamia. *Microfinance and Its Discontents: Women in Debt in Bangladesh*. Minneapolis: University of Minnesota Press, 2011.
Karnani, Aneel. "Mirage at the Bottom of the Pyramid." *Business Standard*, September 22, 2006. www.business-standard.com/article/opinion/aneel-karnani-mirage-at-the-bottom-of-the-pyramid-106092201109_1.html.
Keane, Webb. *Christian Moderns: Freedom and Fetish in the Mission Encounter*. Berkeley: University of California Press, 2007.
Kevane, Michael, and Bruce Wydick. "Microenterprise Lending to Female Entrepreneurs: Sacrificing Economic Growth for Poverty Reduction?" *World Development* 29, no. 7 (July): 1225–36.
Khawaja, Noreen. *The Religion of Existence: Asceticism in Philosophy from Kierkegaard to Sartre*. Chicago: University of Chicago Press, 2016.
King, David. "The New Internationalists: World Vision and the Revival of American Evangelical Humanitarianism." *Religions* 3, no. 4 (2012): 922–49.
Kish, Zenia, and Justin Leroy. "Bonded Life: Technologies of Racial Finance from Slave Insurance to Philanthrocapital." *Cultural Studies* 29, nos. 5–6 (2015): 630–51.
Kondo, Marie. *The Life-Changing Magic of Tidying Up: The Japanese Art of Decluttering and Organizing*. Berkeley, CA: Ten Speed Press, 2014.
Kramer, Paul. *The Blood of Government: Race, Empire, the United States, and the Philippines*. 2nd ed. Chapel Hill: University of North Carolina Press, 2006.
Kreider, Kenneth J. *A Cup of Cold Water: The Story of Brethren Service*. Elgin, IL: Brethren, 1991.

Kruse, Kevin. *One Nation under God: How Corporate America Invented Christian America*. New York: Basic, 2015.

Kuchler, Andreas. "Do Microfinance Programs Change Fertility? Evidence Using Panel Data from Bangladesh." *Journal of Developing Areas* 46, no. 2 (Fall 2012): 297–319.

Lazzarato, Maurizio. *The Making of the Indebted Man*. Los Angeles: Semiotext(e), 2012.

Leatherman, Sheila, et al. "Integrating Microfinance and Health Strategies: Examining the Evidence to Inform Policy and Practice." *Health Policy and Planning* 27, no. 2 (March 2012): 85–101.

Levy, Jonathan. *Freaks of Fortune: The Emerging World of Capitalism and Risk in America*. Cambridge, MA: Harvard University Press, 2013.

Li, Yiyun. *Dear Friend, from My Life I Write to You in Your Life*. New York: Random House, 2017.

Lipartito, Kenneth. "Reassembling the Economic: New Departures in Historical Materialism." *American Historical Review* (February 2016): 101–39.

Lofton, Kathryn. *Consuming Religion*. Chicago: University of Chicago Press, 2017.

Logemann, Jan L. "From Cradle to Bankruptcy: Credit Access and the American Welfare State." In *The Development of Consumer Credit in Global Perspective: Business, Regulation, and Culture*, edited by Logemann, 201–19. New York: Palgrave Macmillan, 2012.

Love, Heather. "Truth and Consequences: On Paranoid Reading and Reparative Reading." *Criticism* 52, no. 2 (2010): 235–41.

Maira, Sunaina. *Boycott! The Academy and Justice for Palestine*. Berkeley: University of California Press, 2018.

Mallette, Wendy. "Lesbian Feminist Killjoys, Negativity, and Living in a Sinful World." PhD diss., Yale University, May 2022.

Malone, Noreen. "Sexual-Harassment Claims against a 'She-E.O.'" *New York Magazine*, March 17, 2017. https://www.thecut.com/2017/03/thinx-employee-accuses-miki-agrawal-of-sexual-harassment.html.

Mankekar, Purnima, and Akhil Gupta. "Intimate Encounters: Affective Labor in Call Centers." *Positions* 24, no. 1 (2016): 17–43.

Marx, Karl. *Capital: A Critique of Political Economy*. Vol. 1. Translated by Ben Fowkes. New York: Penguin, 1976.

Marx, Karl. *Economic and Philosophic Manuscripts of 1844*. In *The Marx and Engels Reader*. 2nd ed. Edited by Robert C. Tucker. New York: W. W. Norton, 1978.

Marx, Karl. "The German Ideology: A Contribution to the Critique of Hegel's Philosophy of Right: Introduction." In *The Marx-Engels Reader*. 2nd ed. Edited by Robert C. Tucker, 146–200. New York: W. W. Norton, 1978.

Marx, Karl. "On the Jewish Question." In *The Marx-Engels Reader*. 2nd ed. Edited by Robert C. Tucker, 26–46. New York: W. W. Norton, 1978.

Masuzawa, Tomoko. *The Invention of World Religions, or How European Universalism Was Preserved in the Language of Pluralism*. Chicago: University of Chicago Press, 2005.

Mauss, Marcel. *The Gift: Forms and Functions of Exchange in Archaic Societies.* New York: Routledge University Press, 2002.
May, Elaine Tyler. *Homeward Bound: American Families in the Cold War.* New York: Basic, 1988.
May, Henry. *Protestant Churches and Industrial America.* New York: Harper and Row, 1967.
McAlevey, Jane. *No Shortcuts: Organizing for Power in the New Gilded Age.* New York: Oxford University Press, 2016.
McAlevey, Jane. *Raising Expectations (and Raising Hell): My Decade Fighting for the Labor Movement.* Brooklyn, NY: Verso, 2012.
McAlister, Melani. *Epic Encounters: Religion, Media, and US Interests in the Middle East since 1945.* 2nd ed. Berkeley: University of California Press, 2005.
McAlister, Melani. *The Kingdom of God Has No Borders: A Global History of American Evangelicals.* New York: Oxford University Press, 2018.
McAllister, Carlota, and Diane M. Nelson. "Aftermath: Harvests of Violence and Histories of the Future." In *War by Other Means: Aftermath in Post-Genocide Guatemala*, edited by McAllister and Nelson, 1–46. Durham, NC: Duke University Press, 2013.
McGerr, Michael. *A Fierce Discontent: The Rise and Fall of the Progressive Movement in America 1870–1920.* New York: Free Press, 2003.
McIntosh, Craig, and Bruce Wydick. "Competition and Microfinance." *Journal of Development Economics* 78, no. 2 (2005): 271–98.
Melamed, Jodi. "Proceduralism, Predisposing, Poesis: Forms of Institutionality, in the Making." *Lateral: Journal of the Cultural Studies Association* 5, no. 1 (Spring 2016). https://doi.org/10.25158/L5.1.10.
Melamed, Jodi. *Represent and Destroy: Rationalizing Violence in the New Racial Capitalism.* Minneapolis: University of Minnesota Press, 2011.
Meta, Sushmita, and Caitlin Sanford. "My Turn to Speak: Voices of Microfinance Clients in Benin, Pakistan, Peru, and Georgia." SMART Campaign, February 2016. http://smartcampaign.org/storage/documents/Synthesis_Report_ENG_FINAL.pdf.U.S.
Meyerowitz, Joanne. *A War on Global Poverty: The Lost Promise of Redistribution and the Rise of Microcredit.* Princeton, NJ: Princeton University Press, 2021.
Mills, Charles W. *The Racial Contract.* Ithaca, NY: Cornell University Press, 1997.
Mills, Charles W., and Carole Pateman. *Contract and Domination.* Cambridge, MA: Polity, 2007.
Mink, Gwendolyn. *The Wages of Motherhood: Inequality in the Welfare State, 1917–1942.* Ithaca, NY: Cornell University Press, 1995.
Mittelstadt, Jennifer. *From Welfare to Workfare: The Unintended Consequences of Liberal Reform, 1945–1965.* Chapel Hill: University of North Carolina Press, 2005.
Mivera, Bheryl. "Move Slow and Break Things: A Guide to Workplace Sabotage." *Lux Magazine* 4 (2022): 13–16.
Montgomery, David. *Citizen Worker: The Experience of Workers in the United States with Democracy and the Free Market during the Nineteenth Century.* New York: Cambridge University Press, 1993.

Moreiras, Alberto. *The Exhaustion of Difference: The Politics of Latin American Cultural Studies*. Durham, NC: Duke University Press, 2001.

Moreton, Bethany. *To Serve God and Wal-Mart: The Making of Christian Free Enterprise*. Cambridge, MA: Harvard University Press, 2009.

Morgan, Jennifer L. "Archives and Histories of Racial Capitalism." *Social Text* 33, no. 4 (December 2015): 153–61.

Morgan, Jennifer L. *Laboring Women: Reproduction and Gender in New World Slavery*. Philadelphia: University of Pennsylvania Press, 2004.

Moten, Fred. *In the Break: The Aesthetics of the Black Radical Tradition*. Minneapolis: University of Minnesota Press, 2003.

Muhammad, Khalil Gibran. *The Condemnation of Blackness: Race, Crime, and the Making of Modern Urban America*. Cambridge, MA: Harvard University Press, 2010.

Muñoz, José. *Cruising Utopia: The Then and There of Queer Futurity*. New York: New York University Press, 2013.

Muñoz, José. "The Sense of Brownness." In "Dossier: *Theorizing Queer Inhumanisms*." *GLQ* 21, no. 3 (2015): 15–25.

Murphy, Michelle. *The Economization of Life*. Durham, NC: Duke University Press, 2017.

Mycoskie, Blake. "A New Model of Philanthropy." *Stanford Social Innovation Review*, December 9, 2011.

Mycoskie, Blake. *Start Something That Matters*. New York: Spiegel and Grau, 2011.

Narciso, Rubén, et al. "Totonicapán 2013: caracterización departamental." Instituto Nacional de Estadística, Gobierno de Guatemala, December 2015. www.ine.gob.gt/sistema/uploads/2015/07/20/EfsWFqUtoEkcXfE2PB1sVbSpfVPHbJVY.pdf.

Nash, Jennifer. *Black Feminism Reimagined: After Intersectionality*. Durham, NC: Duke University Press, 2019.

Nasrallah, Laura, and Melanie Johnson-DeBaufre. "Beyond the Heroic Paul." In *The Colonized Apostle: Paul through Postcolonial Eyes*, edited by Christopher Stanley, 161–74. Minneapolis: Fortress, 2011.

Nelms, Taylor C., Bill Maurer, and Lana Swartz. "Social Payments: Innovation, Trust, Bitcoin and the Sharing Economy." *Theory, Culture, and Society* 35, no. 3 (2018): 13–33.

Nelson, Candace, et al. *Village Banking: The State of the Practice*. New York: Small Enterprise Education and Promotion Network and the United Nations Development Fund for Women, 1996.

Nelson, Deborah. *Tough Enough: Arbus, Arendt, Didion, McCarthy, Sontag, Weil*. Chicago: University of Chicago Press, 2017.

Nguyen, Mimi Thi. *The Gift of Freedom: War, Debt, and Other Refugee Passages*. Durham, NC: Duke University Press, 2012.

Nietzsche, Friedrich. *On the Genealogy of Morality*. Translated by Carol Diethe. Cambridge: Cambridge University Press, 1997.

Nolt, Steven M. "Globalizing a Separate People: World Christianity and North American Mennonites, 1940–1990." *Mennonite Quarterly Review* 84, no. 4 (October 2010): 487–506.

Nolt, Stephen M. "Self Help Philosophy and Organizational Change: The Origins and Development of SELFHELP Crafts." *Pennsylvania Mennonite Heritage* (1991): 14–27.

O'Connor, Alice. *Social Science for What? Philanthropy and the Social Question in a World Turned Rightside Up*. New York: Russell Sage Foundation, 2007.

Olmos, Raúl. "La mafia financiera de los Legionarios de Cristo." *Armando Info*, November 6, 2014. https://armando.info/la-mafia-financiera-de-los-legionarios-de-cristo.

O'Neill, Kevin Lewis. "Caught on Camera." *Public Culture* 29, no. 3 (2017): 493–515.

O'Neill, Kevin Lewis. *Secure the Soul: Christian Piety and Gang Prevention in Guatemala*. Berkeley: University of California Press, 2015.

Ozeki, Ruth. *The Book of Form and Emptiness*. New York: Viking, 2021.

Pateman, Carole. *The Sexual Contract*. Palo Alto, CA: Stanford University Press, 1988.

Pease, Donald, and Robyn Weigman. "Futures." In *Futures of American Studies*, edited by Donald Pease and Robyn Weigman, 1–44. Durham, NC: Duke University Press, 2002.

Penslar, Derek. *Shylock's Children: Economics and Jewish Identity in Modern Europe*. Berkeley: University of California Press, 2001.

Peretti, Jonah. "My Nike Media Adventure." *Nation*, April 9, 2001. https://www.thenation.com/article/archive/my-nike-media-adventure.

Peteet, Julie. *Landscapes of Hope and Despair: Palestinian Refugee Camps*. Philadelphia: University of Pennsylvania Press, 2005.

Peters, Jacob. "Mennonites in Mexico and Paraguay: A Comparative Analysis of the Colony Social System." *Journal of Mennonite Studies* 6 (1998): 198–215.

Phelan, Hayley. "The Second Coming of Guru Jagat." *Vanity Fair* 64, no. 1 (2021): 118.

Phillips-Fein, Kim. *Invisible Hands: Making the Conservative Movement from the New Deal to Reagan*. New York: W. W. Norton, 2009.

Pietz, William. "The Problem of the Fetish, I." *RES: Anthropology and Aesthetics* 9 (Spring 1985): 5–17.

Pietz, William. "The Problem of the Fetish, II: The Origin of the Fetish." *RES: Anthropology and Aesthetics* 13 (Spring 1987): 23–45.

Pietz, William. "The Problem of the Fetish, III: Bosman's Guinea and the Enlightenment Theory of Fetishism." *RES: Anthropology and Aesthetics* 16 (Autumn 1988): 105–24.

Pitkin, Daisy. *On the Line: A Story of Class, Solidarity, and Two Women's Epic Fight to Build a Union*. Chapel Hill, NC: Algonquin Books, 2022.

Postel, Charles. *The Populist Vision*. New York: Oxford University Press, 2007.

Povinelli, Elizabeth. *The Cunning of Recognition: Indigenous Alterities and the Making of Australian Multiculturalism*. Durham, NC: Duke University Press, 2002.

Povinelli, Elizabeth. *Empire of Love: Toward a Theory of Intimacy, Genealogy, and Carnality*. Durham, NC: Duke University Press, 2006.

Prahalad, C. K. *The Fortune at the Bottom of the Pyramid: Eradicating Poverty through Profits*. Upper Saddle River, NJ: Wharton School Publishing, 2004.

Prahalad, C. K., and Stuart L. Hart. "The Fortune at the Bottom of the Pyramid." *Strategy+Business* 26 (January 2002), https://www.strategy-business.com/article/11518?gko=9a4ba.

Prahalad, C. K., and Kenneth Lieberthal. "The End of Corporate Imperialism." *Harvard Business Review*, August 2003. https://hbr.org/2003/08/the-end-of-corporate-imperialism.

Puar, Jasbir. *Terrorist Assemblages: Homonationalism in Queer Times*. Durham, NC: Duke University Press, 2007.

Radakrishnan, Smitha. *Making Women Pay: Microfinance in Urban India*. Durham, NC: Duke University Press, 2020.

Rawls, John. *Political Liberalism*. New York: Columbia University Press, 1993.

Reddy, Chandan. *Freedom with Violence: Race, Sexuality, and the US State*. Durham, NC: Duke University Press, 2011.

Reich, Robert. *Saving Capitalism: For the Many, Not the Few*. New York: Alfred A. Knopf, 2015.

Rieger, Joerg. *No Rising Tide: Theology, Economics, and the Future*. Minneapolis, MN: Fortress Press, 2009.

Robinson, Cedric J. *Black Marxism: The Making of the Black Radical Tradition*. Chapel Hill: University of North Carolina Press, 1983.

Robinson, Louis Newton. *Ten Thousand Small Loans: Facts about Borrowers in 109 Cities in 17 States*. New York: Russell Sage Foundation, 1930.

Robinson, Louis N., and Rolf Nugent. *Regulation of the Small Loan Business*. New York: Russell Sage Foundation, 1935.

Rockman, Seth. *Scraping By: Wage Labor, Slavery, and Survival in Early Baltimore*. Baltimore: Johns Hopkins University Press, 2008.

Rodgers, Daniel. *Atlantic Crossings: Social Politics in a Progressive Age*. Cambridge, MA: Harvard University Press, 1998.

Rodkey, Evin. "Disposable Labor, Repurposed: Outsourcing Deportees in the Call Center Industry." *Anthropology of Work Review* 37, no. 1 (July 2016): 34–43.

Roediger, David. "Making Solidarity Uneasy: Cautions on a Keyword from Black Lives Matter to the Past." In Roediger, *Class, Race, and Marxism*, 157–88. New York: Verso, 2019.

Roper, Laura, ed. *Change Not Charity: Essays on Oxfam America's First 40 Years*. Boston: Oxfam, 2011.

Rose, Kevin. "Living Green: The Neoliberal Climate of Protestant Environmentalism," PhD diss., University of Virginia, 2022.

Rossinow, Doug. "Letting Go: Revisiting the New Left's Demise." In *The New Left Revisited*, edited by Paul Buhle and John Macmillan, 241–54. Philadelphia: Temple University Press, 2009.

Roy, Ananya. *Poverty Capital: Microfinance and the Making of Development*. New York: Routledge, 2010.

Roy, William G. *Reds, Whites, and Blues: Social Movements, Folk Music, and Race in the United States*. Princeton, NJ: Princeton University Press, 2010.

Ryan, Kay. "The Job." In *The Best of It: New and Collected Poems*, 193. New York: Grove, 2010.

Salaita, Steven. *The Holy Land in Transit: Colonialism and the Quest for Canaan*. Syracuse, NY: Syracuse University Press, 2006.

Salinger, Sharon. *"To Serve Well and Faithfully": Labor and Indentured Servants in Pennsylvania, 1682–1800*. New York: Cambridge University Press, 1987.

Sawatsky, Harry Leonard. *They Sought a Country: Mennonite Colonization in Mexico*. Berkeley: University of California Press, 1971.

Schacher, Yael, and Rachel Schmidtke. *Harmful Returns: The Compounded Vulnerabilities of Returned Guatemalans in a Time of Covid-19*. Refugees International. June 2020. https://www.refugeesinternational.org/reports/2020/6/16/harmful-returns-the-compounded-vulnerabilities-of-returned-guatemalans-in-the-time-of-covid-19.

Schmitt, Carl. *The Concept of the Political: Four Chapters on the Concept of Sovereignty*. Cambridge, MA: MIT Press, 1988.

Schreiner, Mark. "PPI for Guatemala 2014." Poverty Probability Index. 2018. www.povertyindex.org/country/guatemala.

Schuster, Caroline. *Social Collateral: Women and Microfinance in Paraguay's Smuggling Economy*. Berkeley: University of California Press, 2015.

Scott, Dareick. *Extravagant Abjection: Blackness, Power, and Sexuality in the African American Literary Imagination*. New York: NYU Press, 2011.

Sedgwick, Eve. *Touching Feeling: Affect, Pedagogy, Performativity*. Durham, NC: Duke University Press, 2003.

Sexton, Jared. "Affirmation in the Dark: Racial Slavery and Philosophical Pessimism." *The Comparatist* 43 (October 2019): 90–111.

Sexton, Jared. *Amalgamation Schemes: Antiblackness and the Critique of Multiracialism*. Minneapolis: University of Minnesota Press, 2008.

Sexton, Jared. "The Social Life of Social Death: On Afro-Pessimism and Black Optimism." *InTensions* 5 (Fall/Winter 2011): 1–47.

Shahani, Nishant. "The Future Is Queer Stuff: Critical Utopianism and Its Discontents." *GLQ* 19, no. 4 (2013): 545–58.

Sharma, Aradhana. *Logics of Empowerment: Development, Gender, and Governance in Neoliberal India*. Minneapolis: University of Minnesota Press, 2008.

Sharpe, Christina. *In the Wake: On Blackness and Being*. Durham, NC: Duke University Press, 2016.

Sharpe, Christina. *Monstrous Intimacies: Making Post-Slavery Subjects*. Durham, NC: Duke University Press, 2010.

Silva, Denise Ferreira da. *Toward a Global Idea of Race*. Minneapolis: University of Minnesota Press, 2007.

Simpson, Audra. *Mohawk Interruptus: Political Life across Borders of Settler States*. Durham, NC: Duke University Press, 2014.

Sklansky, Jeffrey. "The Elusive Sovereign: New Intellectual and Social Histories of Capitalism." *Modern Intellectual History* 9, no. 1 (April 2012): 233–48.

Sklansky, Jeffrey. "Labor, Money, and the Financial Turn in the History of Capitalism." *Labor* 11, no. 1 (2014): 23–46.

Smith, Carol A. "The Militarization of Civil Society in Guatemala: Economic Reorganization as a Continuation of War." *Latin American Perspectives* 17, no. 4 (1990): 8–41.

Smith, Christian. *Resisting Reagan: The US Central America Peace Movement*. Chicago: University of Chicago Press, 1996.
Social Performance Management Center at the Grameen Foundation. *Piloting the PPI: A Handbook for First-Time Users of the Poverty Probability Index (PPI)*. Institute for Poverty Action, 2012. www.povertyindex.org/materials-piloting-and-implementing-ppi.
Spillers, Hortense. "Mama's Baby, Papa's Maybe: An American Grammar Book." *Diacritics* 17, no. 2 (1987): 64–81.
Srinivasan, Amia. "Would Politics Be Better Off without Anger?" *The Nation*, November 16, 2016. https://www.thenation.com/article/archive/a-righteous-fury/.
Stanley, Amy Dru. "Contract." In *Keywords for American Cultural Studies*, edited by Bruce Burgett and Glenn Hendler, 60–64. New York: NYU Press, 2014.
Stanley, Amy Dru. *From Bondage to Contract: Wage Labor, Marriage, and the Market in the Age of Slave Emancipation*. Cambridge, MA: Cambridge University Press, 1998.
Steinfield, Robert. *Coercion, Contract, and Free Labor in the Nineteenth Century*. New York: Cambridge University Press, 2001.
Stuelke, Patricia. *The Ruse of Repair: US Neoliberal Empire and the Turn from Critique*. Durham, NC: Duke University Press, 2021.
Taussig, Michael. *The Devil and Commodity Fetishism in South America*. Chapel Hill: University of North Carolina Press, 1981.
Taylor, Keeanga-Yamahtta. *Race for Profit: How Banks and the Real Estate Industry Undermined Black Homeownership*. Chapel Hill: University of North Carolina Press, 2019.
Tokumitsu, Miya. "What a Start-Up's Scandal Says about Your Workplace." *New York Times*, March 23, 2017. https://www.nytimes.com/2017/03/23/opinion/thinx-what-a-startups-scandal-says-about-your-workplace.html.
Tonstad, Linn. "Ambivalent Loves." *Literature and Theology* 31, no. 4 (December 2017): 472–89.
Tsing, Anna. *Friction: An Ethnography of Global Connection*. Princeton, NJ: Princeton University Press, 2004.
Turshen, Meredeth. *Privatizing Health Services in Africa*. New Brunswick, NJ: Rutgers University Press, 1999.
Tyrell, Ian. *Reforming the World: The Creation of America's Moral Empire*. Princeton, NJ: Princeton University Press, 2010.
Tzul Tzul, Gladys. "Communal Strategies for Controlling Microfinance in Chuimeq'ena' Guatemala." *South Atlantic Quarterly* 115, no. 3 (2016): 625–31.
Valenze, Deborah. *The Social Life of Money in the English Past*. New York: Cambridge University Press, 2006.
Viego, Antonio. *Dead Subjects: Toward a Politics of Loss in Latino Studies*. Durham, NC: Duke University Press, 2008.
Villanueva, Edgar. *Decolonizing Wealth: Indigenous Wisdom to Heal Divides and Restore Balance*. Oakland, CA: Berrett-Koehler, 2018.

Von Eschen, Penny. *Satchmo Blows Up the World: Jazz Ambassadors during the Cold War*. Cambridge, MA: Harvard University Press, 2004.

Wassam, Clarence Wycliffe. *Salary Loan Business in New York City: A Report Prepared under the Direction of the Bureau for Social Research, New York School of Philanthropy*. New York: Charities Publication Committee, 1908.

Weaver, Alain Epp. "Mennonites, Exile and the Palestinian Right of Return." *Journal of Mennonite Studies* 32, no. 1 (2014): 139–49.

Weeks, Kathi. *The Problem with Work: Feminism, Marxism, Antiwork Politics, and Postwork Imaginaries*. Durham, NC: Duke University Press, 2011.

Weiss, Margot. "'Reinvigorating the Queer Political Imagination': A Roundtable with Ryan Conrad, Yasmin Nair, and Karma Chávez of Against Equality." *American Quarterly* 64, no. 4 (2012): 845–49.

Weld, Kirsten. *Paper Cadavers: Archives of Dictatorship*. Durham, NC: Duke University Press, 2014.

Weiner, Annette. *Inalienable Possessions: The Paradox of Keeping-While-Giving*. Berkeley: University of California Press, 2002.

Wenger, Tisa. *Religious Freedom: The Contested History of an American Ideal*. Chapel Hill: University of North Carolina Press, 2017.

Wenger, Tisa. *We Have a Religion: The 1920s Pueblo Indian Dance Controversy and American Religious Freedom*. Chapel Hill: University of North Carolina Press, 2009.

Westad, Odd Arne. *The Global Cold War: Third World Interventions and the Making of Our Times*. Cambridge: Cambridge University Press, 2005.

Wiegman, Robyn. "The Times We're In: Queer Feminist Criticism and the Reparative 'Turn.'" *Feminist Theory* 15, no. 1 (2014): 4–25.

Wilderson, Frank B. *Red, White, and Black: Cinema and the Structure of US Antagonisms*. Durham, NC: Duke University Press, 2010.

Winant, Gabriel. *The Next Shift: The Fall of Industry and the Rise of Health Care in Rust Belt America*. Cambridge, MA: Harvard University Press, 2021.

Wright, Thomas C. *Latin America in the Era of the Cuban Revolution*. Westport, CT: Praeger, 1991.

Yoder, Glee. *Passing on the Gift: The Story of Dan West*. Elgin, IL: Brethren, 1978.

Yunus, Muhammad. *Banker to the Poor: Micro-Lending and the Battle against World Poverty*. New York: PublicAffairs, (1998) 2008.

Yunus, Muhammad, with Alan Jolis. *Banker to the Poor: Micro-Lending and the Battle against World Poverty*. New York: PublicAffairs, 1999.

Zizek, Slavoj. *The Fragile Absolute; or, Why Is the Christian Legacy Worth Fighting For?* London: Verso, 2000.

Index

Page locators in italics indicate figures

abolitionists, 55
accelerationism, 146–47
Acción Democrática (Venezuela), 84
ACCION International, 14–15, 81–88, 90–93, 204n10; Center for Financial Inclusion (CFI), 98, 121–22; and Compartamos microbank, 97–98, 119–20; early volunteer service model, 83–85, 204n15; "solidarity lending" by, 87–88; and US borrowers, 117–18
accounting, capitalist humanitarian, 15–16
accumulation by dispossession, 5–6, 39, 108
addiction literature, 205–6n32
adoption tropes, 164, 168, 172–73
Adorno, Theodor, 186
advertising, 33, 53–55, *54*, 56, 64–65, *72*; of ministerial gifts, 68–71
agency, 178, 212n8; of commodity, 57–61, 64, 65; passive voice used to evade, 42
Agrawal, Miki, 69–71
Ahmed, Sara, 212n5
algorithms, 146
alienation, 8, 14, 55, 57–60, 64, 66, 206n38; of affect, 180–81, 197n36

alternatives: to not misuse existence, 186–87, 190; refusal of, 185–87, 214n23
American Academy of Religion (AAR), 78
Americans for Community Cooperation with Other Nations. *See* ACCION International
Amity Assets, 143–50
Anabaptists, 4, 32–34, 42–43
anger, 124, 138, 212n5
anticapitalist dissent, 12, 14, 54, 81, 101, 218n16
appropriation, 27, 55, 62–63, 219n7
archive, 3, 12–13, 213–14n23; and efficiency, 146–47; history of capitalism approach to, 46–47; of Ten Thousand Villages, 33–34
archives, capitalist humanitarian: archivists of, 142–49; assessment surveys, 135–38, *137*; bureaucracy, 146–47; client satisfaction surveys, 131, 150–54; consent forms, 139–41; contracts, 139–42; data collection, cultures of, 15–16; data-collection missions, 143; self-management by subjects, 150–55; synchronous documents, 141–42. *See also* capitalist humanitarianism; consent, manufactured

artisanal forms, preservation of as capitalist humanitarian focus, 1–2, 13, 34–35, 43, 172
asceticism, 4, 6, 32, 34
assessment surveys, 135–38, *137*
austerity, 5, 12, 17, 100, 119, 167, 172
authenticity, 27, 30, 35, 43, 60, 104, 198n5
automobile companies, 116

Banco Solidario (BancoSol, Bolivia), 97
Banker to the Poor (Yunus), 91
banking: Compartamos (Mexican microbank), 97–98, 119–20; health care attached to, 165–67; and medical clinics, 165–68, 216n6; "philanthropic," 15, 109–17, 119; predatory inclusion, 15; "solidarity banking," 82, 90–91, 101; "unbanked," 15, 107, 109, 111, 140. *See also* Grameen Bank
Bartel, Rebecca, 216–17n11
benevolent supremacy/soft power, 4, 31, 45, 81
Berlant, Lauren, 177–78, 218n24
Bernanke, Ben, 120
Betancourt, Rómolo, 83–84
black freedom legacy, 22
Blatchford, Joe, 82–85
blood metaphor, 53–54, *54*
Bolivia, 93–97
"bottom of the pyramid" (BOP), 118–20; World Economic Pyramid, 106–8, *107*, 210n36
boycott, divestment, and sanction (BDS) movement, 55
boycotts, 53–54
Brazil, 85
Bread for the World, 96
Brown, Wendy, 164
Brusco, Elizabeth, 216n11
"bureaucracy," neoliberal criticisms of, 146–47
"Business of Spirituality: On Money, Branding, and Other Taboos, The" (Harvard Divinity School), 68–71
Business process outsourcing (BPO) firms, 152

Butler, Judith, 73
"buy one, give one" model, 65–66, 202–3n22
Byler, Edna Ruth, 31–32

Café Nica (Equal Exchange), 56–57
call centers, xii, xv, 129–31; in Guatemala, 131, 150–53
capital, as "energy," 73
Capital (Marx), 58
Capital for Change (CFC) tour, 162–82
capitalism: "conscious," 4–5, 12; history of, as disciplinary subfield, 46–48; industrial, 89–90; Protestantism associated with, 6; as religious form, 8; as solution to capitalism, 1–2, 211n1; tycoon, 157, 209n26. *See also* neoliberalism; racial capitalism
capitalist humanitarianism: accounting, 15–16; commodity reformulated as instrument of emancipation, 59–61; competitors, 62–63; "double bottom line," 5; evolution of, 13; as expression of neoliberal institutionality, 3; free market, hopes for rehabilitation of, 4–5; gendered assumptions of, 170–71, 214n24, 216–17n11; human of, 123–27; indebtedness, narratives of, 36, 39–40; "knowing the history," 27, 30–31, 34, 35–36, 44–46; narratives of, 23, 36–42, 36–44, 59; optics used in, 106–9, *107*; as political theological discourse, 6–7; promises to customers, 54; prosperity rhetoric, 17, 89, 163–65; Protestant affinities with, 77–78; public reflection on history as central to, 1–2; racialized giving, 65–66; reinvestment, 3, 5, 10, 73, 171; self-critique as idiom of, 1–3, 13–14, 40–41, 99–100, 186; social boundaries transformed by indebtedness, 167–68; as theological approach, 6–7. *See also* archives, capitalist humanitarian
Catholic Church, cultural power of, 8
celebrity academics, 19–20
Center for Financial Inclusion (CFI), 98, 121–22

Central America solidarity movement, 3, 56, 79, 80–82, 87, 93; transition to microfinance, 80–81. *See also* Latin America; sanctuary churches; solidarity
Chakravartty, Paula, 120–21
Chávez, César, 37–38
child, idealized figure of, 218–19n25, 218n24
child labor, 16, 169–70, 174–79, *175*, 218–19n25; as figure for social reform, 177–79; maquiladoras, "socially responsible," 176–77; Nike scandal, 177; sentimental responses to, 178–79; "somewhat-better-off," 179; as "youth empowerment," 16, 165, 174–77
children: "adopted" into family of neoliberal labor, 164, 168, 172; as credit and debt, 166; fixation on rescuing, 177–78; hope transferred to "next generation," 164, 166, 173, 182, 215n2, 218n24
Christianity, 6, 196n18; Catholic Church, cultural power of, 8; kinship networks, 110–17; Pentecostal, 6, 216–17n11; plot structure of, 157–58; pro-business evangelical organizations, 6, 45, 77, 157–58, 176; Protestant secularism, 6, 16; salvation, concept of, 6, 16, 27, 115, 172–73, 217n14, 218n16. *See also* Left Christians; Mennonite Central Committee (MCC); Mennonites; sanctuary churches
Christian start-ups, 78
Chu, Michael, 97
"Church of New Capital," 5, 73, 74
Citizen Consumer Summit (Equal Exchange), 21–24, 27, 35–39, 49, 198n5, 200n26
citizenship, 15, 111–17; consumer, 4, 21–24; expulsion from, 118, 121, 124; privatized domesticity and assimilation, 113
citizen-subjectivity, 109
civil rights movement, 23
Clarke, Jean, 94–96
class conflict, 46, 90
class unconsciousness, 178
client satisfaction surveys, 131, 150–54
Clinton, Hillary, 117

commodity: affective bonds with material objects, 50–52; agency of, 57–61, 64, 65; collective degradation by, 59; conscious, 14, 61, 63; as elemental violence of bourgeois capitalism, 59; enchanted, 14, 59–64, 67, 68; exchange value, 55, 57–58; fantasies projected onto, 64; as gift exchange, 55, 64; industry for fighting attachment to, 51–52; laborer as, 60–61; Marxian understanding of, 55; reformulated as instrument of emancipation, 59–61; resistance by, 61; and slavery, 60–61; "speaking," 60–61; spectacle of loan recipient as, 170; use value, 20, 57
commodity fetish, 55, 57–60, 73, 202n7; retheorization of, 14, 57; spiritual and wellness entrepreneurs' inversion of, 73
Compartamos (Mexican microbank), 97–98, 119–20
competitors, 62–63
complicity, 2, 20, 44, 55, 82, 87, 133, 190
confession, 2, 14, 39
Congress, 81, 96
"conscious capitalism," 4–5, 12, 45
conscious consumer practice, 4, 14, 54–55; and Overseas Needlework and Crafts Project, 31–32; as solidarity, 23
consensus, 75, 196–97n29; neoliberal, 4, 10, 15, 17
consent, manufactured, 15–16, 134–39, 212n7; and contract liberalism, 139–40. *See also* archives, capitalist humanitarian
consumer citizenship, 4, 21–24
consumer power, theories of, 53–54
Consuming Religion (Lofton), 9–10
consumption: as civic involvement, 21; "ethical," 2, 25, 62, 64; as modern religion, 9; spiritual potential linked with, 14, 60
contact centers, 152–53
context, 3, 8, 11–12, 17
contract labor, 140, 212n8
contracts, 139–42, 212nn7,8, 212–13n9
Cooper, Melinda, 16, 216n10
cooptation of Left rhetoric and strategies, 5, 22, 37–38, 40, 53–54, 154–55
Cornell University, 46–48

Index   241

corporations: appropriation of alternative trade rhetoric, 27, 55, 62–63; as "families," 90; as religious form, 90
credit: and Christian kinship networks, 110–17; doubling, as theory of history, 98; as "human right," 117; inclusion as system of, 123; Uniform Small Loans Law proposal, 111–12, 208n14. *See also* debt
credit assessments, 113–14
credit officers: home visits and intervention by, 124, 144, 148–50, 164–65, 169–73; and manufactured consent, 134–41
creditworthiness, 163; "talent, accountability, and positive attitude" required, 163–64, 180–82; tied to performance of hope, 5, 16, 114, 124, 163–70, 173, 178–82
critique: optimism as requirement for, 184–85; post-critique, 10; self-critique, 1–3, 13–14, 40–41, 99–100, 186
cruel optimism, 5, 173
Cuban Revolution (1959), 83
Cuernavaca Center for Intercultural Dialogue on Development (CCIDD), 86

Dayan, Ruth, 43
debt: and citizenship, 15, 111–17; collective liability for, 80, 88, 90–91, 97; collective liability for (solidarity groups/social networks), 80, 163; as historically contingent feeling, 66–67; home loans, 116–17; indebtedness, narratives of, 36, 39–40; medical, 166–68; and obligation, 66–67, 82, 92–93; and promises, 66–67; and reproductive labor, 167–68; and "solidarity," 88–100; solidarity as sense of, 92–93; theories of, 66, 82
debt/finance discipline, 6, 16, 83, 92, 101, 126, 163, 166; as "free choice," 140; internalization expected of borrowers, 144–45. *See also* "empowerment" of women; reproductive labor
Decolonizing Wealth website, *72*
Derrida, Jacques, 213–14n23
deservingness, rhetoric of, 96, 109, 117
desire, 10, 64, 66, 89, 150, 154, 206n32; and contract, 139–42; performance of reciprocal, 141; as "personal," 145; as systems of credit, 122–23; temporalization of, 218n24
dispossession, 2, 5–6, 12, 38–39, 108
Disrupt-Her (Agrawal), 70
dissonance, management of, 3, 5, 177–81, 186
Durkheim, Émile, 8–9, 89–91, 196–97n29, 205nn26, 27, 30, 205–6n32, 206–7n38

Edelman, Lee, 218nn24, 25
El Salvador, and solidarity lending, 88, 90–91
Emerson, Jed, 72–73, 203n34
"empowerment" of women, 13, 16, 131, 144–46, 149, 151, 153–54, 175, 177–79; gendered assumptions of capitalist humanitarians, 170–71, 214n24, 216–17n11; and patriarchy, 145–46, 171. *See also* debt/finance discipline
entitlements, curtailing, 84, 118–19
Equal Exchange coffee cooperative, 14, 21–22, 198n5, 200n26; advertising, 2004, 60–61; Café Nica, 36, 56–57; Citizen Consumer Summit, 21–24, 27, 35–39; early advertising, 56–57; founding story, 36–37, 39–40; *History of Authentic Fair Trade* (comic book), *26, 27, 28, 29*; late 1990s advertising campaign, 53–55, *54*
"ethical consumption," 2, 25, 62, 64
ethical urgency, narratives of, 46
evangelical organizations, pro-business, 6, 45, 77, 157–58, 176
exchange value, 55, 57–59, 68–74; of desires, 122; money as "made up," 70–71
exoticism in advertising, *26*, 26–27
extraction, structures of, 108, 127, 139, 217n13

"fairness," as subjective, 59
fair trade: as multinational start-up phenomenon, 61–63; neoliberal appropriation of label, 27; positioned as outgrowth and fulfillment of black freedom struggles, 61; post–World War II missionary roots of, 13. *See also* Equal Exchange coffee cooperative; Ten Thousand Villages
Fairtrade International, 64

"family values," colonial politics of, 16
far-right presidential appointees, ix, 128–29, 184
Faster, Cecy, 94–95
FEDECREDITO, 88, 91
Federal Home Loan Mortgage Corporation, 116
Federal Housing Authority (FHA), 116
Federal Reserve, 120
Federici, Silvia, 8
feminist theory, 8, 31, 50, 73, 197n33, 212n5, 218n24, 219n4
financial crash of 2008, 15, 118–20, 176
financial history, as salvation history, 115
FINCA International, 14–15, 81, 93–96, 98–99
Fortune at the Bottom of the Pyramid: Eradicating Poverty Through Profits, The (Prahalad), 118–21, 210nn36, 37
Foundation for International Community Assistance. *See* FINCA International
founding-story narratives, 30, 36–41
freedom: on already compromised ground, 190; cooptation of, 154–55; merger of humanitarian and capitalist notions of, 119; subjection as, 140–41
functionalist sociology, 9, 206–7n38

Ganz, Marshall, 37–38, 200n27
gendered notions of labor, 169–71, 216–17n11
"Gender lens" investment strategies, 170
Gente Nueva (New People) nonprofit (Mexico), 97
GI Bill, 116
gift, 14, 25, 55–56, 61–68, 202n18; "buy one, give one" model, 65–66, 202–3n22; conspicuous consumption as act of charitable giving, 14
gift exchange: as act of violence, 66; commodity as, 55, 64; racialized giving, 65–66
global South: children of, "adopted" into family of neoliberal labor, 164, 168, 172; financial discipline imposed on, 13; and freedom of multinational corporations, 119; production of as foretaste of utopian freedom, 23; women targeted for microfinance, 121–27, 134–43, 165, 214n24
Goldman Sachs, 9–10
grace, 185
graduate student actions (UNITE-HERE Local 33), ix–xi, xiv, 49–51, 76, 128–29, 183
Grameen Bank, 15, 91–92, 96, 117, 163, 166, 215n5
Grameen Foundation, 135
Gramlich, Edward, 120
Gramsci, Antonio, 8
Great Depression, 116
grief, 20–21, 156–61
grupos solidarios (solidarity groups/social networks). *See* solidarity groups (collective debtors)
Guatemala, 11–12, 15–16; call centers in, 131, 150–53; deportations from US, 152; entrepreneurial millennials relocated to, 61–62
Guatemala City, 124–25
Guatemalan Alliance of Exporters (AGEXPORT), 152

Haiti, 32
Hall, Stuart, 7–8
Ham, Arthur, 111, 112, 113
Hatch, John, 93–94, 96
Heifer International, 31
higher-education workers, 9–10. *See also* UNITE-HERE Local 33
historical consciousness, 1, 13, 66
history, "knowing," 27, 30–31, 34, 35–36, 44–46
History of Authentic Fair Trade (comic book; Equal Exchange), *26, 27, 28, 29*
history of capitalism, as disciplinary subfield, 46–48
History of Capitalism Summer Camp (Cornell University), 46–48
home visits and intervention, 124, 144, 148–50, 164–65, 169–73
Homo economicus, 4

Honduras, 177
hope, 1, 2; creditworthiness tied to performance of, 5, 16, 114, 124, 163–70, 173, 178–82; transferred to "next generation," 164, 166, 173, 182, 215n2, 218n24. *See also* capitalist humanitarianism; reproductive labor
Hope Connection (HC), 150–54
"How Companies Can Align Profit and Purpose" (Yale School of Management), 37–38
human capital, 164, 173
humanities departments, 46
humanity, universal theory of, 115
hunger strikes: eating disorders compared with, 50–51; as "fasts," 76; Local 33, ix–xi, xiv, 49–51, 76
Hurtado, René, 86, 93, 98–99, 100

identification, 90, 178–79
ideology, critique of, 7–8
"Ideology and Ideological Struggle" (Hall), 7–8
imagery: optics used in capitalist humanitarianism, 106–9, *107*; photographic realism, 112–13
impact investing, 37–39, 62, 72–74, 176–77. *See also* microfinance institutions (MFIs); social impact
inclusion, financial: campaign to legalize personal loans for urban working poor, 109–12, 208n14; as expansion of freedom, 140; extraction, structures of, 108, 127; participation requirements, 125, 144–48, 165–66; and philanthropic banking, 109–17, 115, 119; predatory, 15; racialized, 109, 117–23; subprime industry, 117–23; as system of credit, 122–23; "unbanked," 15, 107, 109, 111, 140; usury laws, 110–11, 114–15; women as targets of, 113, 120–27, 164–65
indenture, 140, 212n8
individualism, 89
industrial capitalism, 89–90
industrialization, and suicide rates, 89
"informal economies," 85

initial public offerings (IPOs), 98, 119, 121–22
interactive-voice-response (IVR) technology, 151
international development agenda, 14–15, 81, 88, 163; citizen-subjectivity, discourse of, 109; "solidarity lending," 80, 87–88, 94. *See also* microfinance institutions (MFIs)
International Monetary Fund, 167
Israel: boycott, divestment, and sanction (BDS) movement, 55; Six-Day War (1967), 41–42
Israel Museum, 43

Jackson, Gregory, 113
Jagat, Guru, 69, 203n26
Jerusalem and West Bank, 32
Jewish bankers, racialization of, 114–16

Karani, Aneel, 210n38
Kennedy, John F., 83
Khan Academy, 47
King, Helen, 41–44
kinship, 164, 172; actualized through finance, 114–16; Christian networks, 110–17; practical theory of late-capitalist, 171; spiritual, 112–13
Kondo, Marie, 51, 201n2

labor: of affected performance, 180–81; divisions of, 8; gendered notions of, 169–71, 216–17n11; generational inheritance of, 164, 170–73. *See also* reproductive labor
labor movement, transnational, 9, 207n38. *See also* unions
land-acknowledgment statements, 1, 38–39
Latin America: "informal economies," 85; "microenterprises," loans to, 85–86; organizational deficiency attributed to, 84; religion in, 6; "self-worth" said to be lacking, 88; US imperialism in, 14, 56. *See also* Central America solidarity movement
Left: cooptation of rhetoric and strategies of, 5, 22, 37–38, 40, 53–54, 154–55; cultural studies, absence of, 8–9; Latin American, 81; reification of neoliberalism by, 3, 5, 11, 186, 219n7

Left Christians, 6–7, 13, 76–79, 86–88, 93–96. *See also* Christianity; sanctuary churches
liberalism: authoritarian current of, 141; and consent, 139–41
liberation theology, 3, 6, 72, 86, 94, 100, 158
Lofton, Kathryn, 8–10, 205–6n32
Lundy, Richard, 86, 87, 94, 95, 98–99

"Man and Biosphere" initiative (UNESCO), 103–5, *105*
maquiladoras, "socially responsible," 176–77
Marx, Karl, 8, 55, 57–60; on denaturalization of money, 58, 71–73
masculinity, gendered assumptions about, 169–71, 216–17n11
Maskit (high-end fashion house), 43
Maya astrological calendar, 165
medical clinics, bank-owned, 165–68, 216n6
medicine, money as, 71–72, 74, 203n32
Melamed, Jodi, 108
Mennonite Central Committee (MCC), 27, 29, 32–35, 42
Mennonites, 4, 13, 32–34, 40–43, 198n4
Mexico, microbanks in, 97
microbanks, 88, 97–98, 166
microfinance institutions (MFIs), 211n1; appeal of across constituencies, 101; data collection and knowledge production in, 15–16; FINCA International, 14–15, 81, 93–96, 98–99; "hope for the future" of applicants tied to credit scores, 5, 16; letter-writing campaigns, 96; role in austerity and privatization, 100; "solidarity lending," 80. *See also* ACCION International; international development agenda; solidarity
Middle East, cultural discourse of, 42
"middlemen," rhetoric of, 59, 202n9
missionaries, apologetics in scholarship on, 44–45
modernity, 43, 45, 151; capitalist, 34–35; secular, 4, 6–7, 141, 196n18
money: as abstraction, 70–71; denaturalization of, 58, 71–73; as medicine, 71–72, 74, 203n32; as moral extension of self, 77

Money, a Love Story (Northrup), 69
"Month of Action" (Yale graduate union), 75–76
Morgan, Jennifer L., 214n23
Moreiras, Alberto, 219n7
Moten, Fred, 60–61
multiculturalism, neoliberal, 108
multinational corporations, freedom of, 119
Murphy, Michelle, 164, 167
Mycoskie, Blake, 65–67, 202n19

Nakbah (1948), 41
narratives, capitalist humanitarian, 23, 36–44, 59
National Labor Relations Board (NLRB) process, 128–29, 183
natural gas market, 83
Needlework Project, 31–32, 41–44; multiple narratives of, 43–44
negativity, 9–11, 16, 47; philosophical pessimisms, 186–87, 219n6; politics anchored in, 187
neoliberalism: anticapitalist dissent as a raison d'être, 12; "bureaucracy," criticisms of, 146–47; cooptation of Left rhetoric and strategies, 5, 22, 37–38, 40, 53–54; and gift economy, 64; institutionality of, 3; Left reification of, 3, 5, 11, 186, 219n7; manufactured consensus, 15. *See also* capitalism
neoliberal multiculturalism, 108
New Right, and evangelical Christians, 45
New Yorker, The, profile, 19–21
New York Times, The, 46
Nicaragua, 36, 56–57
Nietzsche, Friedrich, 66, 92
Nike child labor scandal, 177
Nixon, Richard, 85
North American Free Trade Agreement (NAFTA), 177
Northeast Union of Assistance to Small Businesses (UNO), 85
Northrup, Kate, 69–70

obligation, 66–67, 82, 92–93
offshore labor, 116, 152, 164

Index   245

Ohlone Nation, 39
optics, capitalist humanitarian, 106–9, *107*
Overseas Needlework and Crafts Project. *See* Needlework
Oxfam, 31

pain, social inequality equated to, 178
Palestinians in Jerusalem and West Bank, 32, 35, 41–43
participation requirements, 125, 144–48, 165–66
patriarchy: men's productivity delinked from, 217n11; and women's "empowerment," 145–46, 171
Paul, letter to the Galatians, 217n14
Peace Corps, 83, 85
"philanthropic banking/lending," 15, 109–17, 119
philanthropic foundations, 65
photographic realism, 112–13
poverty, longitudinal research on, 135–38
"poverty scorecard," 135–38, *137*, 143
"poverty tours," 162–82
Povinelli, Elizabeth, 39
"Power of Money in Bourgeois Society, The" (Marx), 71
Prahalad, C. K., 118–21, 210nn36, 37
predatory lenders, 110–12, 125–27. *See also* inclusion, financial
Presidential Awards for Excellence in Microenterprise Development, 117
PRIDECO, 88
Prison Notebooks (Gramsci), 8
Program for Investment in the Small Capital Enterprise Study (PISCES), 88, 90–91, 94
Progressive era reformers, 15, 109, 110–13, 209n26
Progress out of Poverty Index (PPI), 135–36, 141, 213n22
prosperity rhetoric, 17, 89, 163–65
Protestant secularism, 6, 16
Puerto Rico, 13, 31–32, 34–35, 199n13
Pulley, Rodmar, 84

Purpose of Capital: Elements of Impact, Financial Flows, and Natural Being, The (Emerson), 72–73

queer theory, 173, 196n20, 197n33, 213nn12, 13, 219n4

racial capitalism, 6, 8, 10, 17, 60–61, 107–8, 196n20; neoliberal multiculturalism, 108; and philanthropic banking, 109–17. *See also* capitalism
racialized financial inclusion, 109, 117–23
racialized sexual-reform projects, 15
Rawls, John, 212n7
Reagan, Ronald, 14, 36, 56–57, 60, 79, 81
Recife, Brazil, 85
redemption, of consumer citizen, 23–24
Regnum Christi (Catholic federation), 97
reinvestment, capitalist humanitarian, 3, 5, 10, 73, 171
religion, 216n10; as convergence between philosophy and action, 8; corporation as form of, 90; Durkheim's view of, 9, 206–7n38; Goldman Sachs as, 9–10; hegemonic dominance, reduction to, 6–8; in historical-material processes, 7–8; in Left cultural studies, absence of, 8–9; liberation theology, 3, 6, 72, 86, 94, 100, 158; spirit, figure of, 7, 140, 196n20; twin patterns in critiques of, 7–8, 196n20; "world religions" model, 9. *See also* Christianity
"Remedial Loans as Factors in Family Rehabilitation" (Ham), 112–13
repair/reparations, 2, 31
reparative reading, 10, 197nn33,34, 219n4
replacement theory, 157–58
reproductive labor, 216n6; adoption tropes, 164, 168, 172–73; as frontier of capital optimization, 167; and indebted labor, 167–68; mandatory family planning classes, 165; offshore sites of, 164; as reparative, 156–58; small family requirements, 166, 167, 173, 215n5; Starfish/Maia Impact, 216n9; surveillance of, 16. *See also* debt/finance discipline; hope

resistance, 140–41
resolution, refusal of, 38, 99, 181, 186, 187
RESULTS, 96
Rha Goddess, 69
Rieger, Joerg, 203n34
Riis, Jacob, 112
"risk," as code for black, brown, and low income, 120
Robinson, Cedric, 8
Romero, Oscar, 86
rotating savings and credit associations (ROSCAS), 91
Russell Sage Foundation (RSF), 111–16, 208n14

Sage, Margaret Olivia, 111–12, 114
Sage, Russell, 111
salvation, 6, 16, 115, 172–73, 217n14, 218n16; false, 27; as genealogical, 172
sanctuary churches, 7, 86–88, 93–96, 98–99; and solidarity, 7, 87, 93; St. Luke Presbyterian Church (USA), 86–88. *See also* Central America solidarity movement
Sandinista government (Nicaragua), 36, 56
Schmitt, Carl, 196n18
secularism, Protestant, 6, 16
Sedgwick, Eve, 10, 197n33, 219n4
self-critique, 1–3, 13–14, 40–41, 99–100, 186
SELFHELP Crafts (SHC), 32–35. *See also* Ten Thousand Villages
self-management by subjects, 150–55
sentimentality, 5, 90, 172, 218n24; and Progressive era reform, 111, 113–14; sentimental solidarity, 178, 186
settler colonial projects, 2, 5–6; and affective production, 44–45; "authenticity" linked to traditions of displaced peoples, 35; innocence, move to, 30; public atonement for genocide, 39
Silva, Denise Ferreira da, 120–21
Six-Day War (1967), 41–42
slavery: afterlife of, 115; laborers as commodity, 60–61; "solving" of through quantitative analysis, 47; transatlantic slave trade, 8; wealth from benefits capitalist humanitarian ventures, 39–40

"Social Capitalism" conference, 76–78
Social Capital Markets (SOCAP), 39, 77
social gospel, 109, 111–13, 116, 209n26
social impact, 1, 5, 131, 150–51, 153, 165, 176. *See also* impact investing
social media, 2, 25, 68
social safety net, 118, 121, 167, 171
social solidarity, 9, 52, 90–91, 196–97n29
solidarity: as as attachment to a majoritarian order, 92–93; conscious consumer practice as, 23; contradictions of, 100–101; free market transactions as, 3, 5; organizers, 82–88; and sanctuary churches, 7, 87, 93; and self-critique, 99–100; as sense of debt, 92–93; sentimental, 178, 186; social, 9, 52, 90–91, 196–97n29; social cohesion as, 89; "solidarity debt," 88–100; *in solido* agreements, 89; as term, 88–89; used to discipline poor, 92. *See also* Central America solidarity movement; microfinance
"solidarity banking," 82, 90–91, 101
solidarity groups (collective debtors), 80, 88, 90–91, 97, 144, 163, 165, 180
solidarity lending: dictatorship, neutral-to-positive references to, 91; El Salvador model, 88, 90–91; justifications for, 92. *See also* ACCION International; FINCA International
"solidarity lending," 80, 87–88, 94
South Africa, international boycott of, 55
speaking commodity, 60–61
spirit, figure of, 7, 140, 196n20
spiritual and wellness entrepreneurs, 68–74
spirituality, advertising of, 68–71
standard of living assessments, 135–38, *137*
Stanley, Amy Dru, 139
state power, 12, 209n26, 214n23
St. Luke Presbyterian Church (USA), 86–88, 93–96, 98–101
"story of now," 38, 200n27
Stuelke, Patricia, 10
subprime industry, 15, 116–17, 117–23
Suicide: A Sociological Study (Durkheim), 89–90
suicide rate, Durkheim's study of, 89–90

surplus value, household as site for production of, 173
"Swinging Ambassadors," 82–83

taboo topics, 68–71
"teddy bear sign," 51–52
Ten Thousand Villages, 4, 13, 25–30, 31–35, 45; history of, 27; inventory decisions, 34; and Six-Day War, 41–42. *See also* SELFHELP Crafts (SHC)
Teresa, Mother, 97, 100
textiles, pawned, 62, *63*
"theology of the social," 216n10
Thinx, 69
TOMS shoes, 65–68, 202n19
tourism, 12, 32, 43, 82–83, 104–6, *105*; Capital for Change (CFC) tour, 162–82
transnational labor movement, 9, 207n38
TUSHY, 69, 70
tycoon capitalism, 157, 209n26

"unbanked," 15, 107, 109, 111, 140
Undoing the Demos (Brown), 4
UNESCO, 103
Uniform Small Loans Law, 111–12, 208n14
unions, 55, 90, 129. *See also* labor movement, transnational; UNITE-HERE Local 33
United Farm Workers, 37–38, 45, 76
United Nations, 31, 210n36
United States: benevolent supremacy/soft power, 4, 31, 45, 81; imperialism of, 14, 56, 115; international development agenda, 14–15, 81; and microfinance, 14–15; moneylenders in, 114–16; post–World War II economy, 31–32; reconstruction, 115
United States Immigration and Customs Enforcement (ICE), 152
UNITE-HERE Local 33, 183, 187–88; hunger strike, ix–xi, xiv, 49–51, 76, 128–29
universities: history of capitalism subfield, 46–47; and land-acknowledgement statements, 38–39

University of Tennessee Vols (Volunteers), 50
USAID, 94–96
use value, 20, 57
US Office of Urban Development, 88
Usurer's Grip, The (film), 111
usury laws, 110–11, 114–16

vampire image: in Equal Exchange advertising, 53, 55; in Marx's writings, 55
Venezuela, 83–84
"Village Banking," 93
Villanueva, Edgar, 203n32
virtue ethic, capitalist humanitarian, 170

welfare recipients, 118
Wiegman, Robyn, 197n34
Williams, Raymond, 7
Wisconsin Coordinating Committee on Nicaragua (WCCN), 80–81
women: "empowerment" of, 13, 16, 131, 144–46, 149, 151, 153–54, 171, 175, 177–79; as targets of financial inclusion, 113, 120–27, 134–43, 214n24
worker corporations, 89–90, 205n30
"Working Capital for Community Needs," 80
World Bank, 12, 31, 97–98, 210n36
World Economic Pyramid, 106–8, *107*, 118, 210n36
world otherwise, dreams of, 10, 11, 140, 185; captured by humanitarian capitalism, 17–18
World Summit on Microfinance, 117–18
worldview, contract as, 139

Yale School of Management, 37–38
Yale University. *See* UNITE-HERE Local 33
"youth empowerment," 16, 165, 174–77
Yunus, Muhammad, 15, 91–92, 96, 117, 119, 124, 163, 166

www.ingramcontent.com/pod-product-compliance
Lightning Source LLC
Chambersburg PA
CBHW070839160426
43192CB00012B/2243